Allan Houser *Drawings*

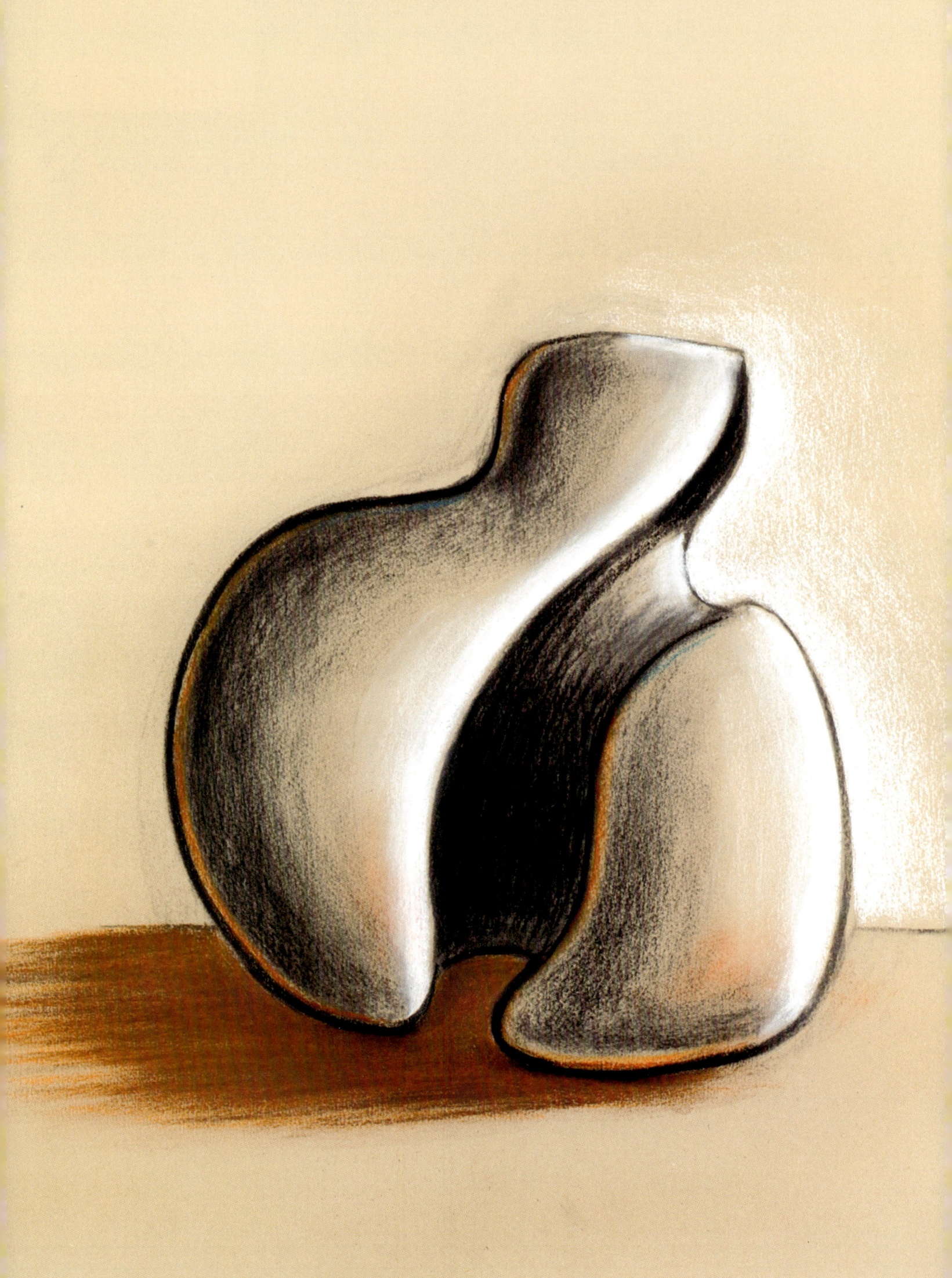

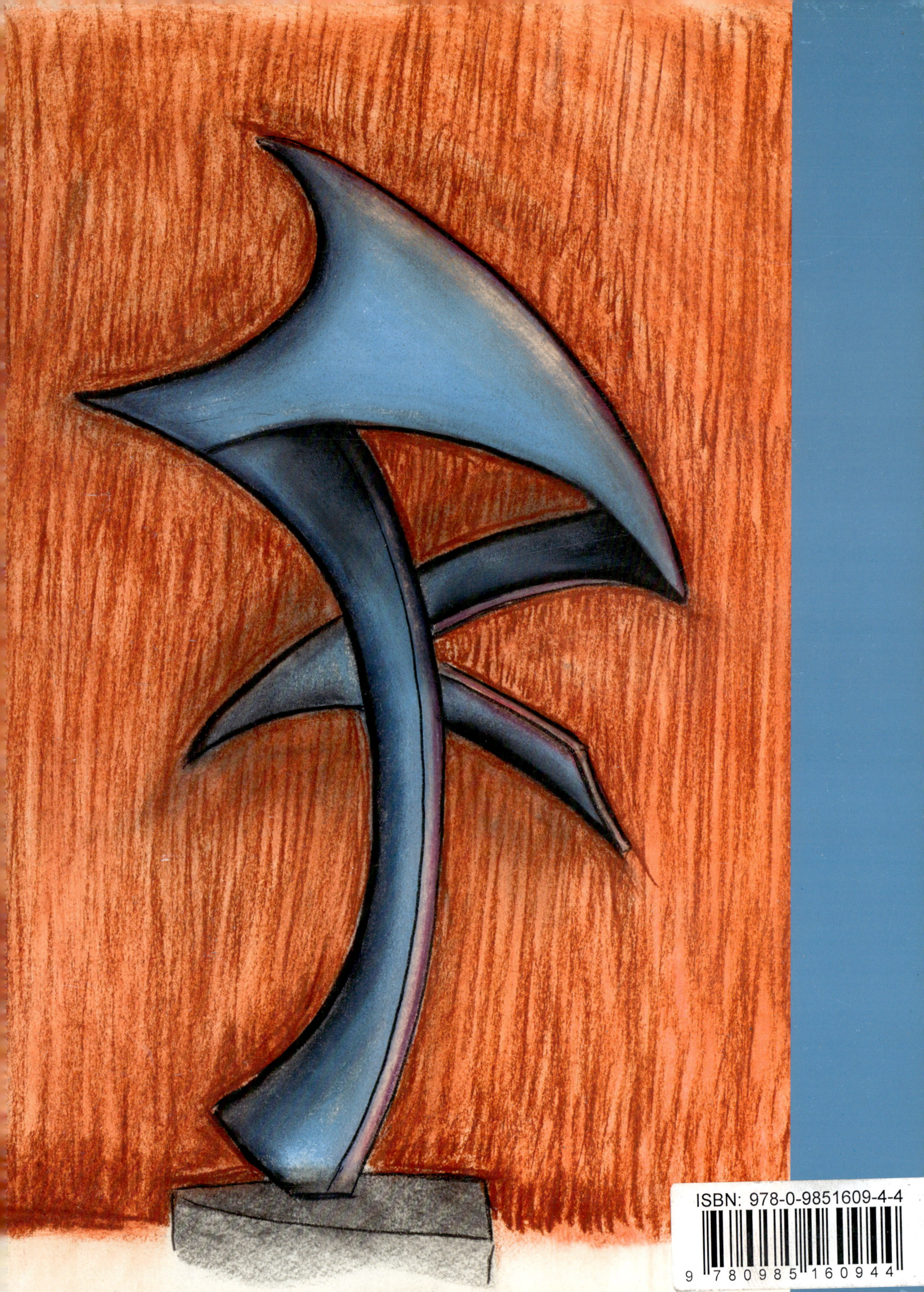

ISBN: 978-0-9851609-4-4

Allan Houser *Drawings*
The Centennial Exhibition

W. Jackson Rushing III

With an Essay by **Hadley Jerman**

Fred Jones Jr. Museum of Art
The University of Oklahoma

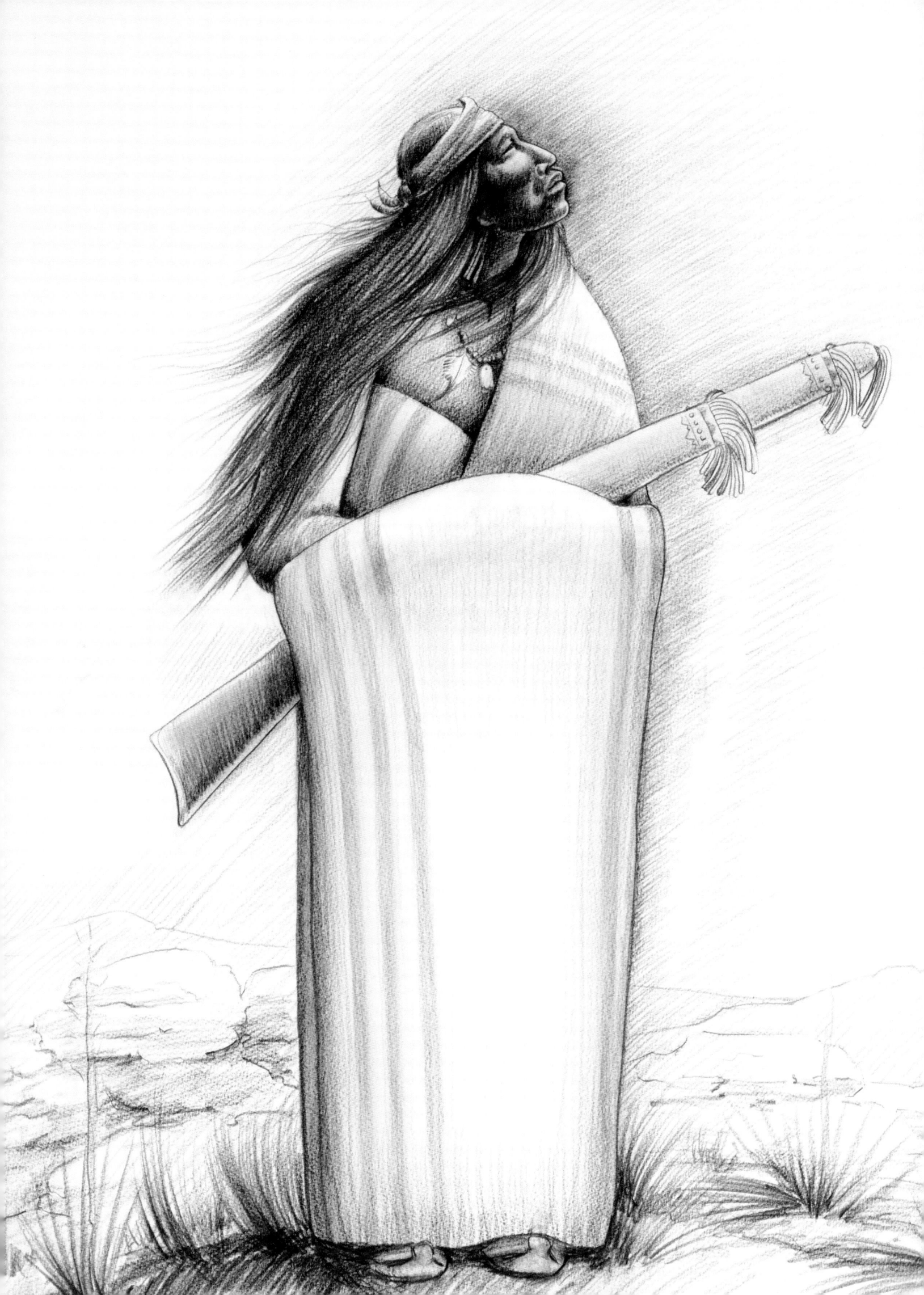

Contents

Foreword

The legacy of Allan Houser (Chiricahua Apache) looms large, not only in art history but also in his native Oklahoma. At present, his sculpture *As Long as the Waters Flow* (1988) greets visitors to the state capitol building, and an image of his *Sacred Rain Arrow* (1988) adorns state license plates. The Fred Jones Jr. Museum of Art (FJJMA) and the University of Oklahoma (OU) also have demonstrated a longstanding interest in his work, which may be found on display both in the museum and elsewhere on university grounds. The museum's founding director, Professor Oscar B. Jacobson, first exhibited Houser's work in the 1930s, and the museum also served as a venue for the important 1992 retrospective *Allan Houser: A Life in Art*. It is only fitting then that the FJJMA has organized the first major exhibition of his drawings, *Allan Houser Drawings: The Centennial Exhibition*, to celebrate the centennial of the artist's birth.

This exhibition would not have been possible without the expertise and passion of two individuals, Ghislain d'Humières and W. Jackson Rushing III. As the former Bill and Wylodean Saxon Director of the FJJMA, d'Humières conceived of a statewide museum celebration of the centennial of Houser's birth, and the realization of this exhibition is a testament to his enthusiasm for both the artist and this project. Guest curator W. Jackson Rushing III, who is the Eugene B. Adkins Presidential Professor of Art History and Mary Lou Milner Carver Chair in Native American Art at OU's School of Art and Art History, brings an incomparable scholarly authority to this project. The excellence of both the exhibition and this publication could not have been achieved without his insight and vision.

Allan Houser Drawings: The Centennial Exhibition also is made possible with the invaluable support of the Houser family and the Allan Houser Foundation, especially David Rettig, Curator of Collections. The exhibition is, moreover, a credit to the excellent work of the FJJMA staff, especially the departments of communications, education, preparation, and registration. The Oklahoma Museums Association and its Executive Director Brenda Granger also deserve accolades for their management of the statewide celebration of Allan Houser. The project would not have been possible without their valuable leadership.

We also owe a special debt of gratitude to Regent Jon R. and Dee Dee Stuart for their generous support of this project and their ongoing patronage of the FJJMA. Finally, I would like to thank University of Oklahoma President David L. Boren and First Lady Molly Shi Boren for their unwavering support of the museum.

It is my belief that this exhibition and publication will contribute significantly to the scholarship on the life and work of Allan Houser, and it is my hope that viewers and readers will gain new insights and appreciation for this important artist.

Mark Andrew White
Eugene B. Adkins Senior Curator
   and Curator of Collections
Fred Jones Jr. Museum of Art
The University of Oklahoma

Preface and Acknowledgments

After training at The Studio of the Santa Fe Indian School in the 1930s, the Chiricahua Apache artist Allan Houser (1914–1994) had both commercial and critical success as a painter and sculptor. In the 1960s and 1970s, for example, he exhibited his paintings at Towne Fine Art in Chicago, and in the 1970s in particular, he made large paintings in a studio he shared in Santa Fe with his son, the artist Bob Haozous. However, shortly thereafter he became disappointed in his efforts to capture movement and vitality in his paintings and largely stopped painting after 1979. His style, he felt, was too static—a lingering influence of the "Studio Style" of his youth, which emphasized flat, linear forms containing discrete zones of color. Unlike some artists, he generally wasn't comfortable working in a painterly (loose, fluid) style. Believing that charcoals and pastels would enable him to intensify the freshness and spontaneity of his imagery, Houser began to focus on drawing.

Houser had always made drawings, of course, but typically only in relation to the development of paintings and sculptures and not to be exhibited for their own sake. He made this clear in a sketchbook entry from 1989:

> I have tried to show the effort I'm making to come up with a style that expresses what feels right for me. I have sketched all throughout my car-rear [*sic*] but only for preparation for painting or sculpture. I have never really drawn for the purpose of selling my work. I have suddenly become interested in developing my drawing skills with the hopes of finding an individual style.[1]

Then, in 1990, Houser built a dedicated drawing and design studio at his compound south of Santa Fe, which included five different surfaces for drawing, where he laid in a cache of quality papers. Encouraged by the quality of the drawings he produced in this new studio, by 1991 he began to envision a body of work

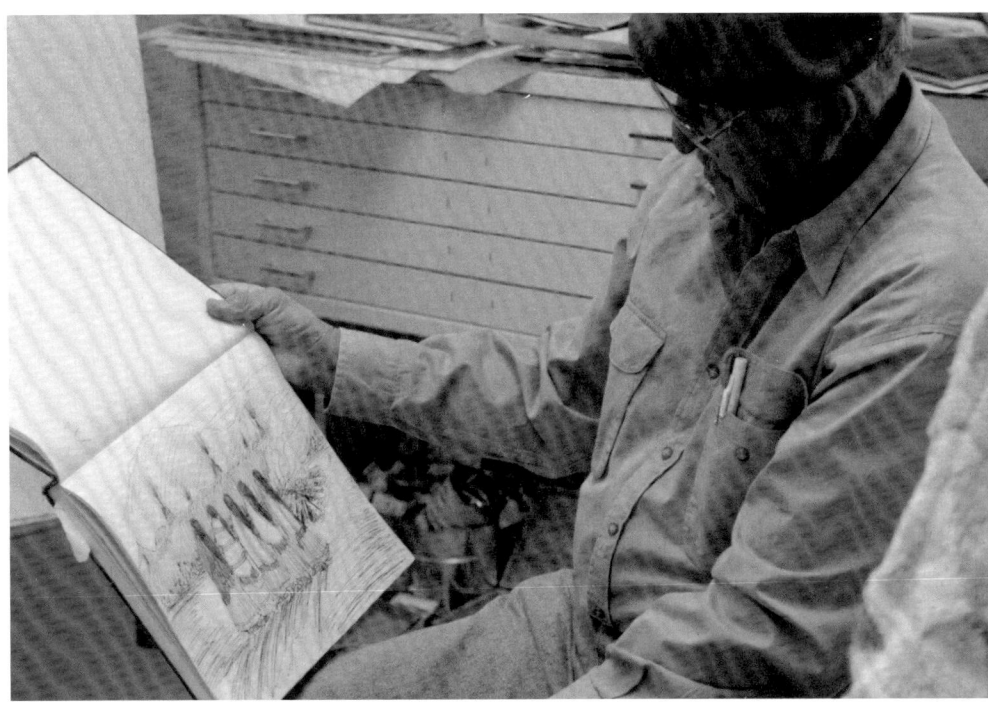

Lee Marmon (U.S., Laguna Pueblo, 1925–)
Allan Houser, 1991
Silver gelatin print, 14 × 11 in.
Fred Jones Jr. Museum of Art, copyright Allan Houser, Inc.
2013.016.010

that would form the basis of an exhibition and book of drawings. From 1992 to 1994 he was especially prolific, and fifty-five outstanding drawings from those years are included in the current exhibition. In January 1994, he was diagnosed with cancer, although in the months that followed he frequently maintained enough strength to keep drawing. By May of that year his interest in exhibiting his drawings had only increased, and he was engaged in conversation with the Fred Jones Jr. Museum of Art about such a project. Sadly, his death in August and the settling of his estate stopped short that process. *Allan Houser Drawings: The Centennial Exhibition* is thus not only a celebration of what would have been his one-hundredth birthday and of his ties to Oklahoma, where he was born, but also the realization of a dream deferred.

Within weeks of my arrival at the University of Oklahoma in late summer 2008, I proposed the idea of this exhibition to Ghislain d'Humières, who embraced it with enthusiasm. It was he who envisioned the exhibition as the centerpiece of a statewide celebration of one of Oklahoma's most cherished Native sons. His support and that of my friend and colleague Mark A. White have been invaluable. Likewise, I am deeply indebted to Mrs. Anna Marie Houser and her sons, Phillip M. Haozous, Bob Haozous, and Stephen V. Houser, for their commitment and cooperation. Their generous loan of ninety-nine historic drawings is greatly appreciated. David Rettig, Curator of Collections at the Allan Houser Foundation in Santa Fe, shared critical information and ideas and provided essential logistical support. I am pleased to thank him for his resourcefulness and professionalism. Hadley Jerman, one of my doctoral students, has contributed to this catalogue a fine essay, which not only makes an important new contribution to the literature on Houser, but also reflects the healthy working relationship between the FJJMA and OU's School of Art and Art History. For their hard work behind the scenes, thanks are also due to the museum staff, especially Susan G. Baley, Michael Bendure, Tracy Bidwell, Selena Capraro, Brynnan Light-Lewis, and Brad Stevens. Kudos to our editor, Alice K. Stanton, and to Julie Rushing, who designed the catalogue. And a special note of appreciation to Jon and Dee Dee Stuart for their ongoing support of the FJJMA.

Allan Houser *Drawings*

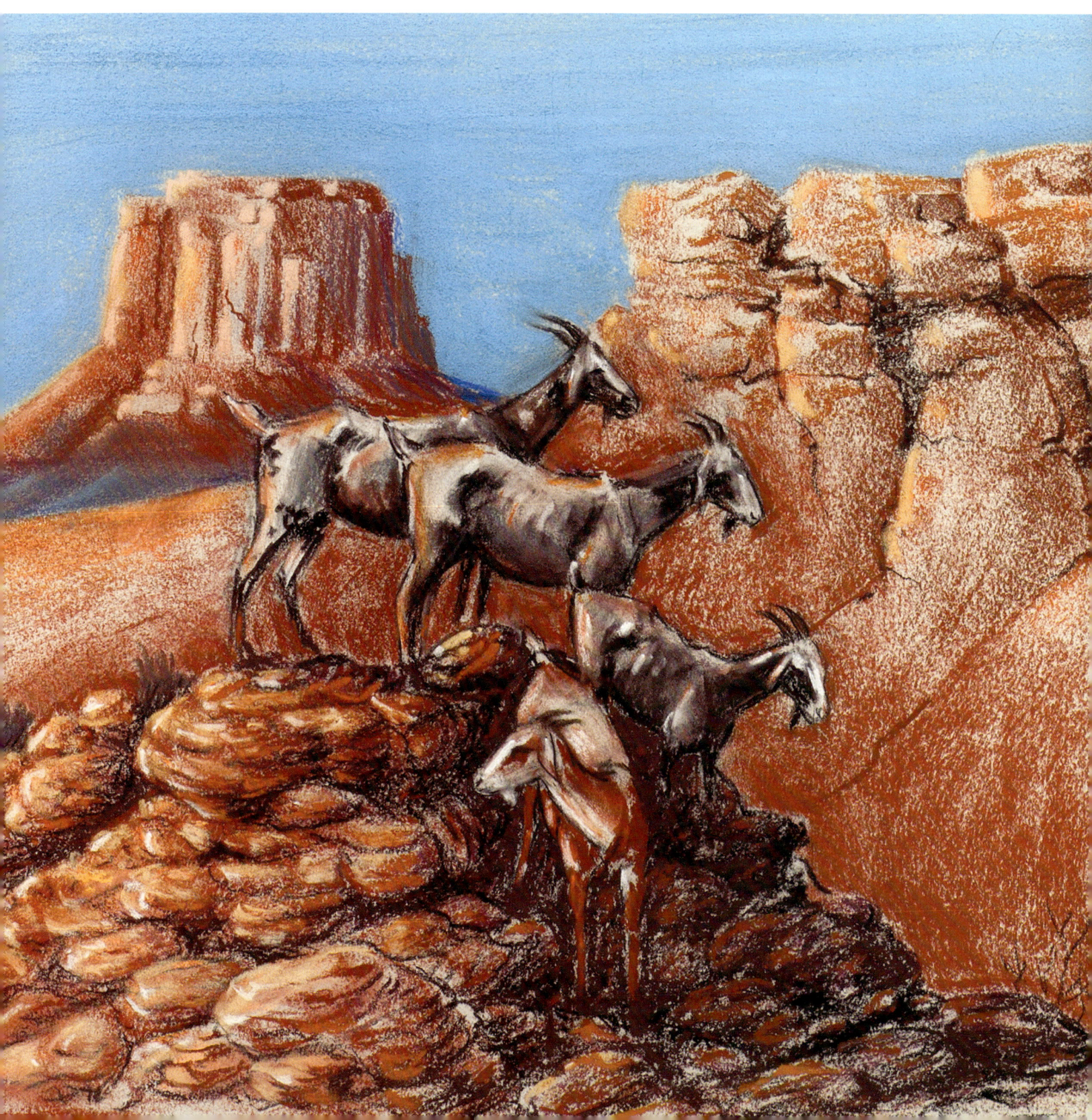

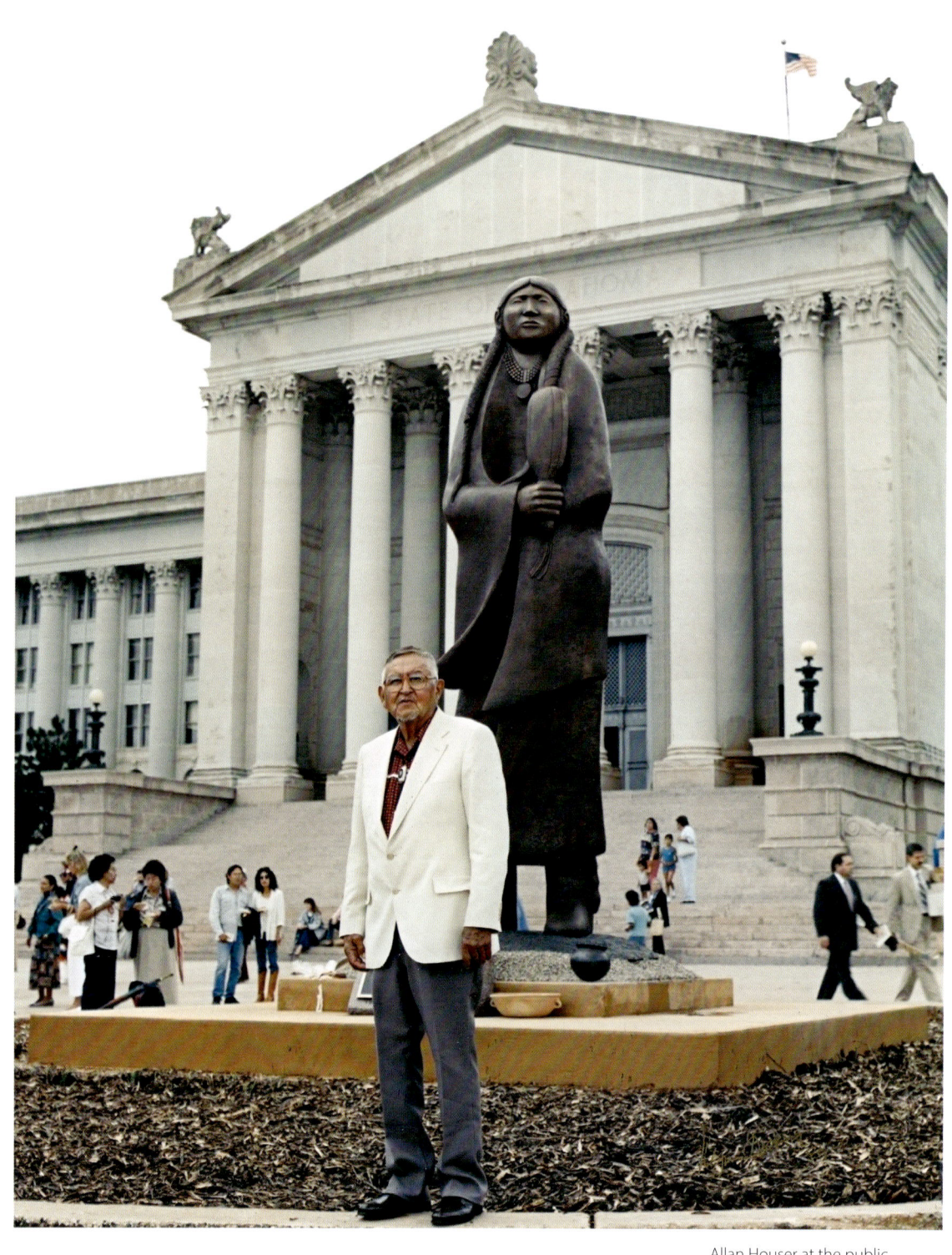

Allan Houser at the public dedication of *As Long as the Waters Flow* (bronze, 1988) at the Oklahoma State Capitol Building, June 4, 1989. Photograph by Lynn Ivory.

Apaches Forever
One Hundred Years, One Hundred Drawings

W. Jackson Rushing III

The year 2014 is the centennial of the birth of Allan Capron Haozous, the distinguished and award-winning Chiricahua Apache modern artist better known as Allan Houser. The son of Sam and Blossom Haozous (see plate 74), he came into the world on June 30, 1914, in Apache, Oklahoma, near Fort Sill, the first Chiricahua child to be born after his people were released following thirty years of captivity.

To help initiate a statewide celebration of this important anniversary, the Fred Jones Jr. Museum of Art (FJJMA) at the University of Oklahoma has organized *Allan Houser Drawings: The Centennial Exhibition*, which seeks to expand our knowledge and appreciation of a much beloved figure, whose art speaks across cultures and generations. Because his life and career have been carefully considered in two monographs,[1] in this essay I will instead offer a précis that sets the stage for an overview of the themes of the exhibition.

After growing up on the Haozous family farm, Houser studied painting under Dorothy Dunn and Geronima Montoya at The Studio of the Santa Fe Indian School (1934–1938), where he achieved early recognition for the quality and authenticity of his work. The year 1939, in particular, was a banner one for the young artist: he was featured in the Golden Gate International Exposition in San Francisco and was commissioned along with Gerald Nailor (Navajo) to paint murals for the Department of the Interior in Washington, D.C. This was also the year he married Anna Maria Gallegos. In 1947, the Thomas F. Gilcrease Museum acquired seven of his paintings, and in 1949 he received both a Guggenheim Foundation Fellowship and the Grand Award in the Philbrook Art Center's 3rd Indian Artists Annual. From 1952 to 1962 Houser was Artist-in-Residence and teacher at the Intermountain Indian School in Brigham City, Utah, and then from 1962 to 1975 he taught at the Institute of American Indian Arts in Santa Fe, serving also as head of the sculpture department.

In the years that followed his retirement from teaching, Houser continued to receive numerous commissions and prizes and was the subject of several solo exhibitions, including *Allan Houser: A Life in Art* (1991–1994), a traveling retrospective organized by the Museum of New Mexico.[2] Some of the many highlights of this period are as follows. In 1979 he was Artist-in-Residence at Dartmouth College, and in 1985 his monumental bronze *Offering of the Sacred Pipe* (1979) was dedicated at the United States Mission to the United Nations in New York City. Yet another monumental bronze, *As Long as the Waters Flow* (1988), was dedicated at the Oklahoma State Capitol in 1989. In 1992 Houser was the first Native American to receive the National Medal of the Arts. In the last decade of his life, major exhibitions of his work were held in Berlin, Paris, Tokyo, and Vienna.[3] He was honored posthumously in 2004 when his work was featured in a two-person exhibition, *Native Modernism: The Art of George Morrison and Allan Houser*, which helped inaugurate the new Smithsonian National Museum of the American Indian on the National Mall in Washington, D.C.[4]

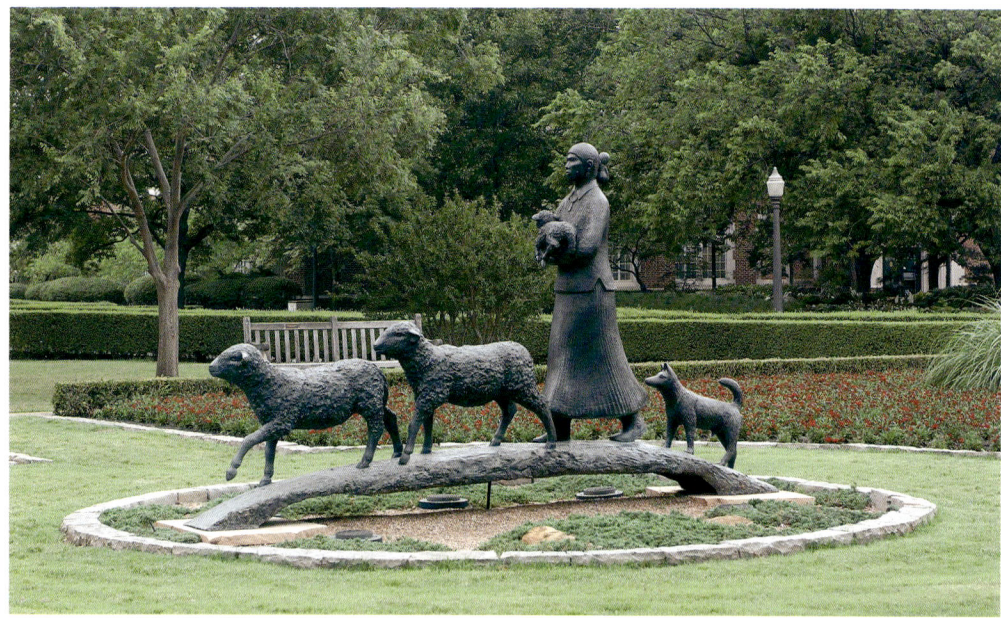

Allan Houser (U.S., Chiricahua
Apache, 1914–1994)
Homeward Bound, 1989
Bronze, 87 ½ × 153 in.
Fred Jones Jr. Museum of Art,
copyright Allan Houser, Inc.
1994.014

Houser began his career in the 1930s as a
Regionalist painter making so-called traditional
Indian paintings in water-based media, later adding
acrylics and oils to his repertoire. As early as 1937
his paintings of historical subjects were exhibited
at the Art Institute of Chicago and the National
Gallery of Art in Washington, D.C., and in 1954 he
was awarded *Les Palmes d'Academique* by the French
government in recognition of his achievements.
Herding Cattle (1940), which was probably produced
for the Works Progress Administration (WPA) and
which the FJJMA acquired in 1942, is a fine example
of the kind of auto-ethnographic painting that the

French Academy found so compelling: a sophisticated
design is rendered with linear clarity; foreshortening
and shifts in scale generate a sense of space; and, in
this case, the narrative vignette is antinostalgic.[5] By
the 1970s Houser was well established as a sculptor,
frequently winning awards—at the Heard Museum
in Phoenix, for example—and receiving significant
commissions—from the Denver Art Museum, for
example—for his inimitable figurative and, later,
abstract sculptures in various media, including wood,
stone, and bronze. Seventeen of his sculptures are
in the FJJMA permanent collection, including the
serenely beautiful bronze *Homeward Bound* (1989).

In addition to his renown as a painter and sculptor,
Houser was always an inveterate draftsman, and his
oeuvre includes thousands of compelling drawings
of a variety of subjects. Always sketching, he filled
239 notebooks with roughly 30,000 sketches, which
are housed in the Allan Houser Foundation Archives
in Santa Fe. In recent years, art historians, curators,
and collectors have become increasingly interested
in sculptors' drawings. Partly because of this, and
because the FJJMA believes that Houser's drawings
give us a direct encounter with his creative process
and thus have a remarkable emotional immediacy,
the museum has chosen to mark his centennial by
exploring this essential aspect of his art.

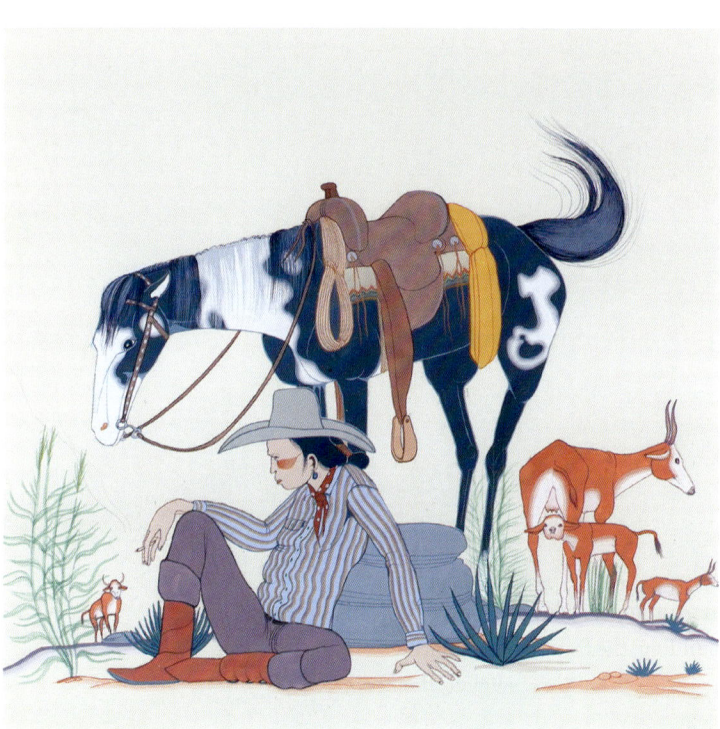

Allan Houser (U.S., Chiricahua
Apache, 1914–1994)
Herding Cattle, 1940
Tempera, 15 × 15 ½ in.
Fred Jones Jr. Museum of Art,
copyright Allan Houser, Inc.
1209

One Hundred Years, One Hundred Drawings

Ninety-nine of Houser's drawings, the vast majority of which are being exhibited and published for the first time, have been lent generously by the Allan Houser Foundation. The works range from small, sketchy studies (1960, plate 10), intimate in nature, revealing the creative process and showing the mind of the artist in its most uninhibited form, to large, finished drawings characterized by dynamic complexity, such as *Pueblo Buffalo Dancer* (c. 1992, plate 72). Some of these large drawings have a high degree of finish and resolution, such as *Apache Singer Kneeling by a Fire* (1985, plate 38). Some are obviously studies for or are related to Houser's sculptures, such as *Abstract Female Figure* (c. 1992, plate 54), while others are autonomous expressions of artistic imagination (1975, plate 29). In them we see both representation and abstraction (c. 1992, plate 89 and c. 1992, plate 63), as well as the impress of "cowboy realism" (1987, plate 40) and the modernism of such sculptors as Constantin Brancusi, Barbara Hepworth, Henry Moore (c. 1992, plate 62), and Francisco Zuniga. The materials Houser used include pastel, charcoal, felt-tip pen, pencil, pen and ink, tempera, and acrylic, all on paper.

Although some of the drawings seem "painterly," the working definition of drawing here is one employed by the Drawing Center in New York City: if it's on paper, it's a drawing.[6] The subjects of these inspiring drawings include mounted warriors and hunters; Navajo pastoral life; musicians and dancers; women and their work; figures and portraits; female nudes; Apache designs; animals, land, and nature (and symbolic forms derived from them, such as plate 18, c. 1965); and drawings for book illustrations, which are examined in Hadley Jerman's essay in this catalogue. Because many of the drawings are unrehearsed, they permit the audience to "look behind the curtain," allowing them to see Houser visually thinking out loud. Viewers are enabled, as such, to track and trace the evolution of his subjects and style, noting both differences and continuities. This is especially true of his representations of Apache Mountain Spirit Dancers (also known as Crown or Ga'an Dancers): he drew (and painted and sculpted) them for sixty years, and the development of these works from decorative and graphic to realistic reveals his evolving awareness and its manifestation in art (1939, plate 3, and 1994, plate 98). The spontaneity of the mind and the imagery that flows from it are clearly visible in a drawing that shows us Houser's world: three freely generated American western vignettes of mounted shepherds, buffalo hunters, and figures on the land are combined with a quasi-abstract figure sculpture based on Henry Moore's response to Pre-Columbian art (1975, plate 32). The total effect of such a drawing might well describe Houser's art in general: a rich, cross-cultural, and visual intertextuality.

Early Works

Warrior with Lance (1934), an untitled charcoal drawing in the FJJMA collection, is perhaps the oldest extant drawing by Houser (plate 1). According to the late Nelson Foss, former curator and archivist at the Allan Houser Foundation, "This was probably the first drawing Allan did at The Studio."[7] Indeed, on its verso side is a note in Dorothy Dunn's handwriting that reads, "(Studio Records) Allan Houser first drawing 1934." Dunn published this drawing many years later in her landmark book *American Indian Painting of the Southwest and Plains Area* (1968) as an example of the Euroamerican influence on Native painting that she wanted her students, Houser in particular, to resist.[8] As I have noted previously, given her ideas about authenticity in Native art, "surely she disapproved of his use of chiaroscuro, which is by no means unsophisticated, or the dynamic torque of the muscular Apache warrior, whose almost Baroque energy is accentuated by the plunging diagonal of the spear in his upraised hand. Fast and naturalistic, this highly personal drawing is diagnostic of the skills and interests he brought with him to Santa Fe."[9]

In 1940, the Department of the Interior's Office of Indian Affairs (forerunner of the Bureau of Indian Affairs) published one of the most important drawings in the current exhibition on the cover of its journal, *Indians at Work*. A bold, black-and-white image, *Apache Ga'an Dancer* (1939, plate 3) is a masterful pen and ink notable for both its dramatic contrasts and visual energy. The dancer's arms and legs, the staves he wields, and the superstructure of his headdress constitute verticals and diagonals that activate space in an exciting way. Similarly, the hard clarity of the carefully contoured forms is balanced by whiplash curves that imply the vigorous motion of the high-stepping dance. In addition to noting the significance of federal government patronage, we should consider also the historiographical importance of two texts that introduced Houser and his drawing to the readers of *Indians at Work*. After explaining that he was engaged in painting murals for the new Department of Interior Building, the frontispiece identified Houser's dancer as a participant "in a religious dance sometimes called the 'Crown Dance,' or more popularly by white people the 'Devil Dance,' because of the fantastic costume worn. The performers, impersonating supernatural beings from the north, south, east and west, dance to bring good fortune to a young Apache girl, who has arrived at maturity." The dancers, the text observed, "wear great headdresses of wooden slats" and "carry a jagged stave, meant, some say, to represent the wooden sword, edged with obsidian, which used to be carried by Indian warriors in Mexico." The black masks covering the dancers' faces "indicate the unimaginable appearance of supernatural beings."[10] In an accompanying article titled "Youthful Descendant of Geronimo Finds Paintings in Stories of His People," Houser's critical reception as an emerging artist was duly noted: solo exhibitions in New Mexico and California; his inclusion in the Oklahoma State exhibit at the New York World's Fair in 1939; and his illustrations for Louise Abeita's *I Am a Pueblo Girl*, published by William Morrow and Company in 1939.[11] Like George Morrison, the Chippewa modernist with whom he is often compared, Houser's youthful interest in drawing was associated with convalescence from an illness, as the article explains: "When in high school . . . he was sick for three months, and it was at that time, Allan says, that he really became interested in drawing. Some friends told him to go to the Indian Service School in Santa Fe. At Santa Fe he received a trophy for his outstanding work in art in 1936, the year before he was graduated. The school sponsored his first one-man show, Allan said, at which he sold all eighteen of the paintings included in the exhibit."[12]

It is not insignificant that fifty-five years after Geronimo's surrender, an article in a federal government publication reported as a positive attribute that "Houser reveals some of the same leadership and determination of Geronimo."[13]

Sketches and Studies

By all accounts, including his own, Houser was constantly drawing. He took a sketchpad with him wherever he went, working freely and quickly, stylizing and playing with form in an effort to find an idea that might work.[14] In some cases, such as *Fancy Dancer* (c. 1985, plate 39), made with a felt-tip pen, the image seems to have coalesced from a freewheeling process akin to surrealist automatic writing. Resisting "closure" or preciosity, Houser's figure appears to be both generated by, and generative of, a whirlwind of impulsive marks. The calligraphic "halo" of linear energy radiating like heat from the dancer's movement is abstract and expressive. In contrast, *Five Masks, Abstracted Ga'an Dancer* (c. 1955, plate 7) is slower,

more studious and elemental, less naturalistic than *Fancy Dancer*. In this instance, the images are more precise, as Houser is rehearsing case studies taken, perhaps, from various cultures. The illustrative quality of these images is deceptive, however, as they reveal Houser's exploration of a universal truth: to masquerade is to be human. Jackson Pollock, we should note, in his sketchbooks of 1939–40, also rehearsed expressive mask imagery inspired by tribal objects, seeking as did Houser to evoke a fundamental stage of human cultural evolution.[15]

The spontaneous and open-ended nature of Houser's creative process is revealed in two drawings in particular. In a pencil sketch we see Houser working out the Plains supplicant seen in his bronze sculpture *Offering of the Sacred Pipe* (1979); surrounding the male figure are series of images: a relatively naturalistic buffalo, seven abstracted buffalo heads, and a disembodied shirt (1975, plate 30). Similarly, on another sheet, we see three studies for sculptural heads next to figures, including an almost pictographic dancer and a horse and rider, as well as notational images of a turkey and a hawk (c. 1965, plate 23). Such drawings make no sense, of course, in terms of narrative or aesthetic unity, nor were they intended to. Call them play, research, practice, or explorations if you will, but certainly what such drawings have in common is their internal freedom. A slightly higher degree of unity is identifiable in *Five Abstracted Figure Studies*, done in charcoal, in which four of the figures—but not the one at bottom right, who is presenting a piece of pottery—are "cubistic." All five of them are joined "atmospherically" by shading that emanates from their bodies like energy or an aura (c. 1992, plate 61).

Drawing Sculpture

In addition to the abstractions discussed below, several drawings in the exhibition relate to Houser's sculpture, including *Three Ga'an Dancers*, a pastel that pictures high-stepping Mountain Spirit Dancers on a base (c. 1992, plate 65). Open and aggressively active, the sculpture group plays with solid and void (positive and negative space). Backlit by firelight, the quasi-abstract bodies of these ritual performers are fairly carefully modeled so as to suggest volumetric form, such that the whole is balanced on the fulcrum between naturalism and mystery. Unframed, the drawing is only two feet high, making it a pendant, although not necessarily intentionally, to the monumental *Study for "Warm Springs Apache Man"* (1991, plate 45), done in charcoal, which is almost five

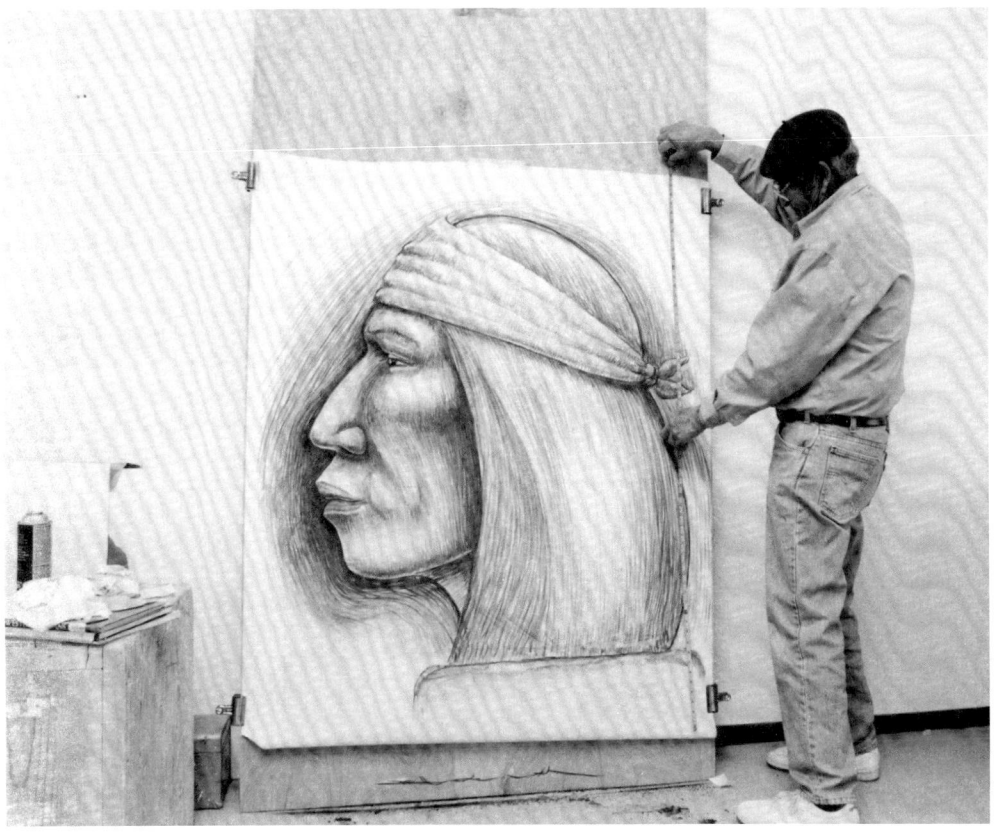

Lee Marmon (U.S., Laguna
Pueblo, 1925–)
Allan Houser, 1991
Silver gelatin print, 14 × 11 in.
Fred Jones Jr. Museum of Art, copyright
Allan Houser, Inc.
2013.016.002

feet high. In fact, the finished bronze (1991) is slightly
smaller, standing forty-nine inches high. Both the
charcoal drawing and the bronze that followed from
it have an irresistible presence, which is only partially
the result of scale. The absolute clarity of ideal form
gives both works of art a handsome gravitas.

Abstract Female Figure (c. 1992, plate 54) also
relates to a sculpture, the smoothly polished bronze
titled *Chrysalis* (1990). The pastel drawing, like the
sculpture, conveys the mystery of female beauty by
distilling it into abstract form. Sleek, elegant, and
both curvilinear and rectilinear, the image seems
to shift back and forth between personhood and
objectness. In this case and in other Houser images as
well, to be wrapped in a blanket is a visual metaphor
for being protected and even for blocked access. The
withholding of information intensifies "her" modesty
and mystery, and thus our curiosity. *Abstract Female
Figure* and *Chrysalis* share their art deco sensibility
with a pastel sculpture study: *Offering to the Great
Spirit* (c. 1992, plate 64). Comparable in some respects
to the figure that constitutes *Sunrise Song* (bronze,
1981), the Plains supplicant in the pastel drawing is
centered iconically on the vertical axis, a placement
that emphasizes balance and symmetry. The
abstracted male body seems ascendant, almost like a
majestic bird rising up into the sky. Narrow at the base

and wider at the top, only the slight turning inward of
the man's hands in the upper register slows down and
subtly halts the graceful vertical thrust of the design.

Study for Reclining Figure, a charcoal drawing
from 1992 (plate 46), belongs to a series of drawings
and sculptures that constitute Houser's sophisticated
engagement with the British sculptor Henry Moore's
Pre-Columbian–inspired primitivism.[16] Through their
investigation of the recumbent female figure, both
artists participated in a Western artistic tradition that
includes Edouard Manet's *Olympia* (1863), Titian's
Venus of Urbino (1538), and *The Three Goddesses* (448–
432 B.C.), the pedimental sculptures on the Parthenon
in Athens. Houser's recumbent females, however, are
identifiably Native and often Navajo in particular, as
in *Reclining Navajo Woman* (bronze, 1992) and in the
drawing considered here, which is a study for *Reclining
Nude III* (bronze, 1992). *Abstract Reclining Nude*, as
I have written previously, "pictures the sculpture on
its base; the body is carefully modeled with light and
shadow, but this effect is made ambiguous by the firm,
dark line that stresses the contours and flattens out the
figure. And like [Henri] Matisse, Houser allows us to
see the processual quality of the drawing by leaving
pentimenti around both shoulders and the left forearm
and elbow. The body is reminiscent of Moore's work,
though—a series of nearly autonomous abstract

parts that look like driftwood, bones, or fragments of excavated sculpture, thus indicating the wedding of organic nature and art history."[17]

Female Nudes

Even though some of Houser's sculptures of female nudes, such as *Hidden Beauty* (marble, 1983) and *By the Water's Edge* (bronze, 1987), are more representational than abstract, they, too, are reductive and "essentializing." In contrast, the life drawings of female nudes selected for this exhibition are neither romanticized nor idealized, but rather naturalistic. And like the Moore-ish recumbent indigenous nudes, the six life drawings in the exhibition, all of which are "titled" *Nude Study*, are candid but not salacious in their depiction of the female body. The two figures seen in plate 35 (1978) have the casual languor that typifies Houser's female nudes; their relative placement on the paper creates a spatial atmosphere, suggesting, perhaps, that we are observing them in nature. The diagonal, upraised figure seen from behind in plate 50 (1992) is more obviously posing for us, and Houser has invested more time in "shadowing" around her form by scrubbing the paper with charcoal. The drawing's sculptural counterpart is *Nude Resting on Elbows* (1993), a bronze notable for its lustrous patination. The contrapposto figure in plate 33 (1978) is rendered delicately with a conte pencil, capturing

with grace and economy the woman's beauty and organic vitality. Although the figure in plate 36 (1982) has breasts that seem anatomically incorrect, overall the image has more "heat" than the others, due perhaps to the expression on her face, the bangs partially covering her eyes, or the fact that she appears to be standing in tall grass. The figure seen from behind in plate 51 (1992) is the most abstract—less about perceptual truth, more about imaginative shapes (her body, apparently, is boneless).

Women and Their Work

In his paintings and sculptures Houser often represented women—their labor and their crafts— and this was a major theme of his drawings as well. *Women in Landscape, Saguaro Cactus* (1962, plate 15) is one of numerous fine-lined pen-and-ink drawings and temperas that were created as illustrations for Ann Nolan Clark's book *The Desert People* (1962), which chronicles the lifeways of the Tohono O'odham (or Papago Indians) of southern Arizona. The strong graphic image reads like a woodcut print and it narrates succinctly a mini-story: upright like the cacti, women, young and old, move in a stately rhythm across the desert floor with their burden baskets, gathering wild foodstuffs. *Woman and Child Cooking* (c. 1992, plate 69), a far less formal genre image, is a richly detailed charcoal drawing that shows a mother and child, both smiling in anticipation of the fry bread in the pan. Note that the mother's arched back does double duty as a mountainous form. Houser often represented Pueblo women and their pottery, as he did in *Woman with Pots Sitting by Horno Oven* (c. 1992, plate 90), which conjoins firing and baking. This carefully shaded charcoal is a more naturalistic treatment of a subject seen in *The Potter* (1982), a quasi-abstract bronze characterized by refined and sensuous art deco curves. Similarly, Houser drew and sculpted women grinding corn on several occasions, as in his lustrous bronze *Corn Grinder* (1982), in the FJJMA collection, which presents a woman with large hands seated with her metate. His charcoal drawing *Woman at Metate* (c. 1992, plate 70) is similar in its evocation of the essence of a woman's dignified work.

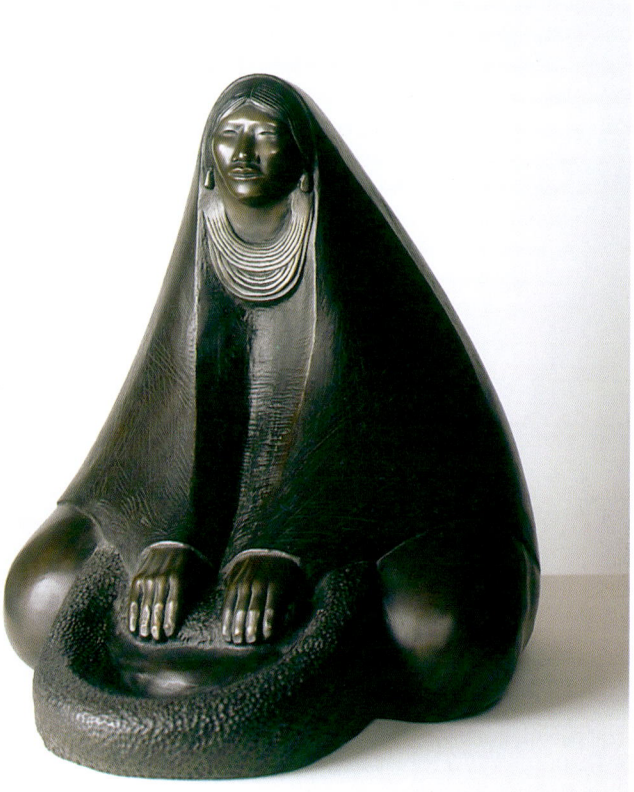

Allan Houser (U.S., Chiricahua
Apache, 1914–1994)
Corn Grinder, 1982
Bronze, 23 × 19 × 25 in.
Fred Jones Jr. Museum of Art, copyright
Allan Houser, Inc.
1996.017/076

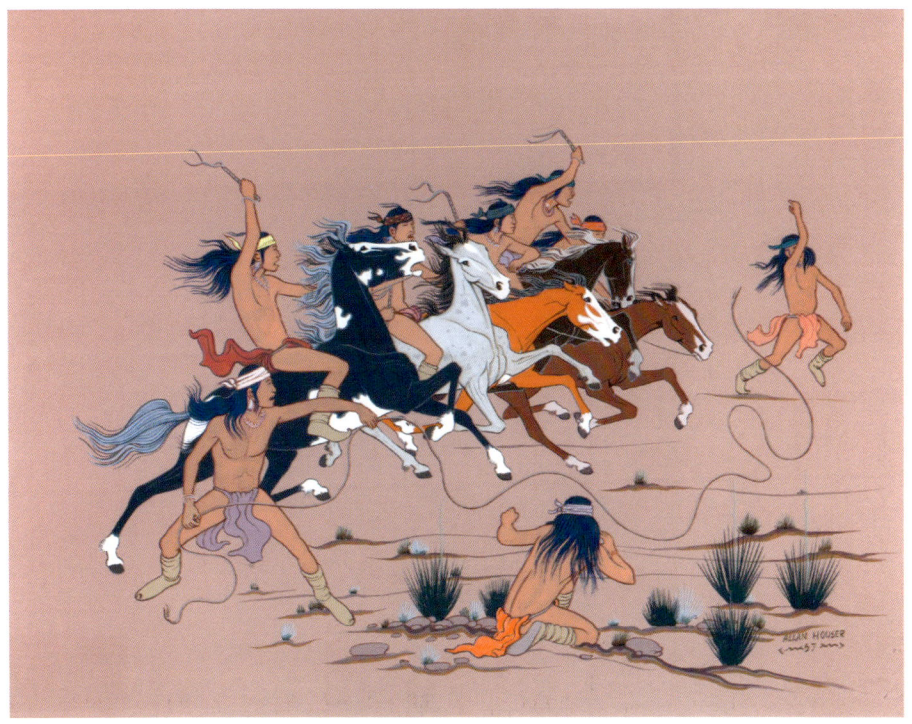

Allan Houser (U.S., Chiricahua
Apache, 1914–1994)
Apache Horse Race, 1957
Watercolor on paper,
22 ¼ × 28 ¼ in.
Fred Jones Jr. Museum of Art
2010.023.0782

Positioned iconically in the center of the picture space, the woman and her metate are basically flat, decorative, abstract shapes, save for her face, which is modeled in exacting detail, using the "white" of the paper as light. Her masklike countenance only heightens the religious connotation attributed here to food preparation. Another charcoal drawing in the exhibition connects with the museum's collection as well: *Navajo Shepherdess* (c. 1992, plate 92) is clearly related to the over life-size bronze figure group *Homeward Bound*, mentioned above, situated near the University of Oklahoma's main library (see page 4). Gathering a lamb as if it were a child, the heroically tall shepherdess in plate 92 moves with pastoral grace through the land, while the bulk of the flock (in the middle register) follows a goat that Houser imbues with no small amount of endearing charm.

Animals, Land, and Nature

Houser was a complex man, who could be described accurately in a number of ways: American artist, modern artist, and Apache or Native American artist. But he was also a *western* artist, one for whom animals, land, and nature were never mere props in his visual stories. On the contrary, they were often *dramatis personae* in their own right, elements with pictorial agency. As I have noted previously, "Houser was always nourished by the flora, fauna, and geography of the Southwest and he took long walks that allowed his creative spirit to imbibe the rejuvenating spirits of nature."[18] Similarly, Foss wrote, "Houser regularly

went on sketching trips with such friends as Bill Prokopief, Doug Hyde, and Dan Namingha. During these trips he honed his skills at landscape painting while broadening his knowledge of the images of his people and their way of life."[19] To this I would simply add that animals—in particular buffalo, horses, and sheep—were and are an important part of the Indian way of life in Houser's American Southwest.

Apaches on horseback—engaged in races, warfare, or hunting buffalo—were a leitmotif of Houser's drawings, paintings, and sculptures; his 1957 watercolor *Apache Horse Race* in the FJJMA collection is a fine example. His *Buffalo Hunt* (c. 1992, plate 77), done in pastel, is pure Native Americana and certainly one of the most exciting drawings in the exhibition. The magnificent bison in the foreground thunders downhill, its massive body surging ferociously forward in an effort to escape the mounted hunter in pursuit. Long, slashing strokes of fiery color activate the space and give the picture a breakneck internal velocity. One would be hard pressed indeed to find another picture that evoked the visceral passion of hunter and hunted as powerfully as this one does. Elsewhere animals are antagonists: in *Ewe Fighting Off Wolf* (1958, plate 9), a pen-and-ink drawing published as a book illustration, the precisely rendered combatants are situated in a realistic landscape realized with velvety blacks, parallel strokes of varying lengths and widths, and tight hatching and cross-hatching.

In contrast to these action images, an altogether different mood prevails in the visual quietude of

Navajo Man on Horseback (c. 1992, plate 75), which recalls classical equestrian monuments of antiquity. Seen in profile, the horse and rider are lifted up by a mound of earth akin to a sculptural base. Landscape forms spaced rhythmically along the horizon in the middle register measure for us the vastness of the open terrain. Formal and contemplative, the silent grandeur of this drawing differs from the more informal but keenly attentive reportage in *Horse and Rider* (1987, plate 40). The former has obviously been staged for us, while the latter reads as a snapshot of "real life." A pair of detailed pastel drawings, *Four Goats in a Landscape* (c. 1992, plate 76) and *Horses Grazing* (c. 1992, plate 95), are convincing in their evocation of southwestern light and color, as they make manifest Houser's love of animals and the dry, rocky land they occupy. Close observation reveals his nuanced application of color to the paper, as he turned the chalk first one way and then another, with varying degrees of pressure, creating the textures of fur, grass, and earth. His charcoal drawing *Eagle* (c. 1994, plate 99) has such riveting specificity in the bird's face that it makes sense to think of this image as a portrait. Standing on a rock (like a sculpture on a pedestal), the eagle leans forward diagonally across the picture space, filling it with its powerful presence, which is established, in part, by its wild eye, sharp beak, and realistically sizable tongue. The work is related to a cast bronze, *Emperor's Eagle* (1994), which in turn Houser modeled on a direct stone carving of an eagle commissioned by the Clinton White House as a gift for Japanese Emperor Akihito.[20]

We find a curious counterpoint to the theatrical naturalism of *Eagle* in a felt-tip pen drawing with the descriptive title *Abstracted Deer by Tree, Two Non-objective Forms* (c. 1965, plate 18). However, I propose that the two surrealistic sculptural forms left of center are *not* non-objective. That is they *are* abstracted from objects (forms) seen in nature. The two deer on the right are not so much by a tree as one with it; the tree seems to be generated by them or perhaps the tree element at bottom left of that configuration represents a deer transforming into a tree. The birdlike elements of the sculptures on the left are based, in part, on the birds in the tree branches at upper right. Thus the two visionary sculptural forms are not invented out of whole cloth but fuse together aesthetic symbols for deer, tree, and bird. Both sets—the sculptures on the left and the tree/deer/bird configuration on the right—share certain formal characteristics, including a dynamic, open, sharp angularity. Although this quirky

drawing lacks the scale or finesse of many of the more finished ones in the exhibition, it is perhaps the most artistically magical.

Figures (and Portraits)

Representing and portraying people in the fullness of their humanity was a primary goal of Houser's art. The dozens of figurative images in the exhibition—some of which are treated in this section, while others are examined in two of the sections that follow—make the case for the importance of this subject matter in his oeuvre. Among these are realistic portraits, including the one of his parents—based on a photograph—which is characterized by their warm, smiling benevolence (c. 1992, plate 74). Although he always remembered them as courageous survivors of colonial hardship,[21] in this detailed drawing Houser presents them not as heroes but lovingly as plain folks. His *Study for Portrait of Stewart Udall* (1975, plate 31), which utilizes the tooth of the paper to conjure up the bristly texture of Udall's crew cut, reveals the tough intelligence and determination of the environmentalist and Native arts advocate. Udall served as Secretary of the Interior from 1961 to 1969, and in 1975 Houser became the first Native American artist commissioned to paint the official portrait of a member of the president's cabinet.[22]

Some of the figures in Houser's drawings, such as the "red man" titled *Male Figure* (c. 1992 plate 88), are quirky and mysterious: the image is elemental, consisting mostly of scrubbed on texture, and it floats ungrounded in an indeterminate space. Others, including *Portrait of a Man and a Woman* (c. 1992, plate 78), done in pastel and acrylic, are powerfully realistic. Rigorously detailed, this work has a compelling figure-ground relationship. The background pattern is telluric, decorative, and variable, as it tightens up the closer it gets to their bodies, creating an atmosphere around them. The modeling of their faces, generating weathered, earthy skin that maps their resilient endurance, is a tour de force. The pentimenti around the man's hat and both shoulders remind us that many of Houser's drawings are the record of the process by which an image is discovered, not copied directly from nature. *Apache Father and Son* (c. 1992, plate 81) is equally gripping in its dramatic realism, even though it uses a "narrative scale" in which the importance of the man in the boy's life is symbolized by his monumentality. The father's physicality threatens the boundaries of the picture space, which can scarcely contain him. While the father is relaxed, calm, and dignified—like classical statuary—the boy is alert, focused intently on something unseen by us in the distance. Houser's application of color here was fast and gestural, resulting in a fluctuant impressionist surface, and the mottled powder blue of the background is frescolike in its suggestion of plaster flaking off a wall. (Perhaps because I have sons of my own or because I count Houser's sons among my friends, the casual grandeur of the paternal-filial bond represented here makes this drawing my personal favorite.)

A quartet of unrelated works exemplifies two tendencies widespread in Houser's drawings. *Three Navajo Men* (1991, plate 44) presents a profile view of three "portrait busts" of the men. For all their detail, they are idealized, if disembodied heads—like monuments on a Mount Rushmore—and they lack narrative context. That is, the only "story" they imply is the fact of their continuing presence, their indigenous ongoingness. As with so many of Houser's beautiful and dignified images of Native peoples, nobility abounds, but savagery is nowhere to be found.[23] Similarly, in *Three Women Talking* (c. 1994, plate 100), a charcoal drawing more than four feet high, the Apache women *might* be speaking, although that is not unequivocally clear, and what actually matters is the unified configuration of their solid forms. The "meaning" of the drawing or at least one of them, I propose, resides in their irrefutable corporeal presence—a trinity of tall, strong, handsome women who are proof positive of their parents' survival.

In contrast, we might consider a pair of genre images—slice-of-life snapshots—that encourages us to imagine a backstory for the figures. In *Man on a Sawhorse* (c. 1992, plate 91), a tall Apache man in contemporary dress dominates, if casually, the picture space. If he decides to stand up, for example, the space Houser has established with the ground plane and the size of the sawhorse will not be able to contain him. Relaxed and gazing off into the distance—whereas the figures in *Three Navajo Men* are likely envisioning the future—he prompts us to wonder, where is he and what is he doing? Taking a break from work? At a powwow, perhaps? What circumstances have brought him here and what does his future hold? Similarly, we might speculate about the large Apache man seen in *Portrait of a Man in a Hat Smoking* (c. 1992, plate 80). An almost cinematic image that fills the picture space, his head appears to emerge from a bulky landform, beneath which the drawing is "unfinished." Immersed in a strawberry-red color field signifying vibrancy and passion, the seemingly autochthonous man remains inscrutable, which makes us all the more curious about

him. In sum, Houser often "figured" people in two distinctly different ways. The first pair of drawings in our quartet stands for a tendency toward idealization and essence—people as signs for the persistence of aboriginality—while the second pair stands in for numerous works that appear based on observation rather than the formalization of indigenous national character.

Music and Dance

Beginning in the earliest days of his career (see plate 3 discussed above), Houser always made drawings and paintings and, later, sculptures of performers. They were simply one of the most common subjects in his expansive oeuvre and for good reason: singing, drumming, and dancing—both social and ceremonial—have been cultural glue for the aboriginal peoples of the Americas since their cultures first developed. According to Barry Ace, an Odawa visual artist and award-winning powwow dancer, for Native nations dance in particular "is an essential collective celebration of life and death, of spirituality and subsistence," one that enacts both "epistemology and worldview."[24] Because I wanted this section of the catalogue to be informed by a Native dancer's perspective, I asked Ace to review and comment on several of the drawings in the exhibition, and I am pleased that his voice is heard in some of the material below.

Houser's representations of Indian performers were diverse in terms of drawing style, scale, materials, and tribal subjects, although the majority of the performers were either southwestern or Plains. The Navajo are cultural cousins to Houser's Apache people, and he always had a fondness for them and an interest in their way of life. One of the artist's closest friends, dating to his student days at the Santa Fe Indian School, was the Navajo painter Gerald Nailor, with whom he shared a studio in the late 1930s. Houser's *Navajo Singer with a Rattle* (c. 1992, plate 67) exemplifies the idea of drawing as the organization of variable marks, including dense cross-hatching in front of the body and long curved strokes made with the broad side of the charcoal along the shoulder and back. The Navajo singer's mouth is open in ecstatic song, and the vital diagonal thrust of his arm and gourd rattle is a visual equivalent of the rhythmic assertion of the beat. Contrast this single charismatic figure, whose form is solid and yet clings to the front of the picture plane, with the group of animated Tohono O'odham performers in *Five Men Dancing* (1962, plate 14), a fine pen-and-ink line drawing published in Clark's *The*

Desert People. Despite being stylized and illustrative, the figures in this work occupy a convincing recessional space that symbolizes "story space."

Two images of singers on their knees, both drawn in 1985, are instructive. In their prayerful posture, together such images form part of what I have described elsewhere as Houser's iconography of religious ecstasy.[25] In terms of clothing and accouterments, *Plains Warrior with Rattle and Fan* (1985, plate 37) is the more "traditional" of the two images and, furthermore, the drawing is related to *Prayer Song* (bronze, 1983), a sculpture that preceded it. Given his illumination by firelight emanating from a source outside the picture space, the figure in *Apache Singer Kneeling by a Fire* (1985, plate 38) has greater intensity and even, to my eye, heightened mystery. Each of the drawings, though, might be described as quietly dramatic, as compared to the robust performativity of some other drawings in the exhibition, including a pair of Pueblo Buffalo Dancers. Made in the early 1990s, one of them, *Pueblo Buffalo Dancer* (1991, plate 43), offers a frontal view of the dancer, while the other, *Pueblo Buffalo Dancer* (c. 1992, plate 72), shows the dancer in profile. Both dancers wear horned buffalo headdresses, shell mosaic pendants around their necks, bells on their legs, and dance kilts decorated with a picture of Avanyu, a horned water serpent associated with lightning and spring water. Likewise, both carry gourd rattles, while one clutches a bow and the other a lightning stick, and their noticeably hard stomping, according to Ace, implies "a herd of galloping buffalo." For Ace, it is important to understand these images as representations of masquerades linked to hunting narratives, which makes them symbols of an all-encompassing cultural imperative:[26]

> For many Native American tribal societies dance is the tribe's calendar and often tied to seasonal change and to solar and lunar occurrences and therefore essential to the survival of the people.... Yet these dances are not mere calendric signposts, but are also deeply rooted in spiritual meaning, imbued with protocol and ceremony, and signify a retelling of tribal histories and lifeways that are passed on and witnessed by the tribe through dance. Reenactment of successful hunts, imitation of unique movements and traits of an animal, and sacred song and intonations for communion with the spirit of the animal are all intrinsic attributes that are imperative to the maintenance of this fragile balance and interdependence.[27]

The eagle, as Ace observes, is a common sacred animal among Native nations of the Americas, "celebrated and respected for its beauty, strength and poise" and revered for "its ability to fly the highest and thus . . . be closest to the Creator."[28] Houser's charcoal drawing *Eagle Dancer* (1992, plate 52) is richly detailed and convincingly naturalistic. With the eye of a visual artist and dancer, Ace has written thoughtfully about this work, noting in particular the "outstretched wingspan—as if the dancer is soaring high in the sky, riding the updraft of the afternoon thermals—in full flight and in the prime of life." And, in a prescient reading, Ace explains how Houser has shown the viewer the dancer's perspective: "This is apparent from the manner in which the eagle dancer is depicted as he crosses in front of the viewer's shallow depth of field with the drummers and spectators fading out in the distance. This is unequivocally how another dancer encounters a fellow participant. One immediately gets the sense that Houser is not concerned with a mere spectator's voyeuristic gaze, but one of a privileged position where the viewer is experiencing the dance of the eagles from the perspective of a dancer."[29] Houser's *Plains Fancy Dancer*, a very large pastel from circa 1992 (plate 86), is a show-stopper—vital, flamboyant, and celebratory. Anyone who has ever been to a powwow will recognize and recall the explosive energy of the Fancy Dance, sometimes called the Oklahoma Feather Dance. Widely performed, the dance in its current form is pan-Indian in style, although Ace traces its roots (as do other scholars) to the (Ponca) Hethuska Society in Oklahoma. Ace admires Houser's revelation of "a dancer in his prime with strong and youthful and well-defined musculature emphasizing the need for intense physical stamina and endurance that is a prerequisite for this fast-paced style of dance. "[30] The drawing is lit up internally with rosy pink and orange, and the vigorously open composition is unified by the repetition of turquoise in the dancer's moccasins, cuffs, and hair wraps. By focusing on a single, charismatic performer, Houser is echoing a tradition of Plains Indian art identifiable in the watercolors and pochoir prints of the Kiowa Five and in the work of numerous ledger-book artists before them.

The dramatic intensity of Houser's Fancy Dancer in plate 86 is matched in the exhibition only by the figure in his gripping *Large Ga'an Dancer in the Glow of a Fire* (1994, plate 98). The drawing is almost life-size, and its scale symbolizes the central importance to Apache life of the Girl's Puberty Ceremony, where the dancers give spectacular firelight performances early each evening during the ceremony's four days. These Ga'an (or Crown) dancers represent mountain-dwelling supernaturals, whose presence and performance are essential to the community's well-being. This coming-of-age ritual for young women has numerous social and symbolic functions, including an affirmation and intensification of Apacheness. The dancers also appear in shamanic curing ceremonies, and in his youth Houser assisted with applying the dancers' body paint on such occasions. He treated this subject dozens of times over a sixty-year period, because he understood that to face and survive the unpredictability of life, the Apache people needed the strength, balance, and stability that the Mountain Spirits embodied.[31] This particular rendition, which the artist double-signed "Allan Houser/Haozous," is virtually on fire with artistic passion, ablaze with visual energy, as the dancer surges left with his high stepping, his body creating a dramatic diagonal line in space.

The Abstractions

In the 1990s Houser increasingly made abstractions in various media, and the exhibition includes a series of fascinating drawings, all of which have tentatively been dated circa 1992. When they were cataloged in 1995, Foss assigned all of them the descriptive title "Non-Objective Form," but in some cases at least that would seem to be a misnomer. Plate 53, for example, is clearly the abstraction of a seated figure, wrapped in a blanket, which casts a shadow. Delicately modeled to imply volumetric form, the "personage" lifts and turns its "head" to the right, as if it were sniffing the air or seeking the nature and origin of some sound in the distance. The wrapping around of the form creates a shadowy enclosure that evokes a cave, a womb, or the interiority of the self. Plate 55 is likewise based on a seated figure, which is becoming or has become an almost surrealistic biomorph. The empty Dali-like space is clearly established for us by a horizontal line "behind" the figure-form and we read clearly also the curvature of the hip and back, but instead of a "head," the form terminates with a bell-like shape that might suggest a musical instrument or a snout of some sort. What is not in dispute, however, is the lyrical, liquid elegance of the image, which flows uninterrupted from its point of origin to its endpoint. The form in plate 58, by comparison, is not figurative, although it, too, implies wrapping and enclosure. Balanced on sharp points, the object is subtly colored and modeled (shades of gray-green and bits of brown that reflect the tablelike base) and is cast into relief by the pink atmosphere of the background. Simultaneously

organic and linear/sharp, in theme it is related to an earlier drawing and also a bronze sculpture, both titled *Seeking Harmony* (1990).

Houser knew the history of modern art well, and certain of his drawings are in conversation with the work of key figures. The totemic form in plate 62 consists of stacked, linked vertebrae-like shapes that remind us, once again, of Houser's admiration for Henry Moore. More finished than sketchy, the drawing is likely a study for *Striving*, a bronze cast in the same year (1992). The angular, silvery cubistic form in plate 56 is reminiscent of David Smith's "Cubi" series—stainless-steel sculptures (1961–1965) that explored geometric form.

A trio of drawings speaks well to the variety of styles and therefore visual metaphors Houser could pursue in a discrete time period. The figure-form in plate 47, with its flowing, curvilinear rhythms, is obviously female in origin. Mounted on a platform, the image makes reference to body parts, falling water, and the sweeping drapery of classical statuary. Thus the sculpture pictured in the drawing does not so much represent a woman but offers instead a semi-abstract equivalent for female beauty. Atypically, this drawing is both (double) signed and dated. The aerodynamic, constructivist sculpture pictured in plate 60 is cousin to a number of Houser sculptures, including *Water Spirit Bird* (bronze, 1980), *Abstract Orange* (painted steel, 1991), and a later work, *Untitled [for Keith]* (bronze, 1994). Situated not on a pedestal/base, but on the top of a mesa—which is a playful, but significant twist on a monumental scale—the pictured sculpture is sketchy, but clear and sharp and establishes a concentrated internal energy that launches the rocket/beak into space. As opposed to this propulsive, airborne quality, the archaic, totemic form in plate 57 appears anthropomorphic and ritualistic. It could be held in the hand—a dance rattle, for example—or it could be an abstract figure dancing. Rather than looking fabricated, it obviously has been carved, and although it is poised on a base, it is dynamic, as if wanting to be used, to be enacted. Although I know of no documentary evidence to suggest a direct correspondence, it seems reminiscent of the Kota reliquary figures that inspired Pablo Picasso and his followers.

Apaches Forever

In this final section I will address eleven drawings, some of which are related to one another in some respects, although the group in its entirety lacks unity in terms of style, chronology, or subject matter. If we

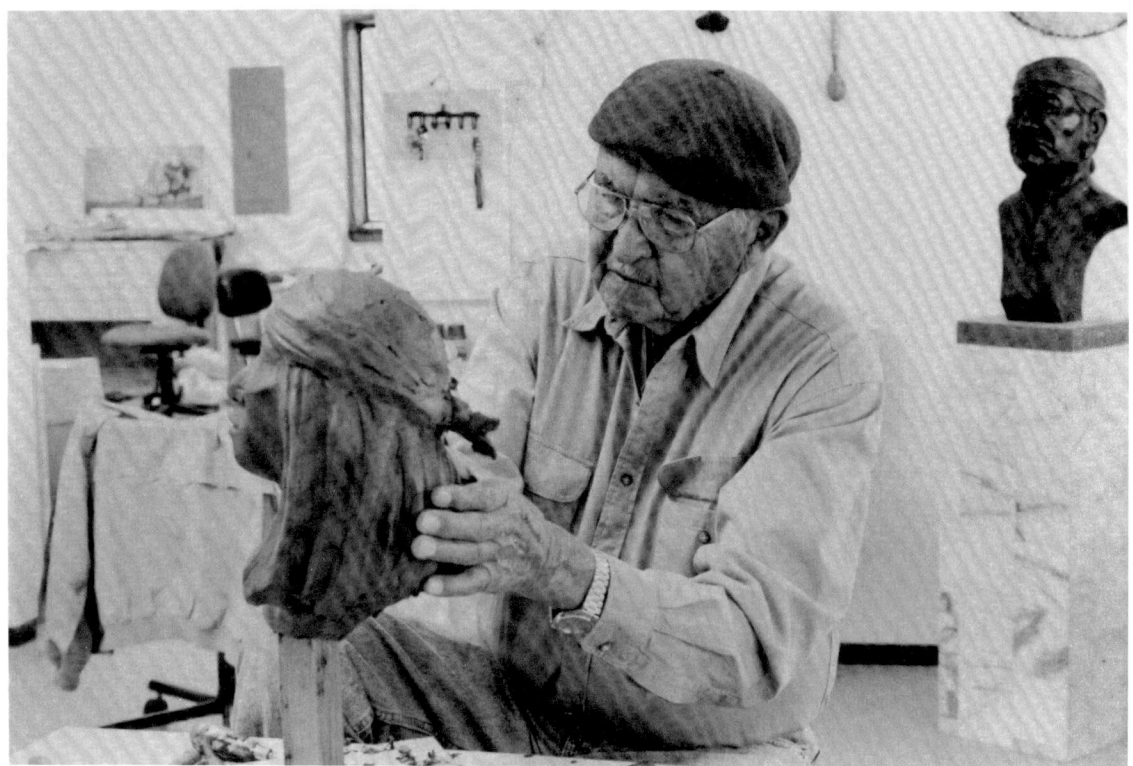

Lee Marmon (U.S., Laguna
Pueblo, 1925–)
Allan Houser, 1991
Silver gelatin print, 14 × 11 in.
Fred Jones Jr. Museum of Art,
copyright Allan Houser, Inc.
2013.016.012

consider them carefully, however, we can see how their variable *content* forms part of a central theme in Houser's art, which is the story of Apache conflict, struggle, and survival. Story was important for Houser and he was always candid about the inspiration he derived from his father's stories in particular. One of his recollections about Sam Haozous is especially poignant vis-à-vis the drawings in this section: "In the evenings we would sit around a big wood stove. He would sing, accompanying himself with an Apache drum, and my mother would join in. People would come from the Apache reservations in Arizona and New Mexico to hear the songs that they had forgotten, that had drifted down, like the stories, through the generations."[32]

This is how we best understand many of Houser's drawings, as visualizations of *stories that drifted down through the generations*. Indeed, storytelling itself was a compelling subject for him. He likely identified strongly with the young boy in *The Old Storyteller* (1961, plate 12), a pen-and-ink drawing published in Clark's *The Desert People*, who sits in front of a fire, captivated by the old man's narrative performance.

A pair of drawings, both dated circa 1992 and both titled *Bust of Geronimo* (plates 73 and 82),

is contextualized for us, once again, by Houser's memories of his father:

> He was a grandson of the Apache war chief Mangus-Colorado and a distant relative of Geronimo. My father was too young to fight in the Apache wars with the U.S. government, but he spent his youth with people who had been on the warpath. After Geronimo's defeat, the tribe was almost destroyed. The survivors lived under military rule in Fort Sill, Oklahoma, virtually prisoners of war. They were promised their own land, but even today many of their claims have not been honored. As I was growing up, my dad and others who had been through the war with Geronimo told stories of those years and of the captivity. My father knew Geronimo's war songs.[33]

In the first of these portraits, Geronimo is hatless and his shoulders and chest read as a mountainous form, out of which his head emerges. His weathered face is set in firm resolve and the linear details are subtle and realistic: the downturn at the corners of his mouth, the puffy skin around his eyes, the wisps of hair and his stubbly chin, and the pinpoint light of his pupils. In the second portrait we notice a delicate leaf pattern on his cap or scarf, the peak of which rises up like a landform. His mountainous visage is marked by furrowed brows and clenched teeth. In both portraits the mostly "unfinished" white space beneath Geronimo's neck heightens the tangibility of his facial features. The second drawing is not unrelated to Houser's bronze portrait bust *Geronimo* (1986), which he created in an edition of twelve busts to commemorate the hundredth anniversary of the surrender of the Chiricahua Apaches. He presented two of the busts, respectively, to the Fort Sill Apache Tribal Center in Apache, Oklahoma, and the National Portrait Gallery in Washington, D.C.

Given the violent military assault on and subsequent dislocation of the Apaches by the U.S. Army, it is not surprising that warfare and Apache warriors, such as Geronimo, would be a near constant subject of Houser's art. It was unusual, however, for him to represent sacred religious symbols in isolation from a narrative context. Three tempera studies, each titled *Geometric Design* (plates 19, 20, and 21), give us a rare glimpse of the artist working directly with traditional symbols. With the exception of a sketchbook page discussed below, the three design studies are virtually unique among the drawings extant in the Houser Foundation's collection. Their rarity, I believe, only enhances their significance. Tentatively dated circa 1965, they may have been studies for applied design, presented perhaps to Houser's students at the Institute of American Indian Arts in Santa Fe to demonstrate the possibilities inherent in recontextualized symbols. The truth is we do not really know how he intended them to function, but their origins are clear. According to Cécile Ganteaume, an Apache curator at the Smithsonian National Museum of the American Indian, the iconographies in these temperas derive from depictions of spiritual beings found on sacred objects. As Ganteaume observes, the Western Apaches refer to such objects as *ke'eschin*, which anthropologist Keith Basso translates as "symbol elements." These symbols are painted on deer hide by *diyin* or "holy men."[34]

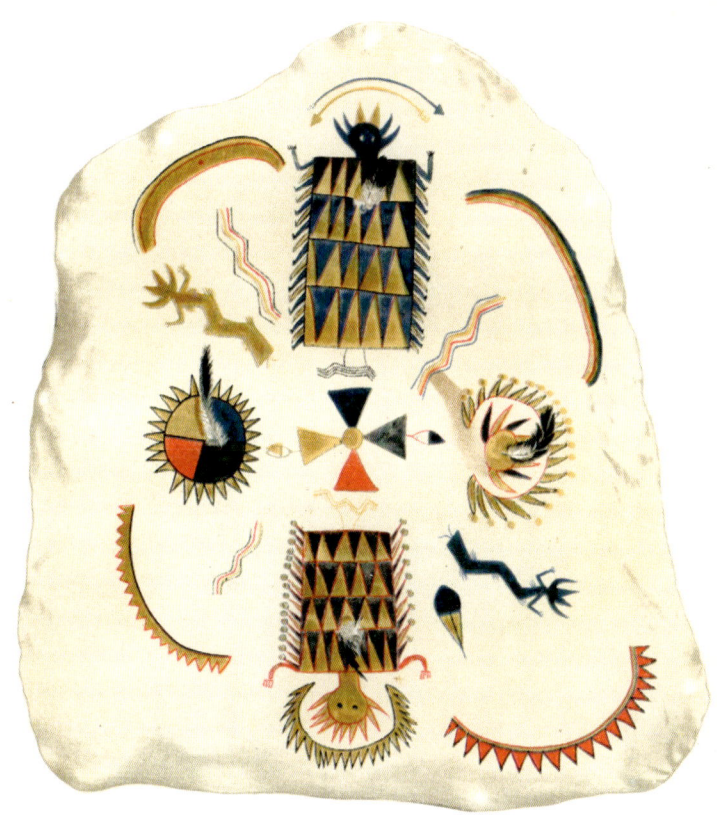

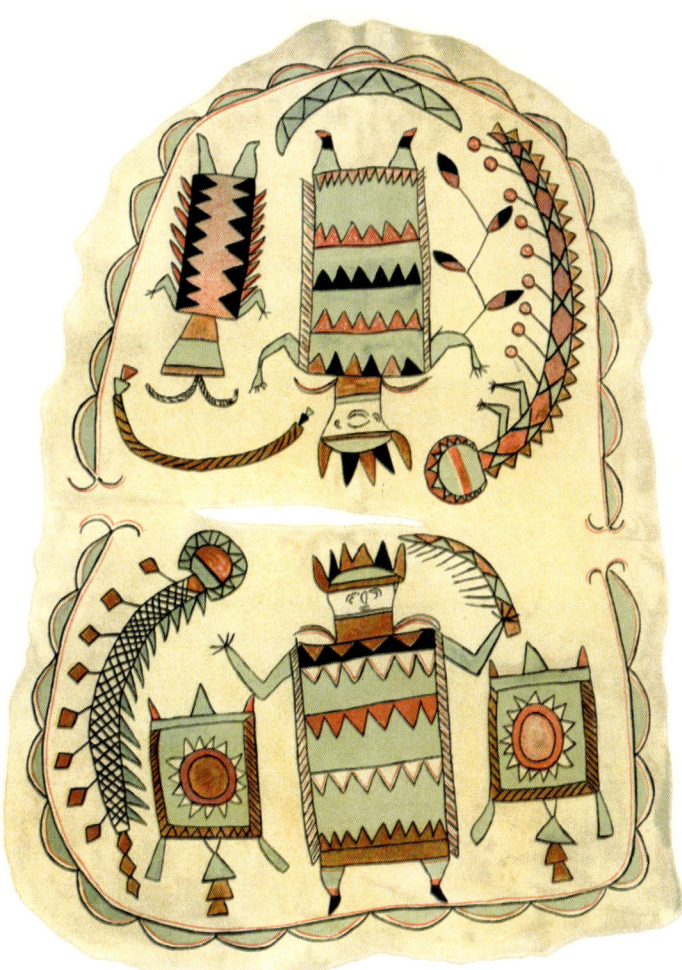

Apache Medicine Shirt, nineteenth century, pigment on hide. Illustrated in John G. Bourke, "Medicine Men of the Apache," in J. W. Powell, *Ninth Annual Report of the Bureau of American Ethnology to the Secretary of the Smithsonian Institution, 1887–1988*. Washington, D.C.: Government Printing Office, 1892, plate VI (*above*) and plate VII (*below*).

The symbolic elements in Houser's three temperas have remarkable correspondence to the iconography found on three Apache medicine shirts (see page 15), reproductions of which were published by John G. Bourke in his essay "Medicine Men of the Apache," in the *Ninth Annual Report of the Bureau of American Ethnology* in 1892.[35] Unfortunately, Bourke did not have much to report about these fascinating medicine shirts, except as follows: "The symbolism is different for each one, but may be generalized as typical of the sun, moon, stars, rainbow, lightning, snake, clouds, rain, hail, tarantula, centipede, snake, and some one or more of the 'kan' or gods."[36] A page from one of Houser's sketchbooks, which shows him "rehearsing" the images and making notes about the color (c. 1965, plate 24), bears an uncanny resemblance to the spirit being and associated symbols depicted in one of Bourke's illustrations. Similarly, Houser used designs like those published by Bourke on war shields that he depicted in an early tempera painting, *Apache Warriors* (1937), which Dunn, in turn, published in her landmark study of southwestern Indian painting.[37] The oral histories (and accompanying illustrations) collected from the Western Apaches by Grenville Goodwin and edited by Basso help us understand the link between the medicine imagery found on shields and charms, the iconography of the medicine shirts Bourke reproduced in his essay, and Houser's design studies.[38] I locate Houser's three studies of symbolic elements in this section to underscore the fact that Apache cultural survival was dependent not only on warriors and storytellers, but on the medicinal practices of holy men and the symbolic forms associated with their practice.

Warrior in a Blanket with a Rifle (c. 1992, plate 84) is the embodiment of vigilance. Columnar and stalwart, the verticality of his body is enlivened by the assertive diagonal of his rifle.[39] We see him in strong profile, on duty and alert to something heard on the wind. The face is carefully modeled to reveal his Athapaskan features, including full lips and high, round cheekbones. Other fine details include faint stripes on his blanket, the leather fringe of his rifle case, and his beaded necklace, decorated with

feathers and an amulet. The strength and dignity of this unconquered warrior are shared by the two imprisoned figures in *Two Apache Warriors in Chains* (1992, plate 66). They, too, are seen in profile, and even in "defeat" they sit upright, strong, healthy, and handsome, gazing calmly and without fear into an uncertain future. The classical calm of these two charcoal drawings is a counterpoint to the explosive visual energy of two pencil drawings from the mid-1960s: *Apache* (c. 1964, plate 16) and *Apaches Forever/ Free At Last* (c. 1964, plate 17). The graphic quality of the images, in tandem with the stencil-like captions— vigorous declarations of Apache sovereignty and self-determination—indicates Houser might have been thinking about comic books or a graphic novel. The first of these, *Apache*, is a dyadic communiqué featuring a pair of signifiers, one visual and one textual, which are mutually complimentary: for Houser, the core of Apacheness is symbolized best by the Mountain Spirit Dancer, who is an overt metonym for a dense cultural matrix of tradition, affirmation, and continuation. The left side (or "page") of *Apaches Forever/Free At Last* reiterates that message but intensifies it with the bold optimism encased in the word "forever." The right half of the drawing—with the words "free at last"—reminds us that Houser was himself "born free" after the Chiricahua Apaches were released following twenty-seven years in captivity at Fort Sill. And I expect it is reasonable to assume we may also be hearing in this drawing an echo of Martin Luther King's 1963 speech on the steps of the Lincoln Memorial in Washington, D.C., thus linking the emergent Red Power Movement to the wider Civil Rights Movement. But freedom, of course, is a journey that never ends, as witnessed by the fact that as I write this essay in August 2013, almost one hundred years after Houser's birth, four Apache tribes are engaged in a protracted negotiation with the American Museum of Natural History in New York City over the repatriation of sacred objects.[40] Houser, it must be said, was not a political activist, but this centennial survey of his inimitable drawings makes clear that he was a dedicated and determined cultural and artistic warrior.

Picturing Home

Allan Houser's Children's Book Illustrations 1952–1962

Hadley Jerman

Between 1952 and 1962, world-renowned Chiricahua Apache artist Allan Houser illustrated seven children's books. Published during the eleven years Houser spent teaching at the Intermountain Indian School in Brigham City, Utah, the books range from picture-driven stories for young readers to intermittently illustrated novels and biographies for adolescents. All feature narratives centered on Native American protagonists, were published by mainstream East Coast publishing houses,[1] and occupy a decade in Houser's art production bound on one end by two-dimensional murals and paintings and, on the other, by three-dimensional sculptures.

Houser's illustrations, especially those published in Edgar Wyatt's *Geronimo, the Last Apache War Chief* (Whittlesey House, 1952) and *Cochise, Apache Warrior and Statesman* (McGraw-Hill, 1953), reflect the artist's own family and tribal history and, in particular, stories he heard from his father, Sam Haozous, while growing up in southwestern Oklahoma.[2] W. Jackson Rushing III describes Houser's oeuvre as "a body of work predicated on the idea of telling true stories."[3] In the case of his book illustrations, the "true stories" involved Mangas Coloradas, Houser's great-grandfather, and Geronimo, the artist's distant relative. Houser recalled, "My dad used to tell stories nightly and sing songs . . . I remember this and a lot of this comes out in my sculpture and painting."[4]

The act of storytelling forms the subject of two closely related illustrations published in Ann Nolan Clark's novel *The Desert People* (Viking, 1962). In both the drawing *The Old Storyteller* and tempera painting *Family around Fire Pit,* which appears on the following spread in Clark's book, a young Tohono O'odham boy sits in rapt attention as an elder weaves a story across the fire-lit room (plate 12).[5] The storyteller raises his right hand in the drawing; his words seem almost visible, mingling with the smoke that drifts up from the fire. Houser delineated the floor in light short strokes radiating outward from the firelight and inked large shadows, cast legend-like, behind the three figures circling the fire. Sam Haozous's stories of traveling as a youth with Geronimo were, for Houser, "the stories that fired a young boy's imagination."[6] In this quasi-autobiographical drawing of three generations, we see a Tohono O'odham boy's imagination being fired, but perhaps Houser's as well. The young boy stands in for Houser; the shadowy figures on the wall serve as symbols for the larger-than-life Mangas Coloradas and Geronimo of his imagination.

In addition to reflecting Houser's Chiricahua and family history, the illustrations also reveal—as Rushing has made clear—the artist's abiding interest in American western art.[7] When Houser arrived at The Studio at the Santa Fe Indian School in 1934, he expressed an interest in creating realistic, action-driven works in the vein of popular American western artists Charles M. Russell and Frederic Remington. However, Dorothy Dunn, the Studio's instructor, deemed such material inappropriate for her Native students.[8] She later criticized Houser in 1968 for his

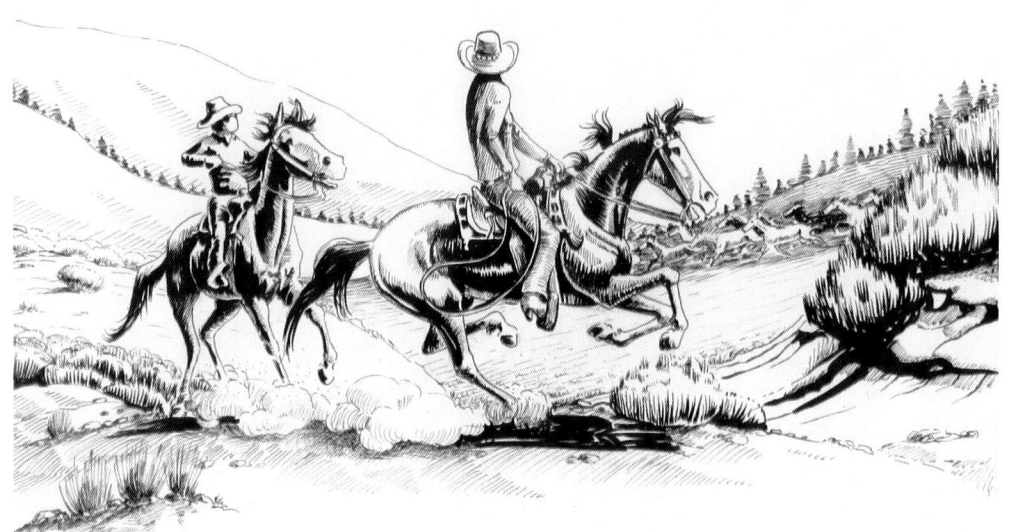

Allan Houser (U.S., Chiricahua
Apache, 1914–1994)
Two Men Herding Horses, 1961,
published in Ann Nolan Clark,
The Desert People (1962)
Pen and ink, 15 × 12 ⁵⁄₁₆ in.
The Allan Houser Foundation
HF1995.1-608.I

"illustrative" images "in the manner of celebrated earlier painters of the Old West."[9] Dunn's comment may as well have been directed at Houser's pen vignettes published a decade earlier in Wyatt's *Geronimo* and *Cochise.* The drawings burst with Russell-esque energy—horses gallop and buildings burn amid neatly rendered southwestern landscapes. Houser's interest in depicting "true stories" and his admiration for the action-driven narrative style of western American art, particularly in the works of Remington and Russell, seem especially evident in his action scenes of Tohono O'odham cowboys riding, roping, and pursuing mustangs in Clark's *The Desert People.*

Houser's enthusiasm for depicting horses in motion is also evident in Clark's *Blue Canyon Horse* (Viking, 1954), where ten illustrations feature galloping horses (plate 6). Houser seems to prefer creating scenes of horses in motion, and their fast gait also reflects the concept of freedom or wildness conveyed in Clark's text: "Then the wild urge like the sting of the whiplash flicks [the mare]. Her nostrils flare. She whirls, turning from the known world to answer the call of the wild unknown."[10] The titular mare and her colt exchange freedom on the canyon's rim for safety and stillness on the canyon floor, under the protection of a young boy. Houser indicates their loss of freedom by rendering the mare and her foal motionless—they stand or graze, confined within the towering canyon walls. (We can hardly read this narrative today without seeing reflections of, in the

words of two prominent scholars, "assimilationist messages stressing . . . submission to federal authority."[11])

Although Dunn may have dismissed Houser's mid-century book illustrations of galloping horses and famed Apache leaders for their realistic depiction of narrative action, she was instrumental during the 1930s and 1940s in selecting Native artists—many of whom were her former students at the Santa Fe Studio—as illustrators for government-published bilingual "Indian Life Readers."[12] Houser's commissions differed in that they were reproduced by mainstream publishers for a general audience and reflect their authors' intent to educate non-Native readers and increase empathy for indigenous peoples, rather than increase literacy rates among Native children. As such, the seven picture and chapter books Houser illustrated between 1952 and 1962 reflect multiple voices: Native and non-Native authors, large publishing houses, editorial staff members, and one Chiricahua artist.

Given these multiple voices, how do Houser's illustrations speak; and what might they mean? How much freedom or control did he exercise during the production process? What is the significance of landscape, an element Houser included, even emphasized, throughout his book illustrations? I first address these questions by investigating Houser's children's book illustrations in the context of his career, paying particular attention to his involvement in the publication process, and then through an analysis of his depiction of landscape in his book illustrations.

Picturing Houser's Book Illustrations at Mid-Century

Seven of the eight children's books that Houser illustrated during the course of his lifetime were published during the eleven years he spent teaching and raising his family at Intermountain Indian School.[13] Although he was already a well-known Apache artist, having achieved success as both a mural painter and sculptor, Houser's familial relationship to Geronimo seems in part responsible for his being selected as the illustrator for his first children's book commission of the 1950s, Wyatt's *Geronimo* (1952). The words "Illustrated by Allan Houser Direct Descendent of Geronimo" appear prominently beneath the author's name on the dust jacket and title page, although Houser was likely Geronimo's second cousin once removed, not a direct descendent. A year later, Houser was recognized as "the distinguished Apache artist" on the title page of Wyatt's *Cochise, Apache Warrior and Statesman,* published by McGraw-Hill in 1953.[14]

Stylistically, Houser's book illustrations of the 1950s and early 1960s reflect the artist's growing interest in sculpture through increasingly modeled forms. Illustrations published in *Geronimo* and *Cochise* (1953) and for Salish Kootenai author D'Arcy McNickle's *Runner in the Sun* (John C. Winston, 1954) consist of simple line drawings of—at times cartoonish—figures in landscape. Afforded little space

in *Geronimo* and *Runner in the Sun*, Houser created small vignettes that accompany the chapter headings or appear wedged between lines of text.

Houser's drawings for *Cochise* contain more accomplished figure renditions than those published in *Geronimo* a year earlier, perhaps due in part to the larger amounts of space afforded them (plates 4 and 5). These line drawings often fill entire pages, and at times span double-page spreads. While given more space in *Cochise,* Houser's extant original ink drawings reveal McGraw-Hill's heavy edits when compared to the drawings published in the book. Not only were Houser's double-page illustrations divided in two with wide margins between them (thus, not true double-trucks), but in some cases only half of the original drawing was published.[15] Most interestingly (or politically), McGraw-Hill excised several of Houser's images depicting Apache warriors engaged in violence. The publisher chose not to publish *Battle Scene,* which features Apache warriors firing on soldiers (and vice versa) and *Apache Warriors Dragging Off Body,* an illustration of warriors galloping away from a fort and dragging a soldier by the neck.[16]

Houser's line drawings for Don Wilcox's *Joe Sunpool,* published by Little, Brown and Company in 1956, like those for *Cochise,* reflect more volumetric forms and accomplished figure drawing. His selection for the commission may have related to his own career success—his fame as a burgeoning sculptor even

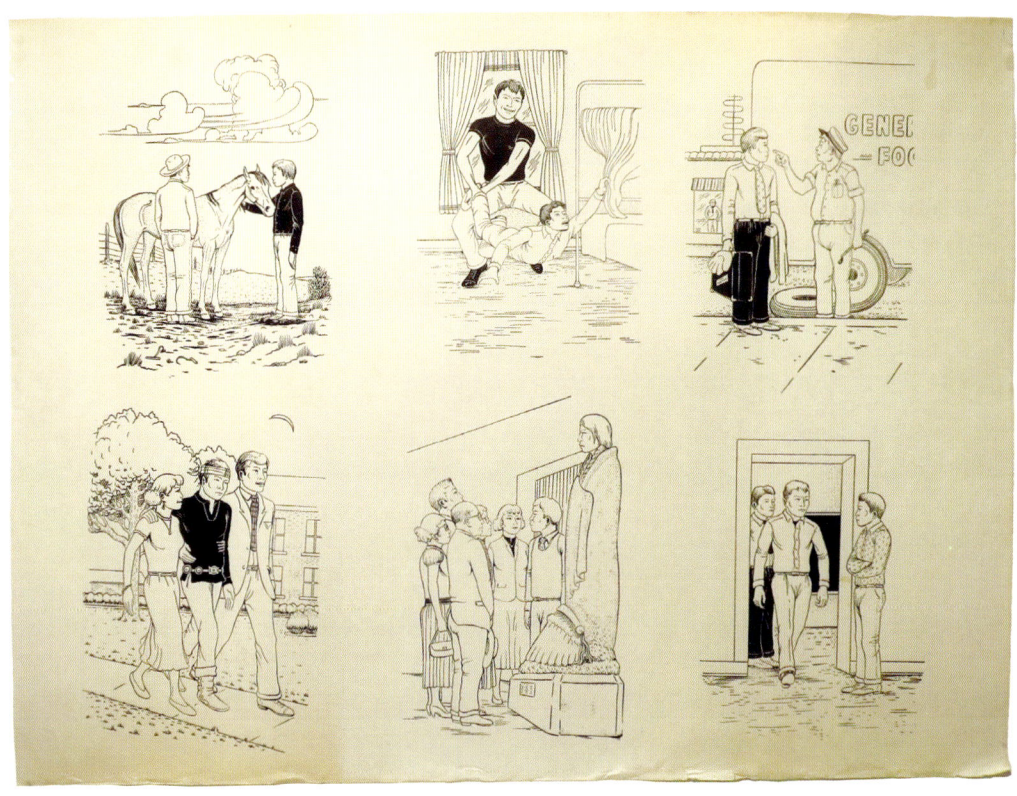

Allan Houser (U.S., Chiricahua Apache, 1914–1994)
Galley proof showing *Comrade in Mourning* (bottom center) published in Don Wilcox, *Joe Sunpool* (1956).
Allan Houser Foundation
HF1995.1-699E.PE

figured into the novel's plot. In one line drawing, Houser depicts the Navajo titular character and his friends viewing Houser's own monumental stone sculpture, *Comrade in Mourning* (1948), at Haskell Institute in Lawrence, Kansas.

Houser's first picture book commission of the decade came in 1954, with Ann Nolan Clark's *Blue Canyon Horse*.[17] Clark, an Indian Day School teacher, was already a prolific author of the Indian Life Readers in collaboration with Willard Beatty. Her relationship with Viking Press began in 1941 when Beatty persuaded the company to publish *In My Mother's House*, which featured Clark's rhythmic prose about Pueblo life and illustrations by Zuni artist Velino Herrera.[18]

In *Blue Canyon Horse,* Houser's double-spread tempera paintings alternate with black India ink drawings printed in sepia. He achieves perspective and the illusion of space through the juxtaposition of thin color washes that suggest distant canyon walls against blocks of opaque orange tempera in the foreground. Houser also submitted an end-page design featuring a Navajo ruglike pattern of stylized orange galloping horses and stepped mountain forms. He scrawled "This is my choice" in the margin; the design appears printed in negative on the end pages.[19] The mare (Clark's protagonist, in a sense) stands on the edge of the canyon, her mane and tail flowing in the wind, in a painting Houser clearly intended for the cover. It bears the notation "Jacket Design" and is the only signed and dated image Houser created for *Blue Canyon Horse*.[20] However, the image was never published, replaced with a painting of the boy and foal peering at each other from either side of the mare. The change in cover image reminds us that while Houser's input was valued, even his picture book illustrations were subject to client and editorial opinion.

Houser's investment in the illustration process for *Blue Canyon Horse* is evidenced by his numerous pentimenti, which indicate careful drawing, and by the large scale and detail of his original illustrations. Houser's original paintings reproduced on double-page spreads in the book are remarkably large—often 18 × 28 inches, and his ink drawings printed on single pages in the published book fill 18 × 12–inch sheets. Pencil marks indicate crop marks and text boxes, page numbers scrawled in blue note the illustrations' placement in the book, and damage from tape residue hints at the paste-up process, reminding us that these finely rendered paintings and drawings served for the publisher as a means to an end. This is not to suggest

that Viking undervalued Houser's work. The publishing house returned his original drawings, and the mailing label for the package demonstrates the economic value Viking ascribed to Houser's work. The label refers to a painting reproduced as a double-truck on pages 10 and 11 of *Blue Canyon Horse* and bears the inscription "Please insure for $200."[21] That Viking may have insured Houser's spread for $200 is significant considering that David Rettig, curator at the Houser Foundation, estimates during the 1950s Houser earned a net of approximately $50 or $60 for paintings sold in galleries.[22]

In 1958, Houser was commissioned to create the fifty-ninth medal for the American Society of Medalists. With their emphasis on contrasting light and dark surfaces, his black-and-white ink drawings for Elizabeth Coatsworth's *The Cave*, published by Viking the same year, mark a departure from his earlier book illustrations. Houser's 1958 drawings build on his work in *Blue Canyon Horse*, but more closely relate to his relief designs for *Apache Buffalo Hunt* and *Apache Fire Dancer,* cast on opposite sides of the medal. On the medal, the figures' protruding surfaces reflect light and stand out against the shadowed background; light and shadow rather than outline delineate the galloping bison, hunter, and dancer. Flowing incised lines beneath the bison hunter create a pattern of light and dark ridges similar in appearance to a woodblock print. Houser's use of texture and shadow rather than outlines alone to define modeled forms, and his juxtaposition of brighter (light-reflecting) figures against darker, solid backgrounds similarly characterize his drawings for *The Cave*, lending the illustrations a sculptured, etching-like appearance (plate 8). Illustrations of Jim, the Navajo protagonist, and of sheep prefigure not only the subject matter but also the modeled surfaces and curvaceous lines that would appear in Houser's abstract sculptural forms in the following decades.

Of all the books Houser illustrated, *The Cave* shows the greatest degree of aesthetic control by the artist. Extant correspondence from Viking and Houser's notes in the margins of his drawings reveal his creative freedom and active input in the production process. In a letter accompanying galleys for the book, the publisher's May Massee wrote, "We hope you'll illustrate [*The Cave*]" and "mark the places where you'd like to make drawings . . . and . . . whether you want the drawings to fill the page or half page."[23] In addition to choosing which aspects of the story *he wanted* to illustrate and emphasize through scale, Houser also designed a jacket image and endpapers for *The Cave*, as he had for *Blue Canyon Horse*. In a letter dated May 9, 1958, Viking's Morris Colman requested that Houser suggest a color for the binding beneath the dust jacket and create an image to be embossed on the cloth binding.[24] Houser responded with a drawing of Jim walking with his ewe and lamb in front of a distant butte. Houser wrote in the left margin, "I hope sketch is not to [sic] detailed if so I will gladly make another."[25] At top left, he painted an orange swatch and labeled it, "my choice for binding color." After Colman indicated Houser's image for the embossment was too detailed to make a die from, Houser created a second, blockier version. However, Viking still made use of the original image; it appears printed in sepia on the back of the dust jacket.[26] Houser's significant input into the *The Cave*'s production is perhaps most evidenced by the fact that he, rather than a production artist, painted the three-color separations on celluloid that together form the vibrant melon, orange, and purple image of Jim, lamb, and cave printed on the book jacket.

Houser created etching-like ink drawings, similar to those he developed in *The Cave*, with the addition of full-color paintings, for his final children's book commission, Clark's *The Desert People*, published by Viking in 1962 (plates 12–15). Houser's illustrations accompany and follow Clark's quiet prose, depicting changing seasons of village life for Tohono O'odham people of southeastern Arizona. Houser's paint colors—blue, orange, green, mauve, and brown—are finely matched by the four overprinted inks that appear in the book. These are richly hued, ornate paintings. Not only are the colors dramatic, but, according to Nelson Foss, late curator of the Allan Houser Foundation, they reflect Houser's deliberate move away from "the rather confining style" of Dunn's Santa Fe Indian School Studio and thus from the "flatter, more subdued pastels Dunn preferred."[27]

Houser's paintings for *The Desert People* are elaborate and indicative of his displeasure with the Studio style, but his ink drawings on wove paper and illustration board are also characteristically large, replete with detail and modeled forms, and carefully rendered despite their eventual significant reduction of size in the book (see, for instance, plate 15). Houser's 8 × 14–inch black ink drawings lost detail and crispness when they were reproduced in sepia and reduced at under 3 × ½ inches in the book's upper margins. And yet Houser's small—if 8 × 14 inches can be termed small—drawings, full of pentimenti and extraordinary detail, indicate no less effort on the

artist's part than is evident in other, larger illustrations in the book.[28]

In addition to his large, detail-filled drawings for *The Desert People*, Houser submitted supplemental illustrations, at least one of which was published in the text. In the margin of a large 13 × 20–inch pen-and-ink drawing of a boy donning cowboy hat, jeans, and boots, standing beside his horse saddled in western tack, Houser wrote, "This could be boys [sic] older brother if you can use it."[29] Viking did, in fact, publish the drawing, much reduced in size, on page 16, above Clark's text, although the image does not really reflect the accompanying description.

Perhaps most impressive of all his children's book illustrations in terms of time and energy invested, and most stylistically distant from Dunn's Studio style, Houser's illustrations for *The Desert People* would also

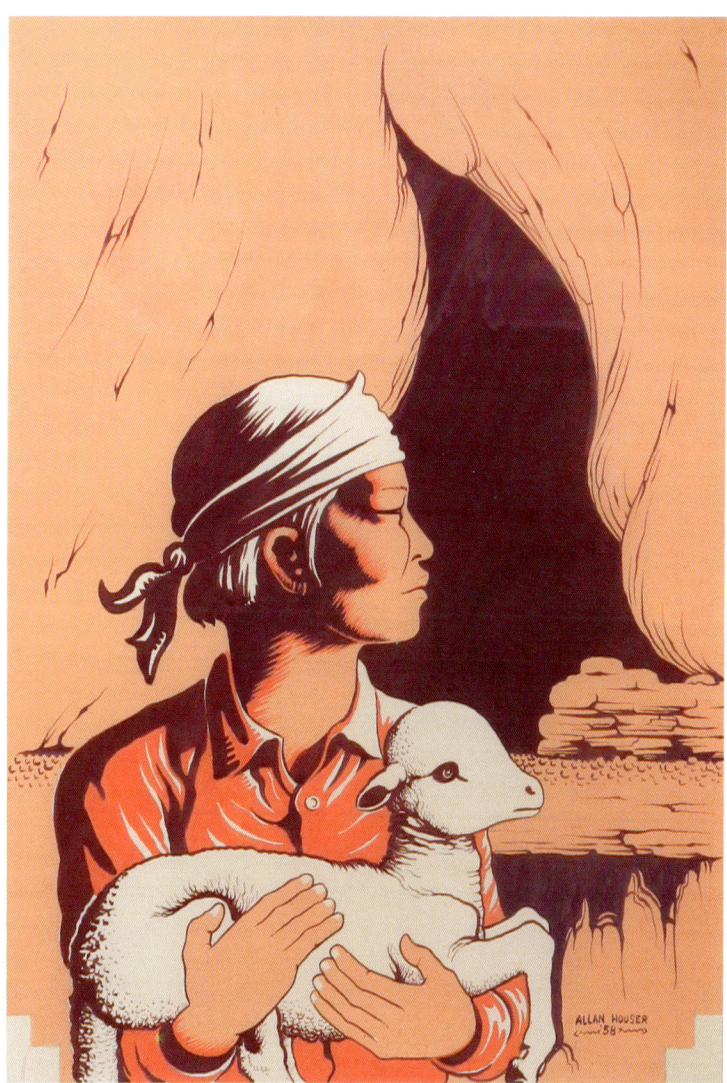

Allan Houser (U.S., Chiricahua Apache, 1914–1994)
Cover art for Elizabeth Coatsworth's *The Cave* (1958)
Tempera, 9 ¼ × 6 ½ in.
The Allan Houser Foundation
HF1995.1-699.BJ

be his last. In 1962, the same year that Viking published *The Desert People*, Houser left Utah—and book illustration—permanently, when he was appointed as the first painting and sculpture instructor at Santa Fe's newly minted Institute of American Indian Arts (IAIA), which replaced the Santa Fe Indian School, where he had studied some thirty years earlier.

That Houser's mid-century book illustrations increasingly suggest three-dimensional sculptural form should come as no surprise; in a later interview Houser acknowledged that as early as the late 1930s, while studying at the Santa Fe Indian School, he wanted to break free from two-dimensional "Indian art" and to create three-dimensional form. Houser took issue with Dunn's limiting view of what constituted Native art. "They call it the Santa Fe Indian School style, flat," he said. "[W]hen you weren't doing that, it wasn't Indian art. That bothered me."[30] His dismay upon learning he would not be taught life drawing or anatomy, or be encouraged to paint in a realistic manner, seems, in part, due to his association of the western artist-illustrators he revered with the "true stories" he hoped to portray.[31] Houser's book illustrations were not only a means for him to step away from the Studio style through color, modeling, and perspective,[32] but also a canvas for him to explore the "truth-telling" realism and action-oriented subject matter inherent in late-nineteenth and early-twentieth-century art of the American West. However, I would argue that when viewed as a whole, it is not galloping horses, famed Apache leaders, or even dramatic narrative that dominate Houser's children's book illustrations. In direct opposition to the backgroundless and "flat" Santa Fe Indian School style, Houser's stage coaches, wild horses, and galloping riders in *Geronimo, Cochise, Blue Canyon Horse, The Cave*, and *The Desert People* travel through complex environments populated by a host of rocks and plants.[33] He eschewed the Studio's preoccupation with flat figures devoid of background, time, and place for realistic depictions of individuals occupying completely rendered natural environments. In fact, Houser's book illustrations at mid-century often seem to be exuberantly *about* landscapes. Furthermore, in *Geronimo, Cochise, Blue Canyon Horse, The Cave*, and *The Desert People* in particular, Houser's drawings and paintings of realistic, memorable landscapes do not merely illustrate the texts they accompany; they visually reinforce concepts of memory, home, and identity, ultimately creating more complicated narratives than what is literally present in the text.

Picturing Landscape and Narrative

Houser's depictions of landforms in book illustrations function in several ways. For *Blue Canyon Horse, The Cave*, and *The Desert People* in particular, Houser drew and painted realistic, memorable landscapes that assume symbolic, metaphorical qualities. In *Geronimo, Cochise*, and *The Desert People*, landscapes primarily serve as a stage for action but also suggest concepts of home and identity. In *Blue Canyon Horse* and *Runner in the Sun,* Houser's repetition of natural forms helps create a familiar place, often a home that protagonists must leave or to which they must return. Anthropomorphized landscapes in *Blue Canyon Horse* and *The Cave* dwarf the characters that pass through them and create psychologically charged places.

Houser's keen interest in landscape in his children's book illustrations is evident in his repetition of specific desert plants and rock formations, his filling the page with landforms rather than focusing only on the action described in the text, and in his depiction of actual places, whether or not specific locations are named in the text. In *Geronimo*, Houser established a canon of landscape elements that would appear throughout his subsequent book illustrations. Here, twisting Juniper trees, fanlike sprays of desert grasses, shafts of yucca, and sandstone rock formations that seem to melt into the landscape make their first appearance.[34] Perhaps Houser repeated these same forms again and again in drawings and paintings for successive books because it was time-effective to do so. However, he was under no obligation to render such complicated scenery in illustrations like A *Knife Flashed and Another Miner Vanished,* one of the few illustrations McGraw-Hill published of Houser's images depicting Apaches engaged in violence.[35] Wyatt's narrative simply states, "If one [miner] wandered into the hills, a brown body dived from a high boulder and crashed upon his back. An Apache knife flashed, and another miner vanished."[36] Houser, while including the elements Wyatt describes—a miner surprise-attacked by a leaping Apache—also inserted a host of plants and rocks, and a rifle grasped clublike in the miner's hands, suggesting the doomed miner is not an innocent or helpless victim of Apache aggression. More pertinent to our discussion of landscape is that Houser refrained from downplaying environment for the sake of action. He could have isolated the two combatants against space in a manner akin to Studio-style murals; he could have created the suggestion of landscape without making it integral to the image. But he did neither. Landscape elements appear both as background and foreground to the action and reinforce the danger at hand. The spiny aloe or yucca beneath the miner directs its dagger-like leaves upward, mimicking the form of the Apache's knife. Two yucca in the middle-left distance lean at odd angles with leaves straight up; they assume the appearance of shocked or anxious bystanders. The humanlike form of a hoodoo in the background towers above the conflict, serving as silent witness to violence in the desert.

Houser also anthropomorphized hoodoos throughout the *Cochise* illustrations he made the following year. In *Cochise*, landscapes again serve as a stage for action while reinforcing the narrative at hand; at times they even serve a narrative function in their own right. In *Warriors Carrying Fallen Comrade*, hoodoos act as witnesses and mimic the human forms of the exhausted and grieving Apache band that travels through them (plate 4). The drawing depicts Chiricahuas transporting a deceased Cochise to his burial site, described in Wyatt's text as "a deep chasm in the rocks."[37] In emphasizing humanlike forms of hoodoos, and visually placing them among the funeral procession, Houser's drawing suggests that the rocks and hills mourn alongside Cochise's people.

While hoodoos, through Houser's pen, become people-like, the plant forms in *Cochise* generally reinforce or visually repeat the narrative at hand, much like his illustration of the Apache-miner conflict in *Geronimo*. A peculiarly placed juniper tree in the foreground resembles the flames barely visible licking the background home of a deceased warrior in *Warrior in Foreground, Mother and Child Fleeing Burning Dwelling* (plate 5). The juniper tree and desert grasses dotting the ground grow diagonally up from left to right, repeating the angle of the distant flames.

Not only did Houser fill his landscape illustrations with anthropomorphized (empathetic) rock formations and vegetation, but he rendered specific desert plants and places. This attention to accurate representation evokes the preoccupation of western art with accuracy while serving the practical function of educating mainstream American audiences about the desert Southwest. (Similarly, Edgar Wyatt sought to educate his readers about Apache history and culture; he went so far as to include a "Guide to Pronunciation of Indian Names" in *Geronimo* and a "Guide to Indian and Spanish Words" at the end of *Cochise*.)

Given that Houser filled 239 sketchbooks with drawings, many of them landscape studies, over the course of his career, it seems no surprise that landscape formed some of the most sophisticated,

realistic, and even at times character-like elements of his illustrations.[38] In his double-page illustrations for *Cochise*, Houser's landscapes are rendered with as much—if not more—detail and specificity as the figures that race through them. An illustration of a stagecoach hurrying across the desert bears the caption "Drivers crossed this stretch with all speed" and contains no less than nine identifiable desert plants. A pair of soaptree yucca leans into the composition at lower left, balanced by a barrel cactus leaning in from lower right. A wild-armed cholla cactus waggles its limbs at center, and beyond the stage expansive saguaro raise their arms alongside what appears to be juniper and distant ocotillo. In contrast to Houser's visual catalogue of desert succulents, Wyatt's text makes no mention of the landscape or vegetation, focusing instead on the potential threat of Apache attack: "Butterfield drivers crossed this stretch of desert with all the speed they could. There was danger here from the roving bands of many Apache tribes."[39] Ironically, Houser includes no suggestion of Apaches or danger in the scene, save for a man perched atop the stagecoach, "riding shotgun." Instead, Houser anthropomorphizes the desert vegetation. The two yucca in the foreground huddle together, inclining their blossoms as if whispering about the quickly passing stage. We recognize them as plants, yet Houser makes us feel as if we are behind them, peering over the yucca's shoulders. In contrast, a saguaro cactus on the right edge of the composition in the distance definitely faces toward the stage and, effectively, toward the viewer, with one arm lifted across its body. The viewer cannot help but read this gesture as one of hand to lips, as if the succulent is surprised (or aghast!) at the intruding Butterfield stage and its armed guardian. Eight other distant saguaros pose with "hands up"—imbuing Houser's landscape with humor as well as irony. While the image lacks the suggestion of "danger" due to many "roving bands" of Apaches, its cast of succulents appears deeply concerned over the intrusion of the stagecoach, its shotgun-bearing drivers, and passengers inside.

Even as Houser depicted specific types of plants in his children's book illustrations, he also imbued landscape with a symbolic quality. This is evident in the anthropomorphic forms of hoodoos, saguaro, and yucca in his *Cochise* illustrations, but the symbolism works even more powerfully in his closing illustration for *Geronimo*, drawn a year earlier. An image of the Apache leader seated on a rock, with hands on his knees, bears the caption, "Geronimo sat in the sun and dreamed of his great battles."[40] At this point in Wyatt's

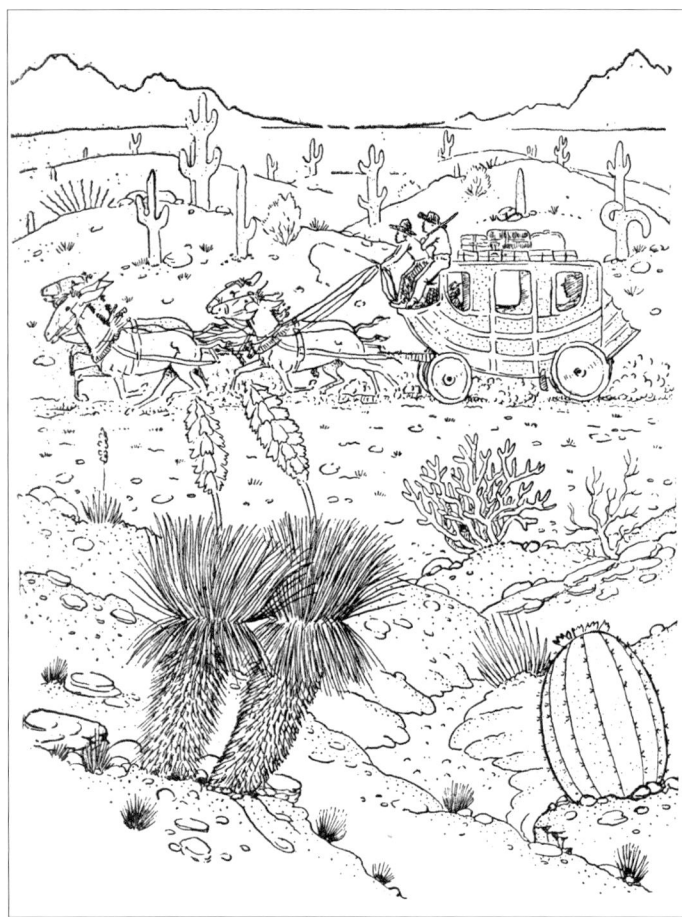

"Drivers crossed this stretch with all speed." From Edgar Wyatt, *Cochise: Apache Warrior and Statesman* (New York: McGraw-Hill Education, 1953), p. 7

narrative, the year is 1894 and Geronimo is sixty-six years old, imprisoned with his people at Fort Sill, Oklahoma. The Apaches would be incarcerated there until 1913–14, four years after Geronimo's death. In Houser's illustration, Geronimo sits on a layered sandstone rock, a small juniper bush behind him. To his left, nine spindly ocotillo arms poke out from behind a rock, and the clumps of desert grasses that populate Houser's paintings and illustrations grow in tufts at his feet. This is one of the sparest illustrations in the book. No clouds scud across the sky, no mountains or hoodoos rise up behind the Apache leader. The plants are small, diminutive, growing. But they are not Oklahoma plants. And Houser, having grown up in arid southwestern Oklahoma, would have known the difference. Houser surrounds the aging Geronimo with the landscape of southern Arizona and New Mexico—the same landscape that surrounds his protagonist throughout the book. No shadowy images of warfare or the "great battles" mentioned in the text encircle him. Rather, the landscape is the sole reference to Geronimo's past. It serves as Geronimo's

memory: "[He] dreamed of his great battles." By surrounding Geronimo with the landscape of his past, Houser suggests that the leader's sense of self is not defined by battles won or lost, but by the land itself. Concerning the stories of Geronimo he grew up hearing from his father, Houser said, "Those memories stayed within my mind through the years and . . . I began to be very interested in who I was."[41] Who Houser was, who Geronimo was, and who the Apaches were, in Houser's depiction, is directly tied to the desert. In the words of Houser's son, the federal government "separated us from the most essential thing to being Apache—our land."[42] This overt connection between landscape and Native identity persists throughout Houser's illustrations published in subsequent children's books.

Picturing Home: Identity and Specific Places

If Houser's landscapes in *Geronimo* and *Cochise* signified the Apaches' homeland, and by extension their identity, in Ann Nolan Clark's picture book *Blue Canyon Horse*, published in 1954, Houser created an even more specific home place using the same canon of rocks, trees, and grasses. In this story of a mare who leaves her young owner and canyon home for the freedom of life with a mustang herd, eventually returning with her foal, repeated forms not only indicate the same *kind* of bush and rock, but *the same* bush and rock. Houser depicts a wizened juniper tree from different angles as the mare climbs, gazes down into, and descends the canyon ledge; the tree orients the reader to the landscape and acts as a signpost. When we see the red-barked tree tenaciously clinging to the ridge, we know with the boy and his mare that they are nearly home.

Just as Houser uses a juniper tree to familiarize readers with the canyon, his rendering of vegetation on the canyon floor gradually invites readers farther into the boy's home. Clark opens the book in her characteristically rhythmic prose: "In lush green fields beside blue water a little mare is feeding, swishing her tail in calm delight and feeding."[43] Houser's accompanying four-color painting depicts the mare reaching for a tuft of grass near a calm stream. Transparent lavender tints suggest the ghostly forms of canyon walls at night, barely visible. A row of distant trees are rendered a bright apple green. Not until eight spreads later does Houser reveal that this row of trees is the boy's orchard; beneath them, stalks of corn grow. Several spreads later, Houser provides a bird's eye view of the canyon floor. The shadow-streaked canyon walls

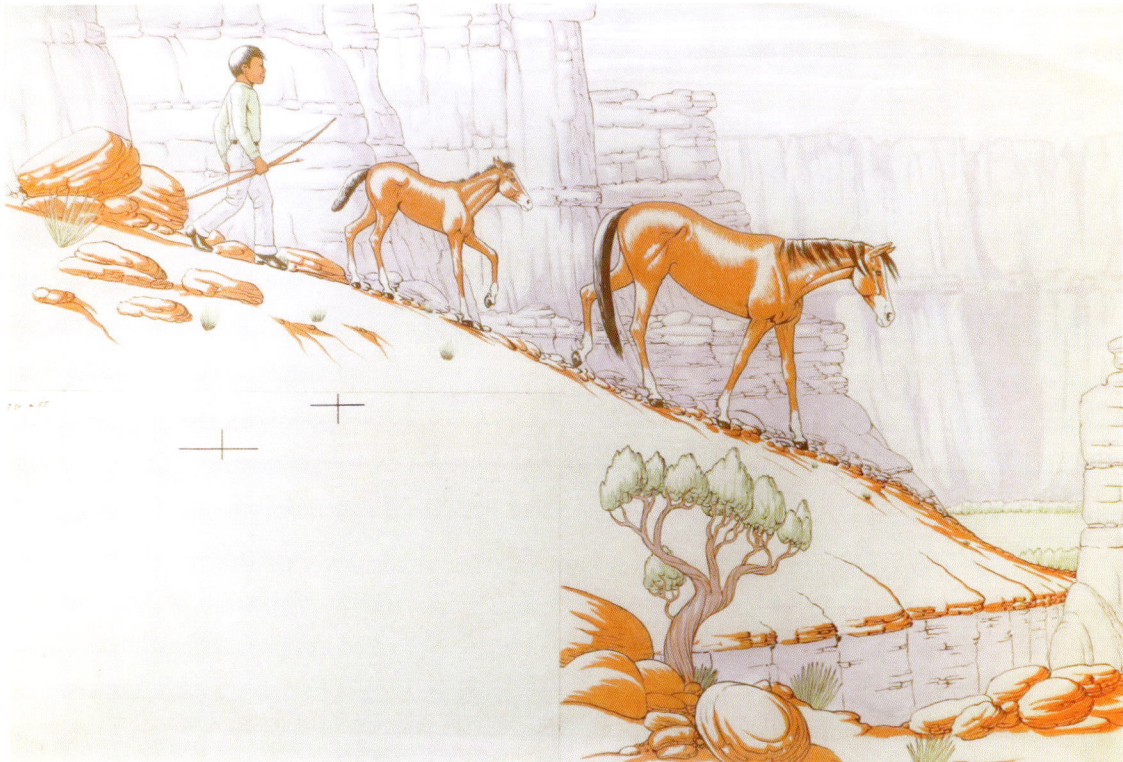

Allan Houser (U.S., Chiricahua
Apache, 1914–1994)
Mare, boy, and foal descending past
juniper tree. Illustration for Ann Nolan
Clark, *Blue Canyon Horse* (1954).
Tempera, 18 × 25 in.
The Allan Houser Foundation
HF1995.1-650-I

loom above rows of corn, trees, dirt road and barbed-wire fence, and house with wisp of smoke lazily spiraling up toward the rim. Houser provides a more specific, more intimate picture of the boy's home than the adjacent text, "On the floor of the canyon the corn is harvested. The cactus fruit is cut. The pinon nuts are gathered. The storerooms of the People are full of food for the winter."[44] After an additional eight spreads, Houser provides the reader a glimpse inside the boy's house as he sleeps, his bridle, boots, and lariat resting on the floor in anticipation of his mare's return. This gradual narrowing of focus familiarizes the reader with the boy's home landscape as a real place, a recognizable place. By the time the mare returns with her foal at the story's close, readers understand what the canyon looks and feels like; for readers, as well as for the mare, the familiar vegetation provides a sort of homecoming.

In *Blue Canyon Horse*, Houser depicted not only a realistic place but a real place. For Houser and those who recognize its steep red walls, narrow spaces, and fertile floor, this is Canyon de Chelly, sacred home to the Navajo people.[45] Clark never names the canyon in the text, nor does she allude to the Navajos' long history there. Unlike the mare's voluntary decision to leave home in Clark's story, the Navajo were forced to leave their homes in the canyon in 1864 and to walk three hundred miles to captivity at Bosque Redondo before eventually being allowed to return in 1868.[46] The significance of the mare's homecoming and the boy's steadfast waiting for her in a canyon that closely

resembles Canyon de Chelly was probably lost on Viking's mainstream audience. But to Houser, and especially to his Navajo students far from home at Intermountain Indian School in Utah, the relationship between place, identity, and home must have been poignantly obvious. In the words of children's books scholar Joseph H. Schwarcz, a child's—or people's—identity is closely related to "a sense of attachment and belonging . . . of being rooted in [a] place."[47]

Although non-Navajo readers may miss the significance of Houser's depiction of Canyon de Chelly in *Blue Canyon Horse*, they could hardly mistake the rock towers looming in the distance of his illustrations for Elizabeth Coatsworth's *The Cave*, published in 1958. Nearly twenty years earlier, John Ford had directed *Stagecoach* amid Monument Valley's iconic rock formations, creating a precedent for a host of western films produced at mid-century in the same iconic landscape on the Arizona-Utah border.[48] Houser's engraving-like illustrations depict Jim, a Navajo boy, and Fernando, a Basque shepherd, guiding Fernando's herd of sheep through this vast open space. By drawing Monument Valley's "Three Sisters" and "Mitten" buttes, Houser situates the story in real

Navajo country. But Houser's renderings of landforms also reinforce the narrative at hand, much as his drawings had in *Cochise* five years earlier. Monument Valley's massive "Mitten" buttes accentuate the danger and drama in the foreground in Houser's illustration of a ewe protecting her lamb from an attacking wolf. Here, the pair of mammoth rock formations in the distance visually parallels the creatures as they face off in a life-or-death struggle in the foreground (plate 9).

Throughout *The Cave*, Houser makes the buttes in this ultra-familiar landscape seem distant, and unsympathetic, in contrast to the empathetic hoodoos of *Cochise*. Houser's representation of the landscape reinforces Jim's psychological state and the sense of dread he feels throughout the story. For Jim, the barren, open space is terrifying because it lacks places to hide. Houser most effectively conveys Jim's anxiety in an image of Jim and Fernando resting at noon. Coatsworth writes, "Fernando and Jim found a little shade beside a rock, with the dogs lying near them. Birds were singing their spring songs and everywhere there were desert flowers."[49] But Houser's illustration contains no flowers or singing birds; instead, simple horizontal lines imply buzzards floating in the distance. Most striking is the looming shape of rock overhanging Jim and Fernando. This rock is not the

benign provider of shade in Coatsworth's text; rather, it overshadows Jim like a dark cloud about to devour him. In fact, Houser's rock visually depicts Jim's mental state described a few sentences later: "The sense of danger [hung] over him."[50]

Later in the story, the real source of Jim's fear, a cave where his ancestors were murdered, proves to be a source of safety. Coatsworth likens the cave's entrance to the "doorway of a Navajo Hogan."[51] In contrast to the rock towers of the valley, the cave appears a safe haven, and Houser makes the opening womblike. With rounded sides narrowing to a leaning point at top, the entrance, in fact, closely resembles Houser's abstract drawings and sculptures of motherly female forms made in following decades. In a large drawing, more than 12×15 inches, Houser places the viewer inside the cave, in safety. Readers and viewers peer out into the wintery scene, past silhouetted sheep and the curving mouth of the cave, to watch (with the ancestors Coatsworth suggests inhabit the cave) Jim and Fernando's approach. Much to his surprise, Jim loses his anxiety in the cave where his ancestors had lived and died; like the mare in *Blue Canyon Horse*, he finds safety and identity in the place he initially sought to avoid. Coatsworth, like Clark in *Blue Canyon Horse*, not so subtly suggests that ancestral homes, not urban areas, are where indigenous people find belonging and identity; Houser, however, shows readers exactly where that "home" is by depicting specific landscapes.

While Houser makes clear links between home, landscape, and identity in *Blue Canyon Horse, Geronimo,* and *The Cave,* his illustrations speak eloquently, and most vibrantly, of individuals' relationship to a specific landscape in his last children's book commission—Clark's *The Desert People.* The book's title and Clark's opening passage allude overtly to the close relationship between Papago (Tohono O'odham, literally "Desert People") identity and their desert home: "I am a boy of the Desert People. . . . White men call me Papago but the wild animals call me Brother because they know me and love me. We call ourselves the Desert People."[52] Houser's elegant ink drawings emphasize the point. On the opening page, nestled amid cacti, mountains, quail, deer,

Allan Houser (U.S., Chiricahua Apache, 1914–1994)
Jim with overhanging rock.
Illustration for Elizabeth Coatsworth, *The Cave* (1958).
Pen and ink, 15⅛ × 12 9/16 in.
The Allan Houser Foundation
HF1995.1-687.1

rabbits, and a lizard, the Tohono O'odham boy appears as much part of his landscape as the rock he relaxes into. Houser delineates his protagonist and surrounding desert creatures with the meeting of light and shadowed forms, creating an effect much like an engraving or bronze relief.

The Desert People, Houser's final contribution to children's book illustration, builds on his work in earlier books. Here, vibrant green, orange, and turquoise paintings of landscape seasons alternating with seasons of village life leap from the page in contrast to Clark's quiet text (plate 13). Here, too, the artist creates real, recognizable places, most notably the historic Mission San Javier Del Bac, outside Tucson, reflecting, as Rushing has pointed out, the fusion of indigenous beliefs with Roman Catholicism in Tohono O'odham religious practice.[53] Although Clark refrains from naming the site in her text, its importance to readers and viewers is evidenced by the fact that Houser's image of the church is his most frequently exhibited children's book illustration. According to Rettig, the image's popularity is primarily due to viewers' familiarity with the historic Spanish mission.[54]

Why did Houser create such specific, real places in his children's book illustrations, especially when no named locations existed in the text? As someone committed to, in Rushing's words, "telling true stories," and concerned with accuracy in his depictions, it seems logical that Houser chose to

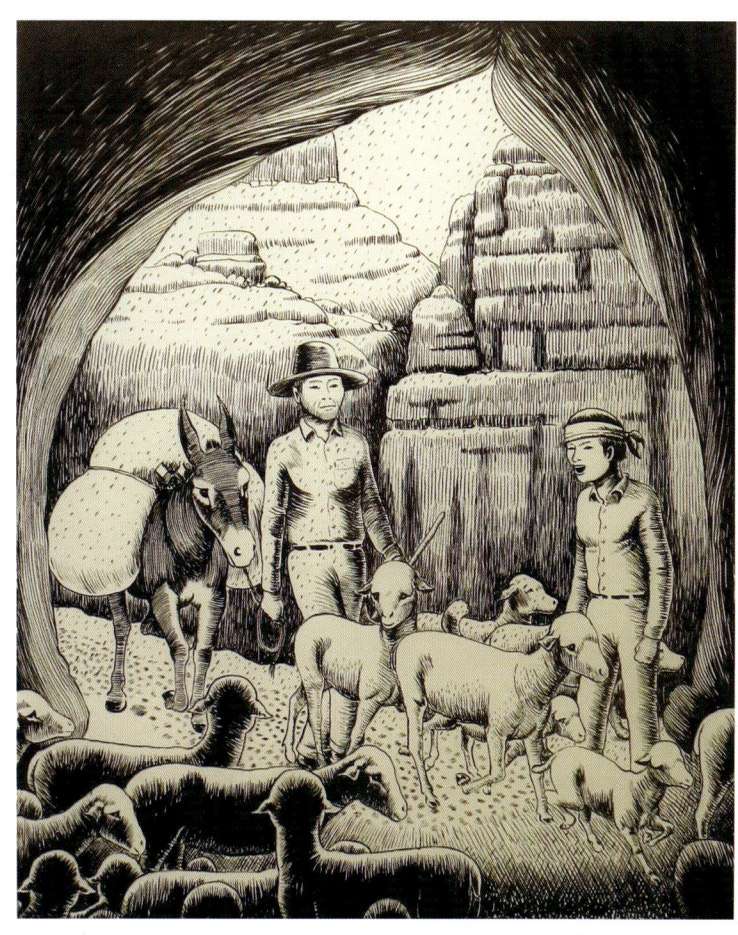

Allan Houser (U.S., Chiricahua Apache, 1914–1994)
Jim and Fernando arrive at the cave. Illustration for Elizabeth Coatsworth, *The Cave* (1958).
Pen and ink, 15 ⅛ × 12 ⁹⁄₁₆ in.
The Allan Houser Foundation
HF1995.1-696.l

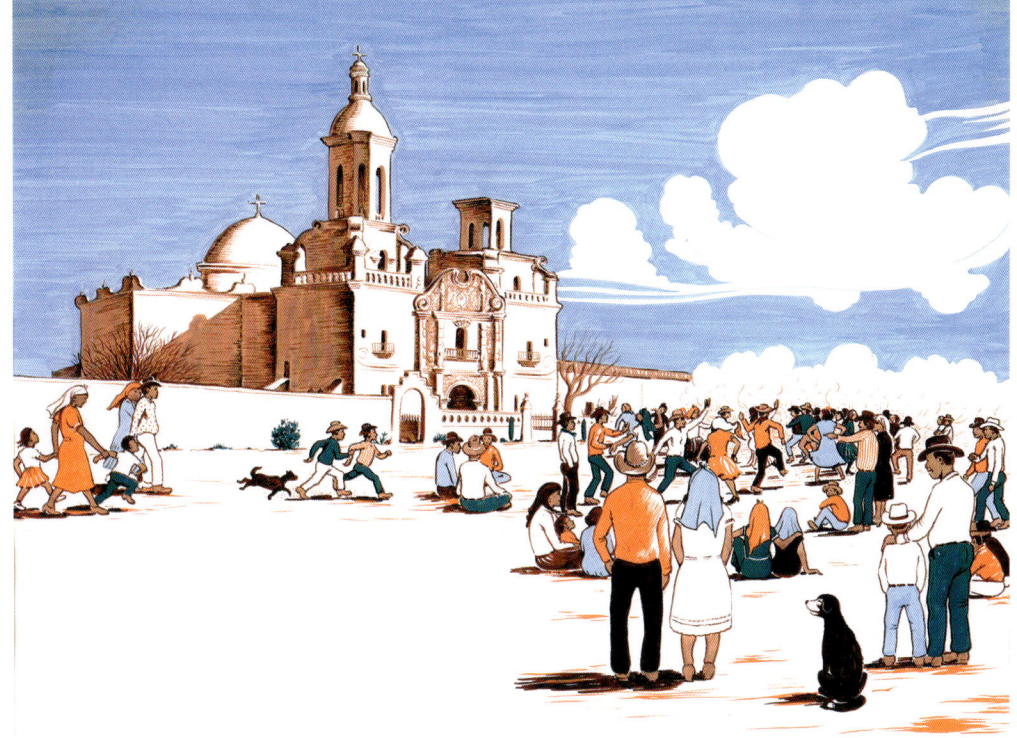

Allan Houser (U.S., Chiricahua Apache, 1914–1994)
Mission San Javier Del Bac, Tucson. Illustration for Ann Nolan Clark, *The Desert People* (1962).
Tempera, 19 ½ × 25 ½ in.
The Allan Houser Foundation
HF1995.1-613.l

situate his characters in real places. Perhaps Houser rendered real landscapes to please both himself and his Navajo students at Intermountain Indian School, who would recognize and know the places he depicted, even if non-Native readers would not.

Houser's emphasis on specific home places seems especially pertinent given that he, too, was far from home during the eleven years he spent illustrating children's books, teaching, and raising his family in Brigham City. In retrospect, Houser's careful rendering of cholla and yucca in books illustrated during his years in Utah seems almost lovingly done, as if enacted partially out of homesickness. In fact, even when Houser lived in Los Angeles during World War II, he continually drew and painted the American Southwest. Similarly, numerous drawings in *Allan Houser Drawings: The Centennial Exhibition* reveal Houser's almost obsessive devotion to depicting land, specifically the arid lands of southwestern New Mexico and Arizona. It also seems pertinent that simultaneous with Houser's reiterations of yucca, cedar, hoodoos, and mesas in drawings, paintings, and illustrations published in children's books at mid-century, the U.S. government encouraged Native people to relocate from reservations to urban areas in a reversal of John Collier's policy of the 1930s.[55] In emphasizing not just landscapes but the land itself, Houser's illustrations reinforce the messages of the books' authors, affirming the importance of indigenous home places following a decade of mass-exodus from reservations following World War II.

In fact, this question—whether to seek employment in Chicago or return home to his Navajo community—is a struggle experienced by the titular character of *Joe Sunpool* throughout Don Wilcox's 1956 novel.[56] Similarly, in D'Arcy McNickle's *Runner in the Sun* (1954), the Anasazi protagonist, Salt, travels deep into present-day South America to obtain a new variety of maize to bring back to his people, who then must leave their ancient homes in order to survive. By contrast, Clark and Coatsworth, whose stories feature characters returning to Native home places—whether the cave in Coatsworth's text or Canyon de Chelly in

Clark's—suggest it is in ancestral homes that their characters ultimately find their identity and sense of belonging.

Contemporary scholars Tsianina K. Lomawaima and Teresa L. McCarty criticize Clark and her colleagues for their celebration of certain "acceptable" indigenous traits published in the Indian Life Readers of the 1940s.[57] Rebecca Benes, on the other hand, views the books Houser illustrated and their predecessors as positive evidence of collaboration between Native illustrators and translators, and non-Native authors and educators for the benefit of, initially, indigenous children.[58] But where does this leave Houser, who, for one decade, invested much energy—more than six months' work in the case of *The Cave*—making ink drawings and tempera paintings to accompany stories for a broad audience of young readers and adolescents? On one hand, book illustration projects provided income during lean years while he taught school and raised his family in Utah. And yet, Houser chose to keep the scrawled-on and tape-damaged drawings that were returned to him. His retention of these drawings, which today still bear the marks of the production process, implies he valued them beyond their immediate economic value. Ultimately, Houser's extant original illustrations made for *Cochise, Blue Canyon Horse, The Cave,* and *The Desert People* bear witness to many voices: Euroamerican authors, East Coast publishing houses, editors, and Houser himself. While themes of home, identity, safety, and change found in the books Houser illustrated at mid-century reflect the authors' responses to federal Indian policy at the time, Houser's voice confronts the reader again and again with plants, rocks, cacti, and land. Whether that land responds to the text in a humorous or ironic way (read cacti surprised by stagecoaches), visibly represents Geronimo's remembered past, or depicts actual places, Houser's book illustrations assert that home and identity are intricately linked not to just any place but to very specific home places, that is, home landscapes, home lands. In "picturing home," Houser depicts not only Navajo and Apache identities, but his own identity.

Allan Houser *Drawings*
Catalogue of the Exhibition

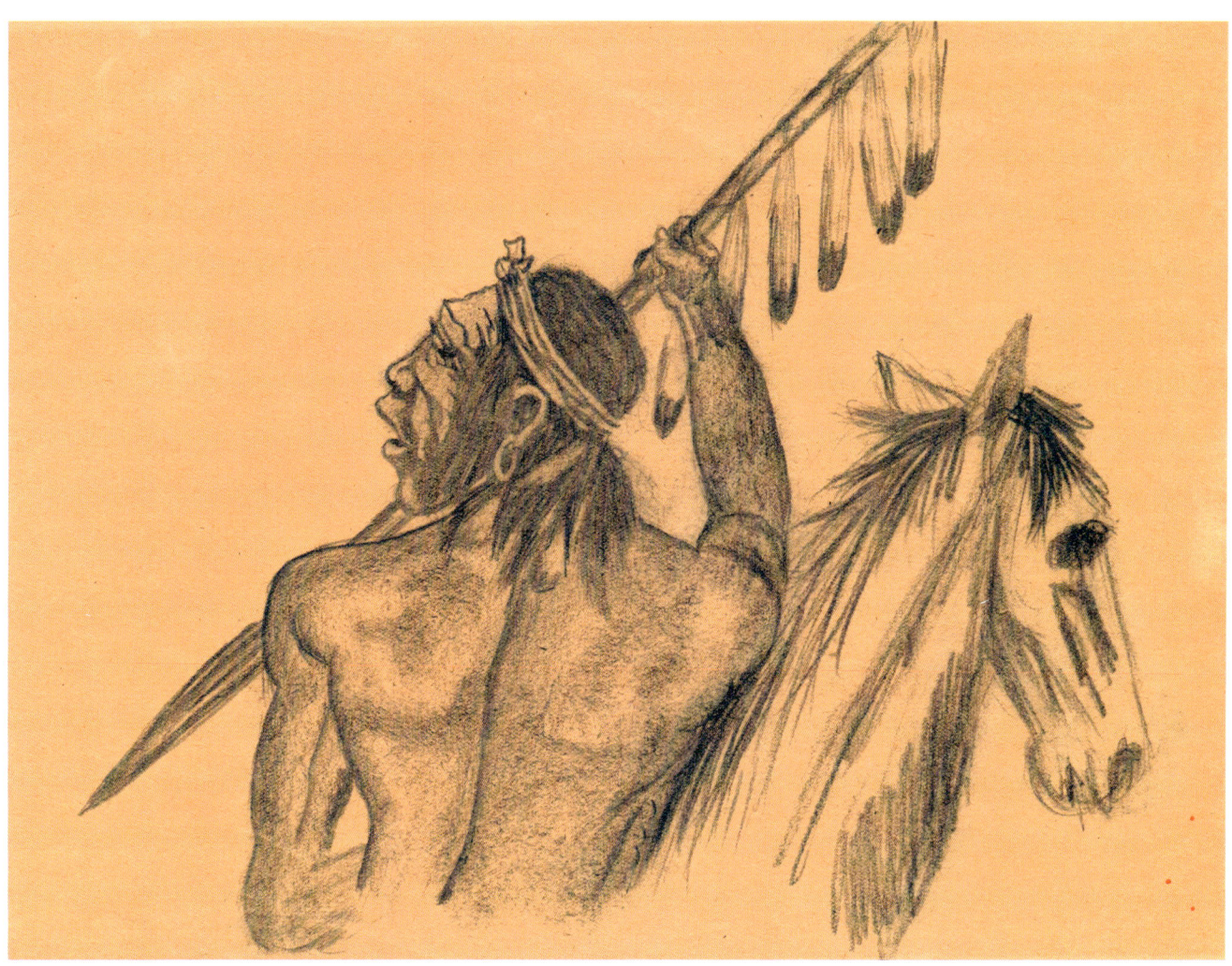

Plate 1
Untitled (Warrior with Lance), 1934
[Signed "Allan C. Houser (Haozous)"]
Charcoal on paper, 8 ½ × 11 ¼ in.
Fred Jones Jr. Museum of Art, University of Oklahoma,
Norman; Gift of Mr. and Mrs. Howard H. Huston in
appreciation of President and Mrs. David L. Boren, 2000
2000.005

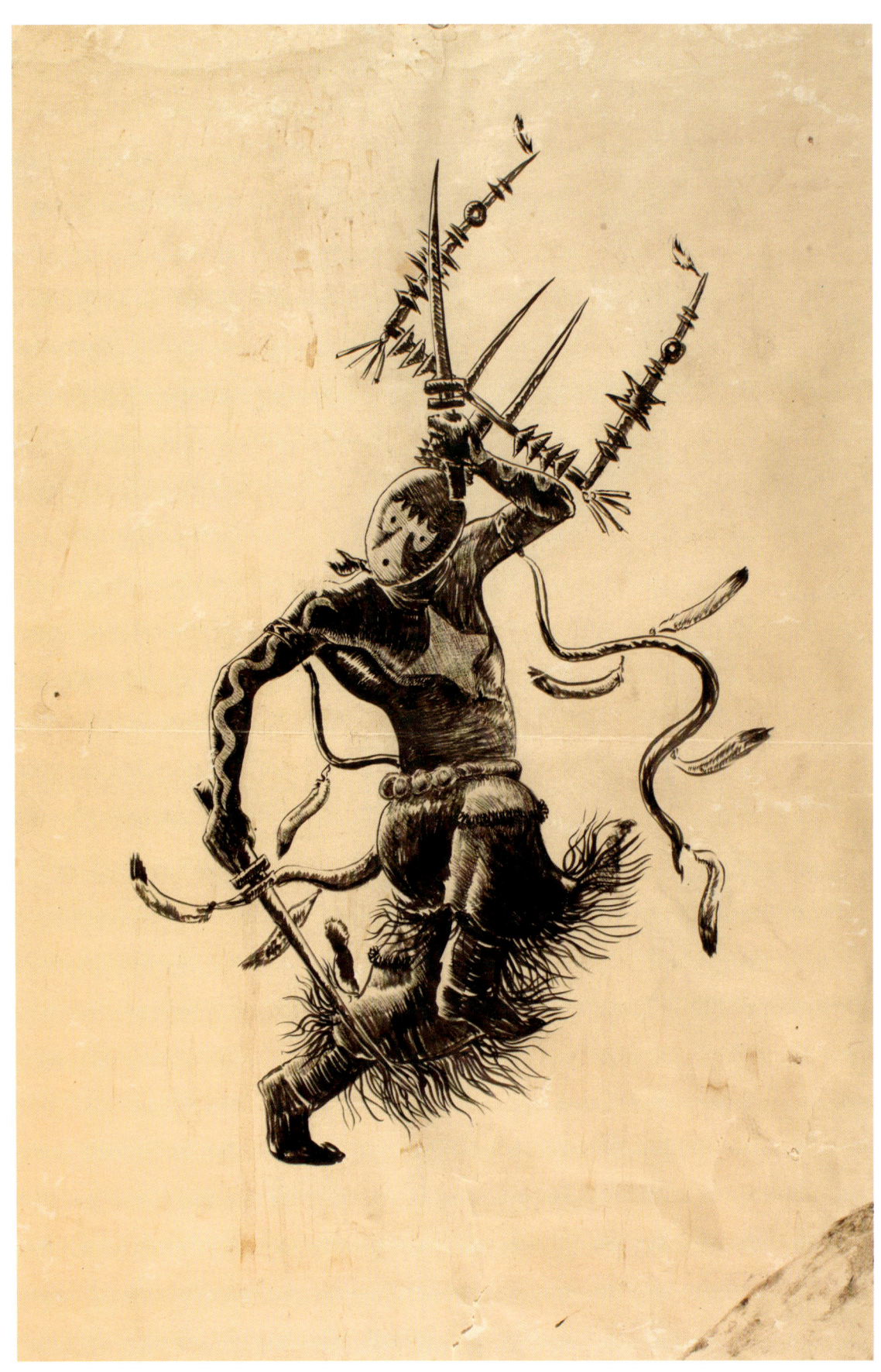

Plate 2
Ga'an Dancer, c. 1938
Black ink, 18 × 12½ in.
The Allan Houser Foundation
HF1995.1-319Bl.a.D

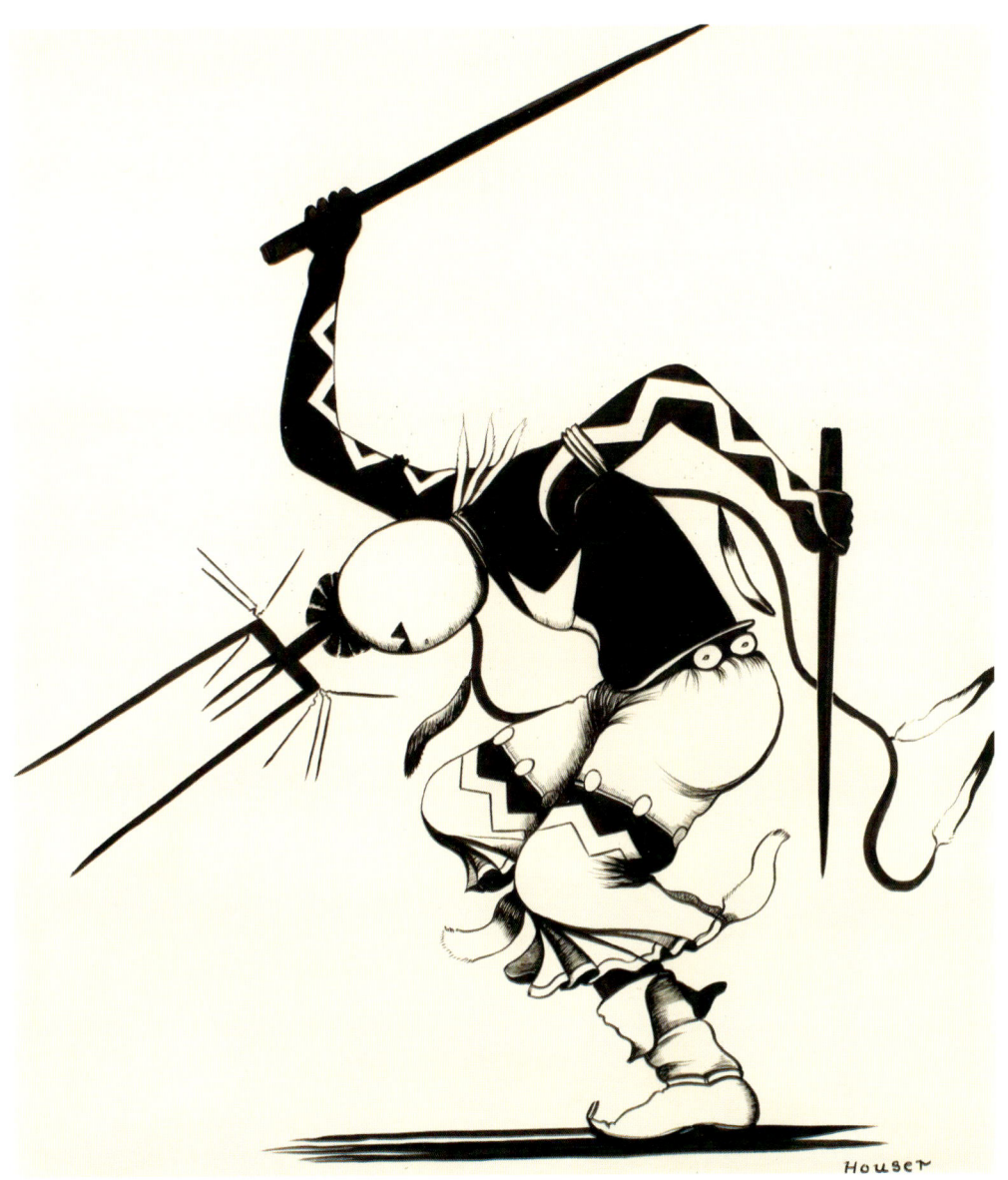

Plate 3
Apache Ga'an Dancer, 1939
Pen and ink, 13½ × 11¾ in.
Allan Houser Inc.
AHI 7276

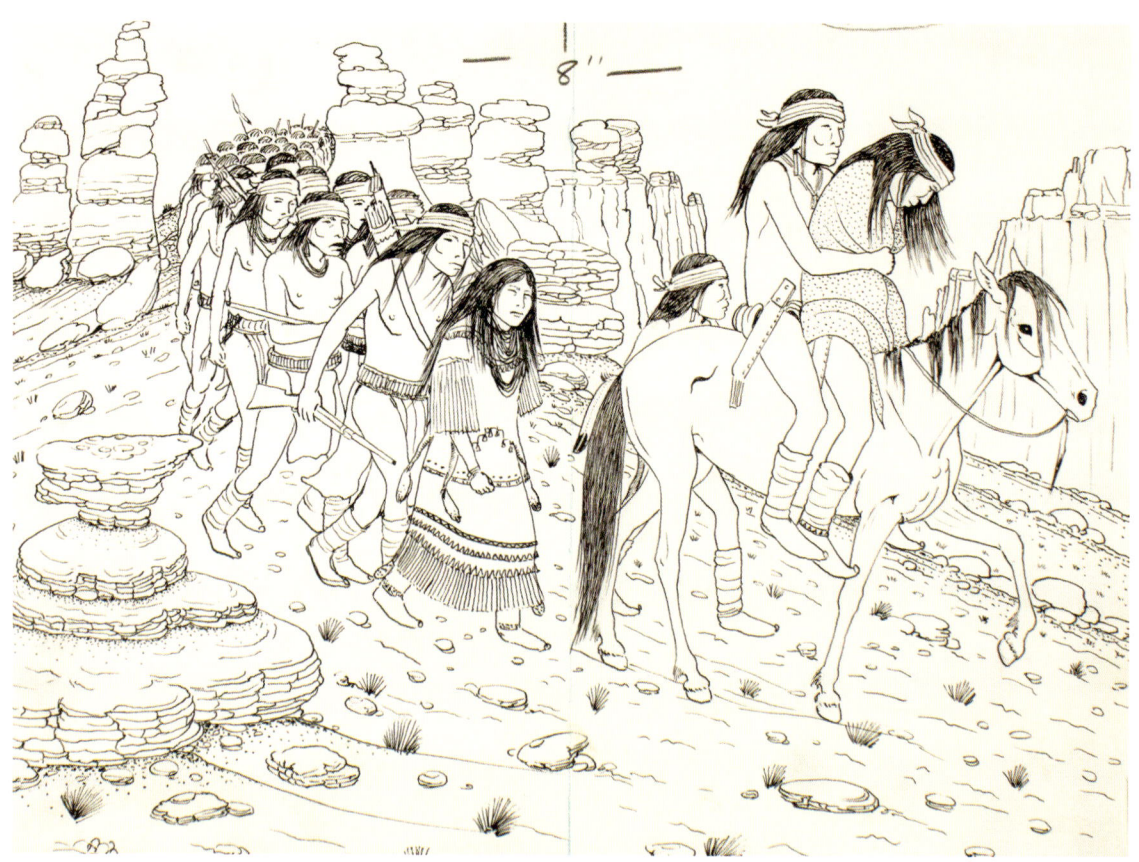

Plate 4
Warriors Carrying Fallen Comrade, 1953
Pen and ink, 8 1/16 × 10 9/16 in.
The Allan Houser Foundation
HF 1995.1-663.S.I

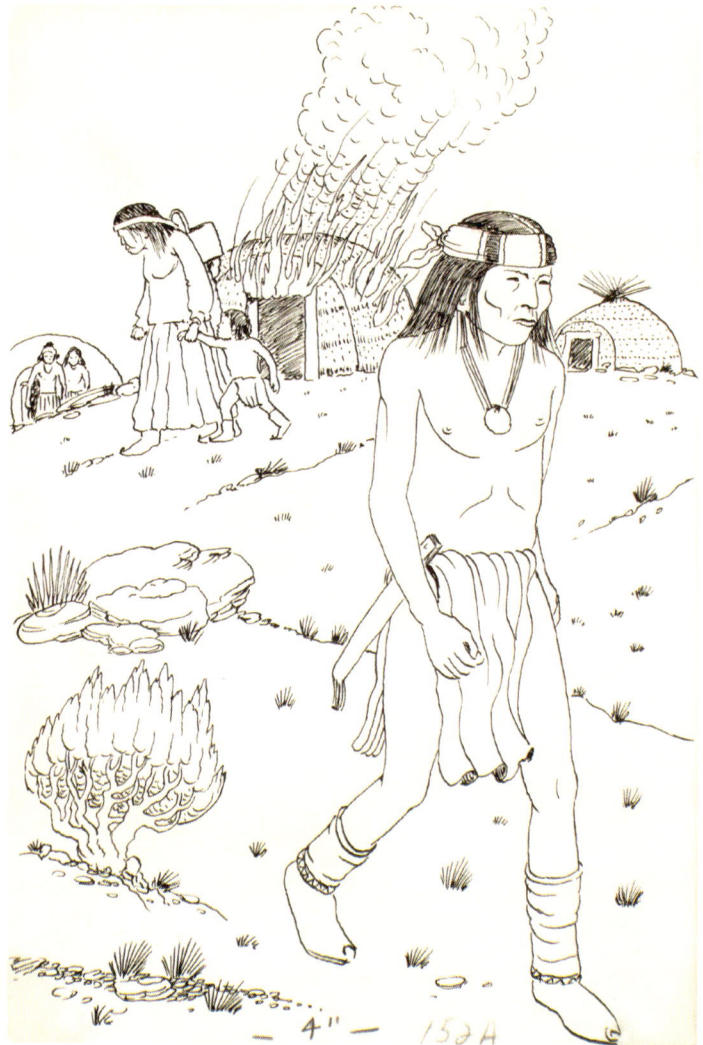

Plate 5
***Warrior in Foreground, Mother and Child
Fleeing Burning Dwelling,*** 1953
Pen and ink, 7 9/16 × 5 1/16 in.
The Allan Houser Foundation
HF 1995.1-663.F.I

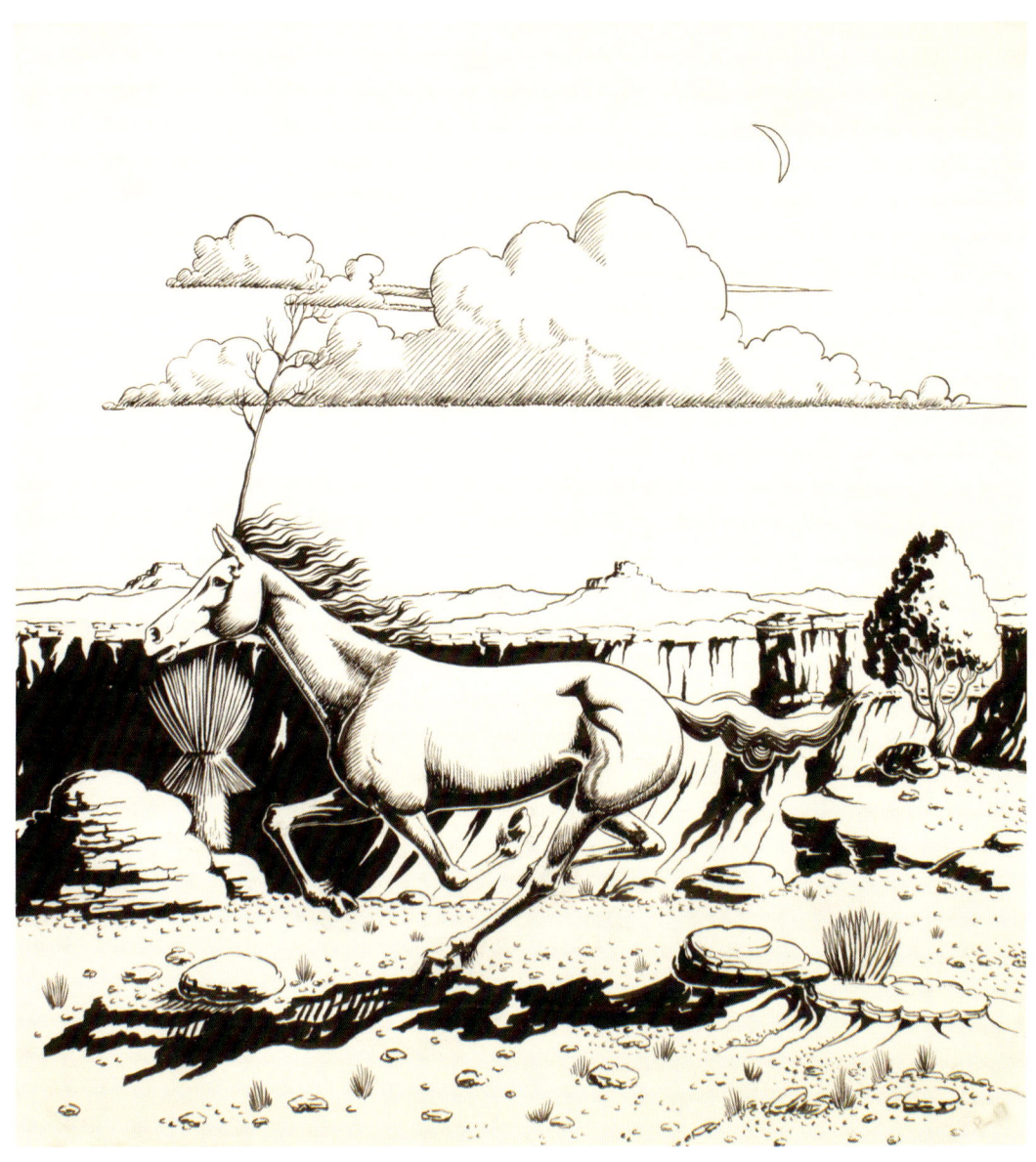

Plate 6
Horse Running in Landscape, 1954
Pen and ink, 11¾ × 11 in.

The Allan Houser Foundation

HF1995.1-635.l

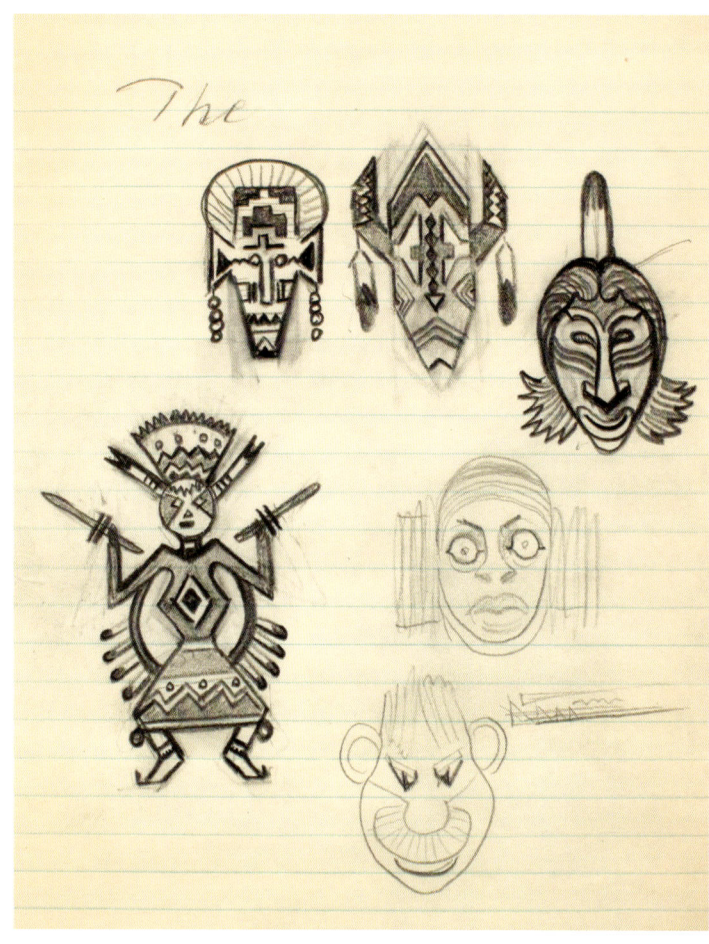

Plate 7
Five Masks, Abstracted
Ga'an Dancer, c. 1955
Pencil, 10½ × 8 in.
Chiinde, LLC.
HF1995.1-319E.D

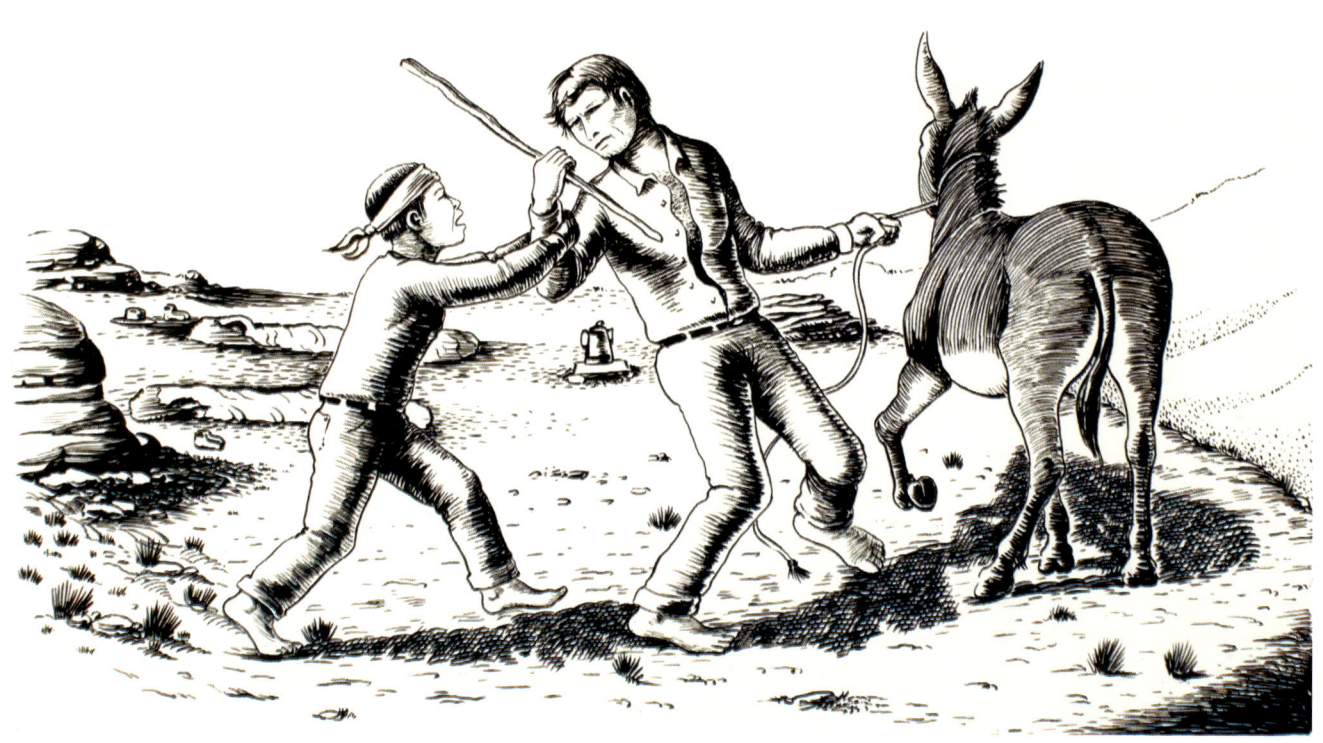

Plate 8
Boy Stopping Man from
Beating Burro, 1958
Pen and ink, 7 15/16 × 12 17/32 in.
The Allan Houser Foundation
HF1995.1-670.I

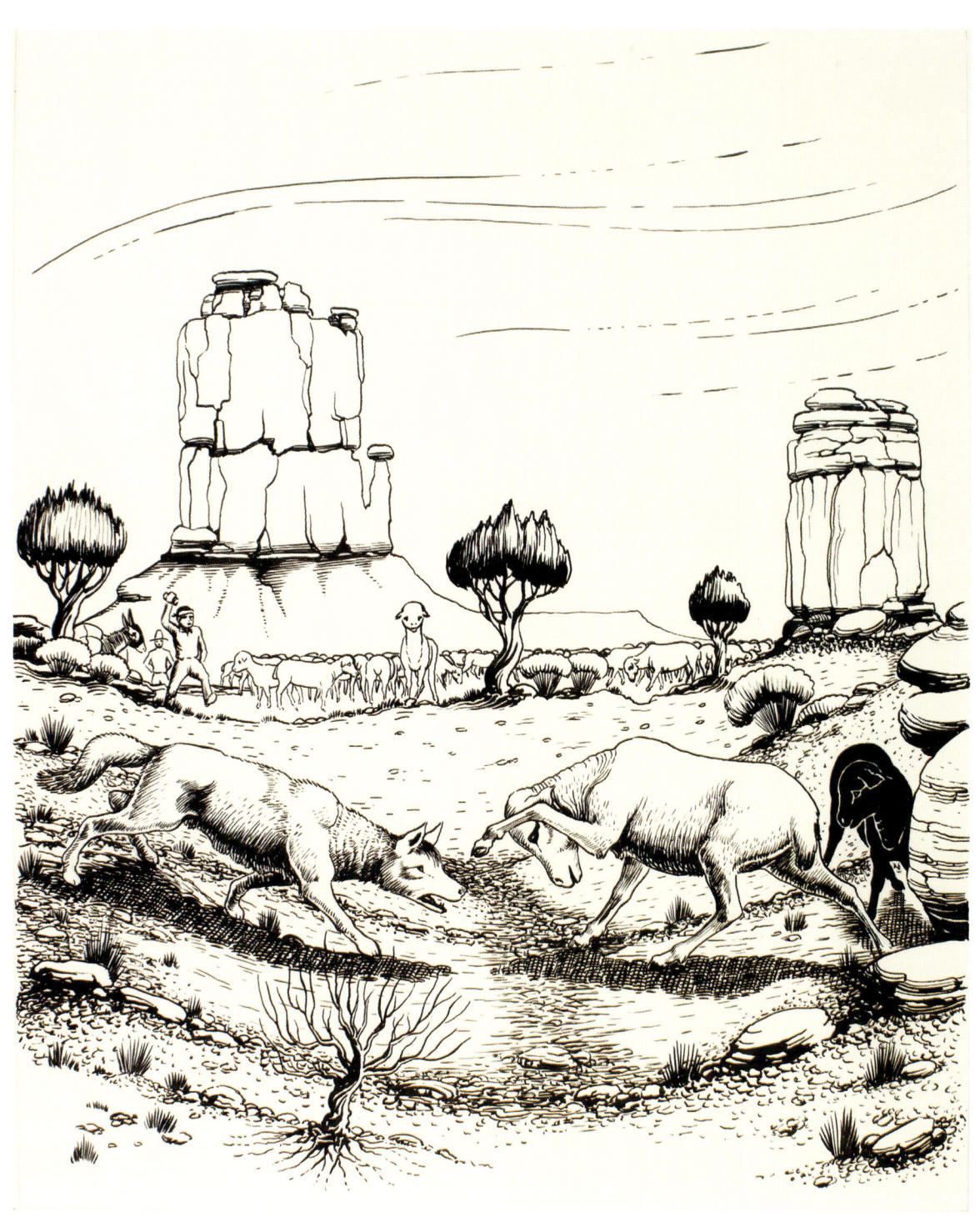

Plate 9
Ewe Fighting Off Wolf, 1958
Pen and ink, 15 ⅛ × 12 ⁹⁄₁₆ in.
The Allan Houser Foundation
HF1995.1-690.J

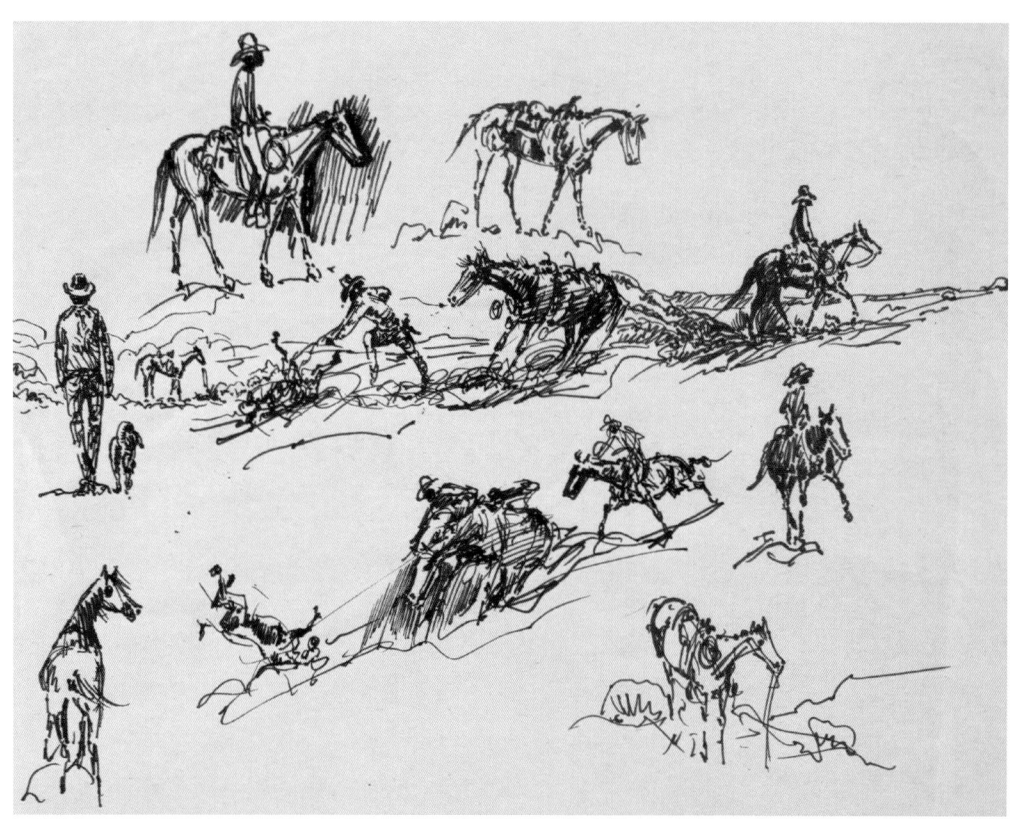

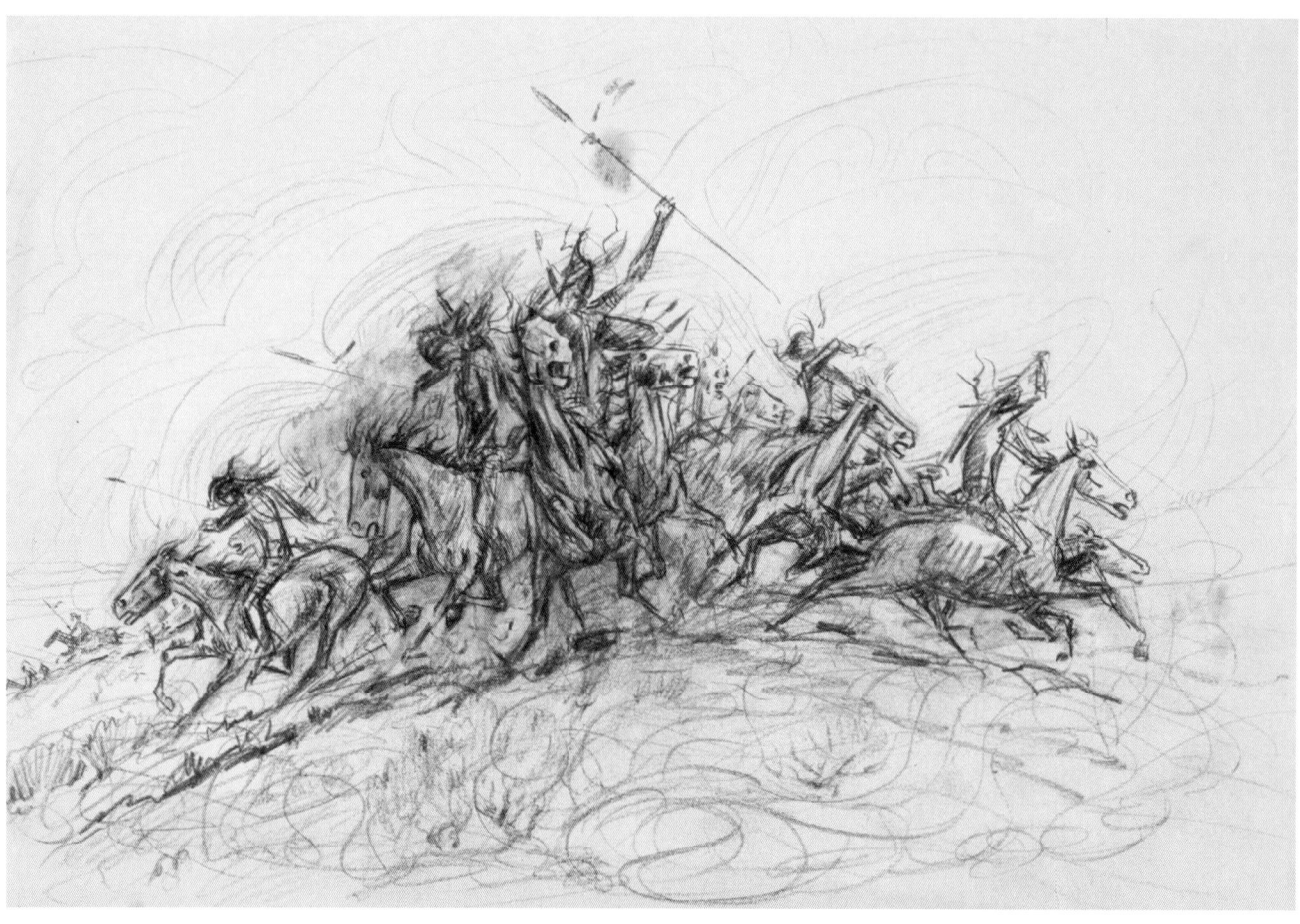

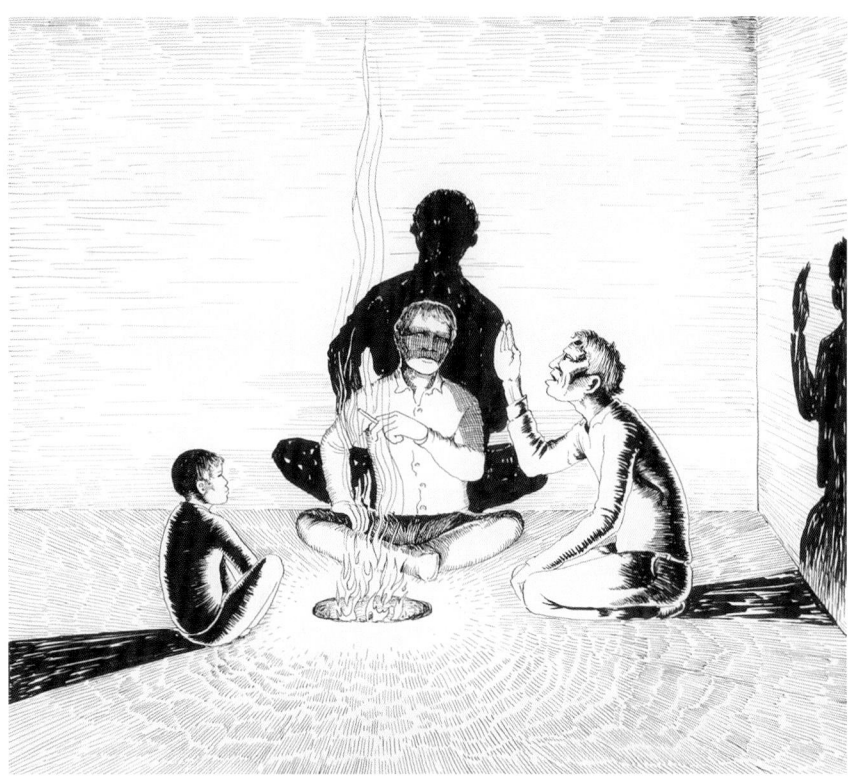

Plate 12
The Old Storyteller, 1961
Pen and ink, 13 ¾ × 13 ³⁄₁₆ in.
The Allan Houser Foundation
HF1995.1-606.A.I

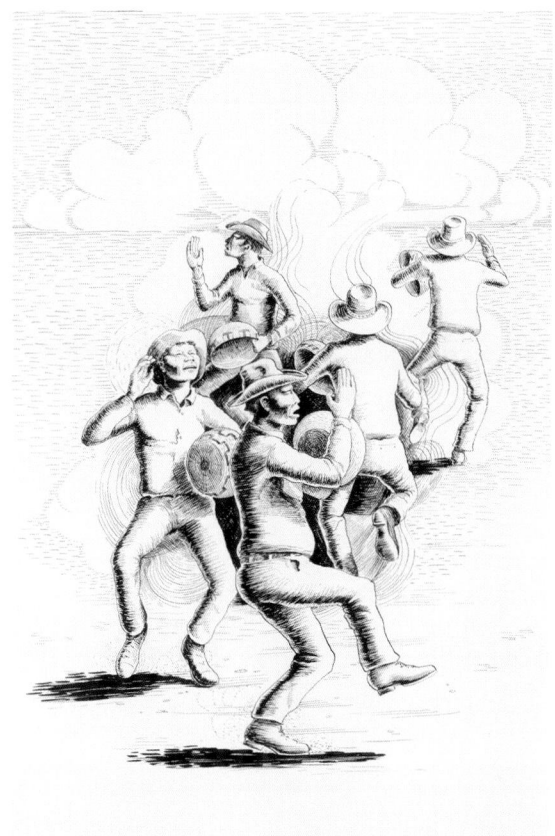

Plate 14
Five Men Dancing, 1962
Pen and ink, 21 ⅝ × 14 ½ in.
The Allan Houser Foundation
HF1995.1-601.I

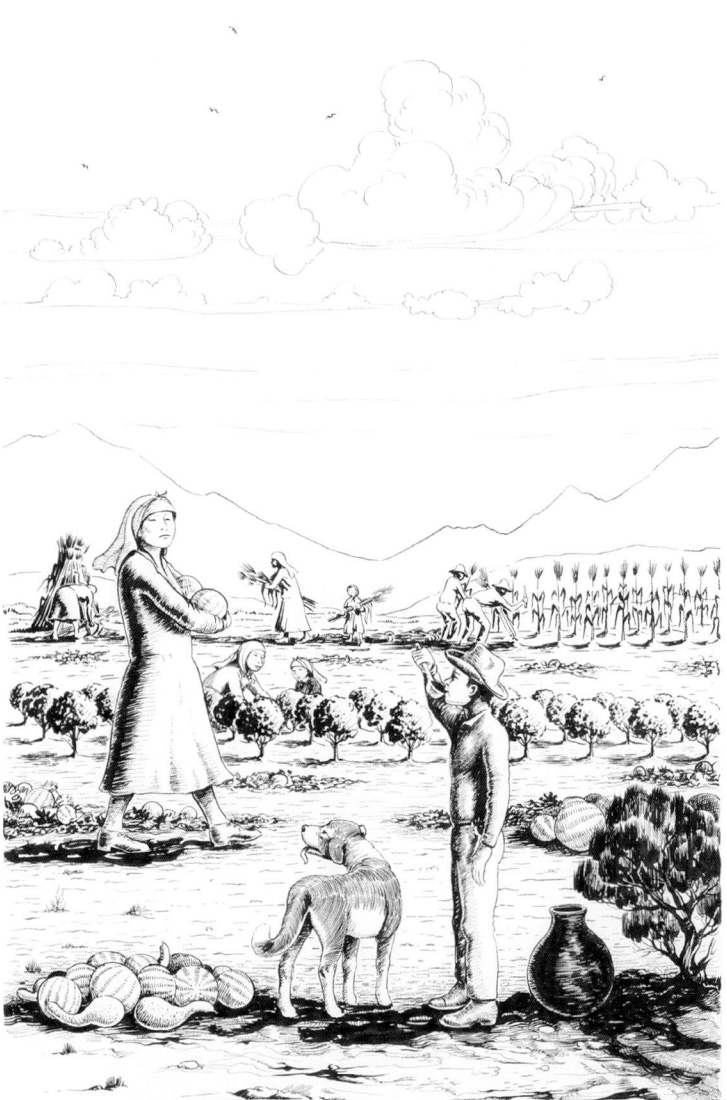

Plate 13
***Landscape with
Boy and Dog,*** 1962
Pen and ink, 22 ¹⁵⁄₁₆ × 15 ⅝ in.
The Allan Houser Foundation
HF1995.1-600.I

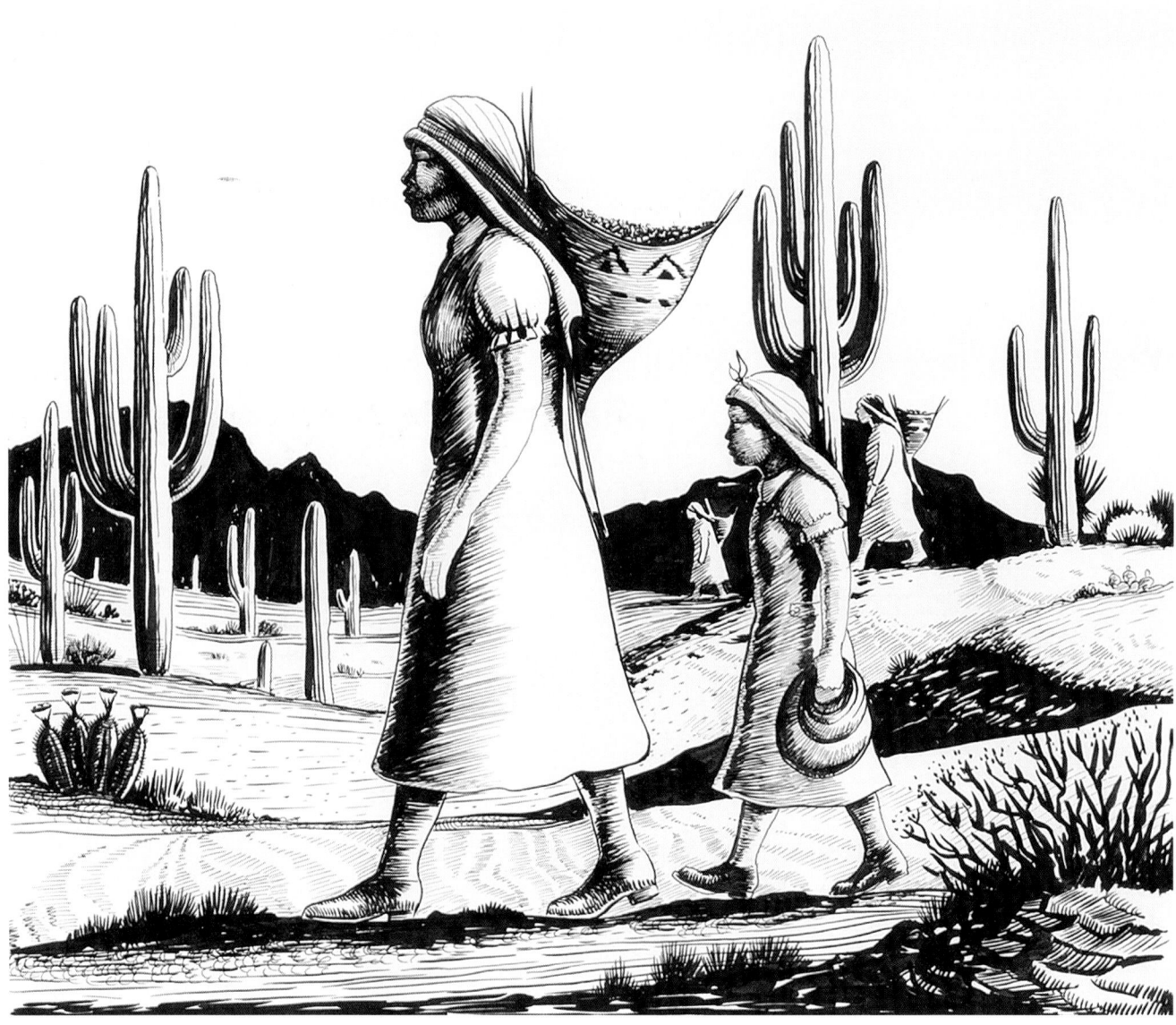

Plate 15
Women in Landscape, Saguaro Cactus, 1962
Pen and ink, 14 ¾ × 16 ½ in.
The Allan Houser Foundation
HF1995.1-607.l

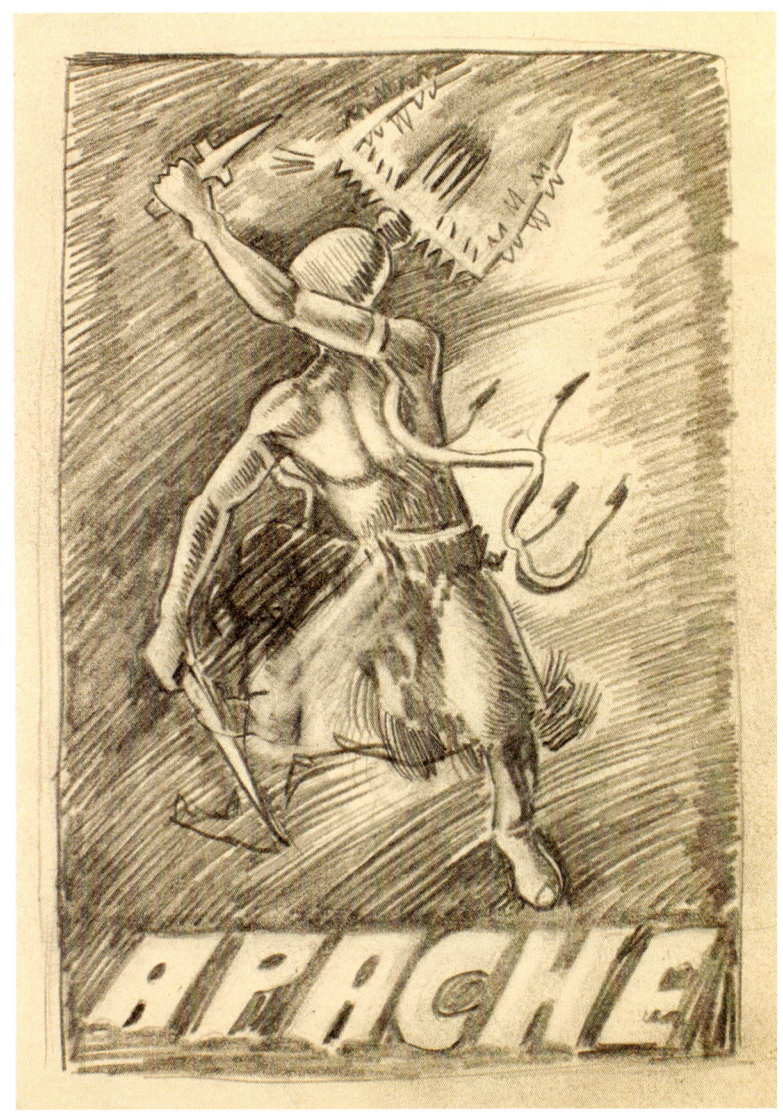

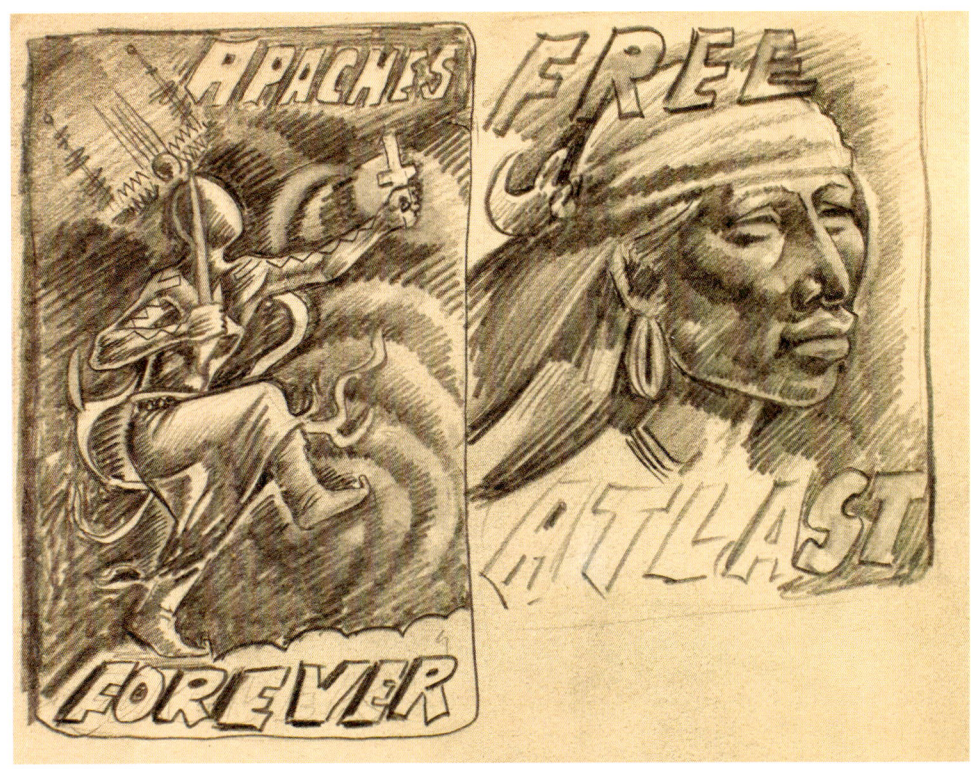

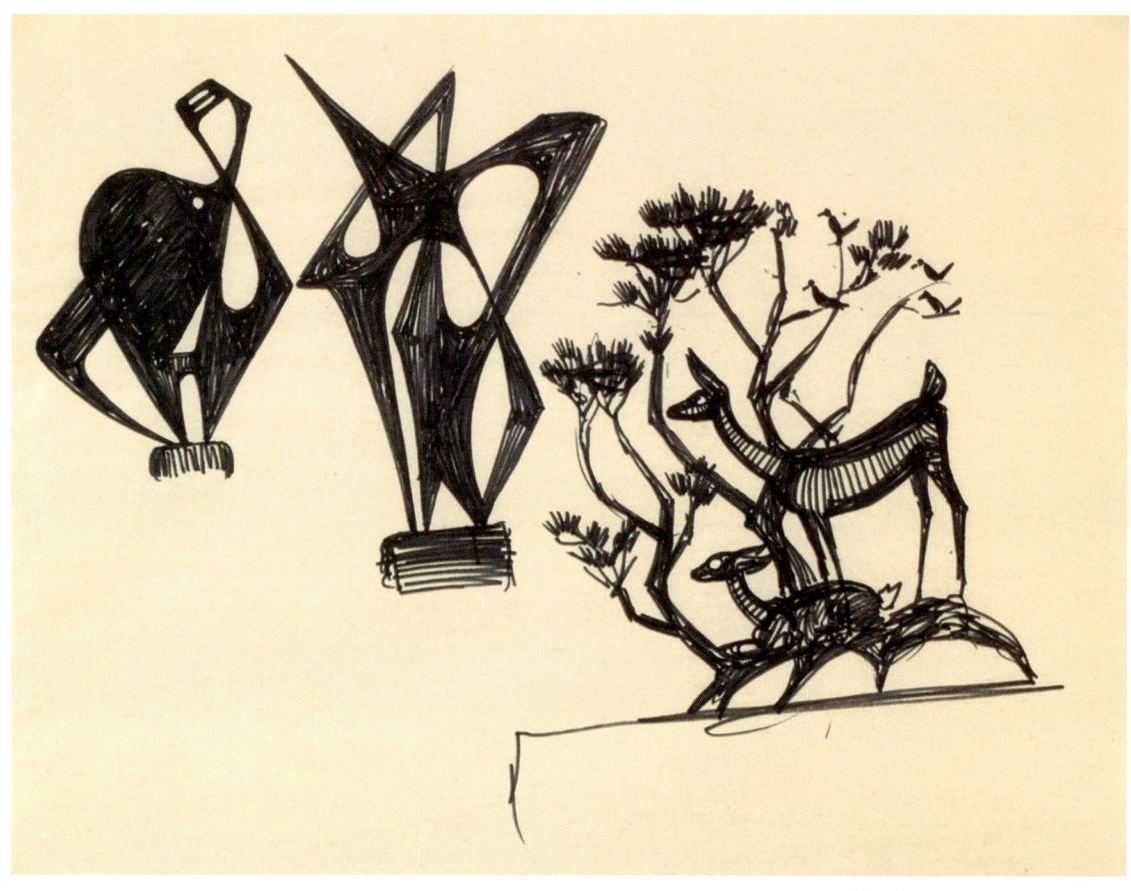

Plate 18
**Abstracted Deer by Tree, Two
Non-objective Forms,** c. 1965
Felt-tip pen, 9 × 12 in.
Chiinde, LLC.
HF1995.1-269O.D

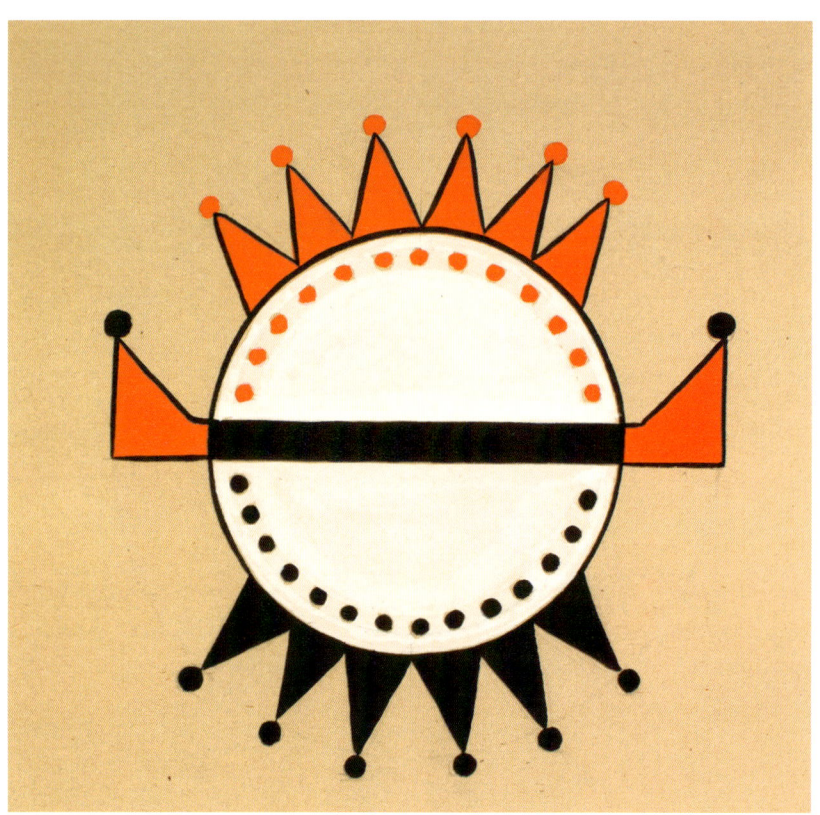

Plate 19
Geometric Design, c. 1965
Tempera, 8 × 9⅞ in.
Chiinde, LLC.
HF1995.1-319AN.a.D

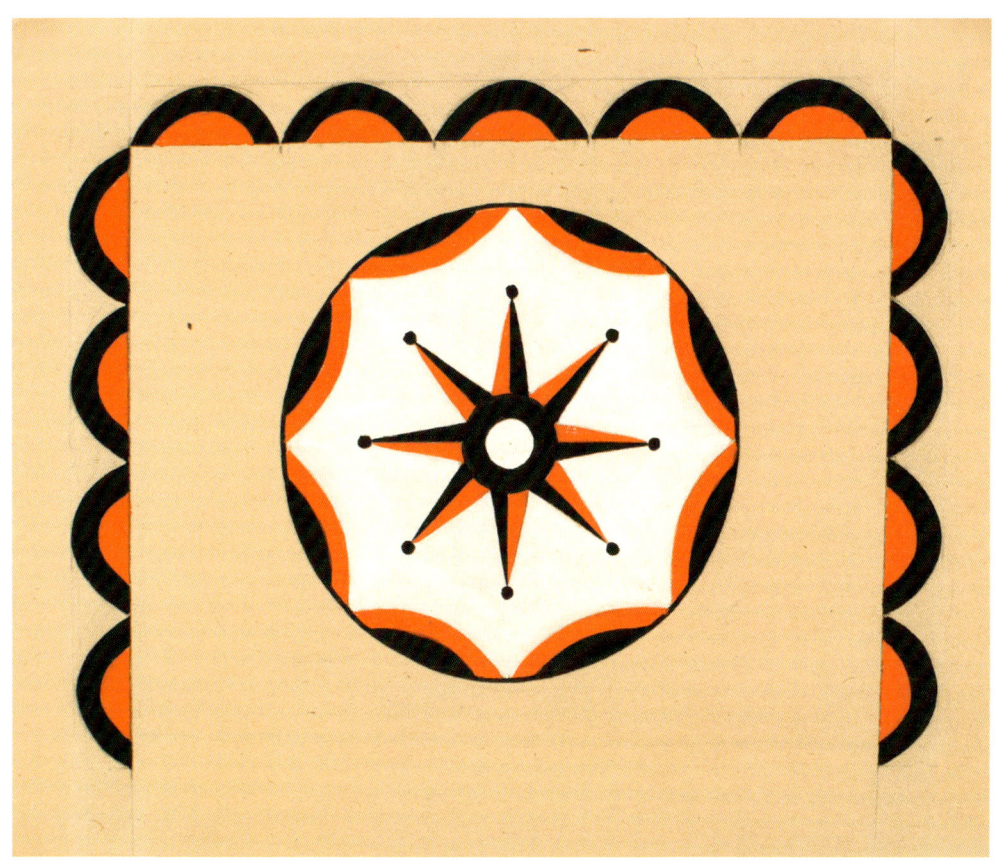

Plate 20
Geometric Design, c. 1965
Tempera, 8 × 8 ¾ in.
Chiinde, LLC.
HF1995.1-319BL.P

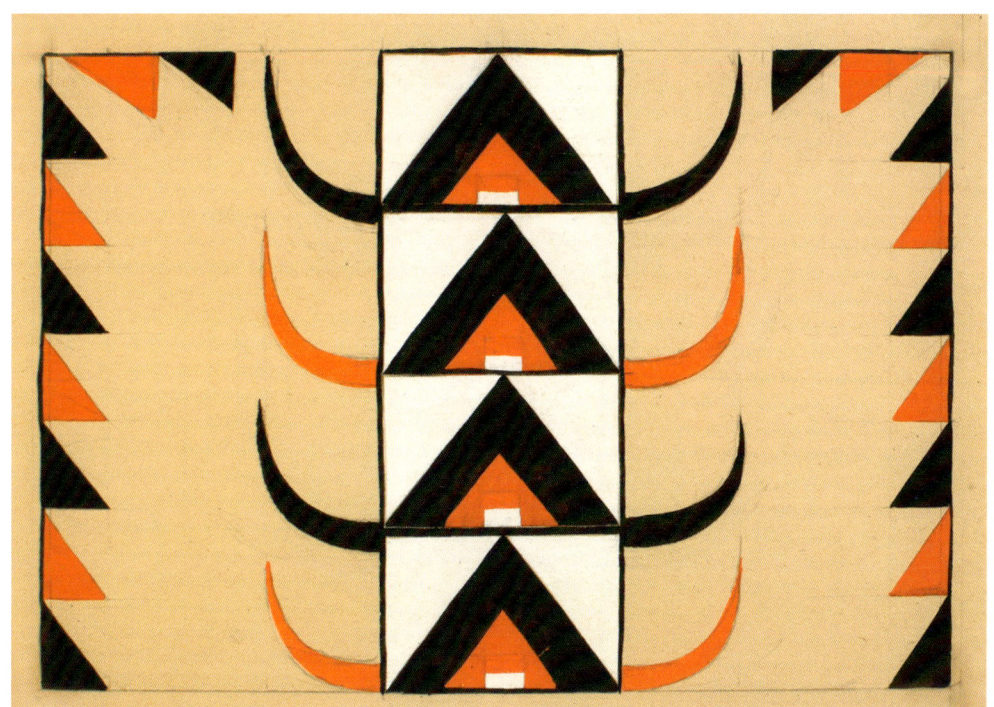

Plate 21
Geometric Design, c. 1965
Tempera, 6 × 8 ¾ in.
Chiinde, LLC.
HF1995.1-319BM.P

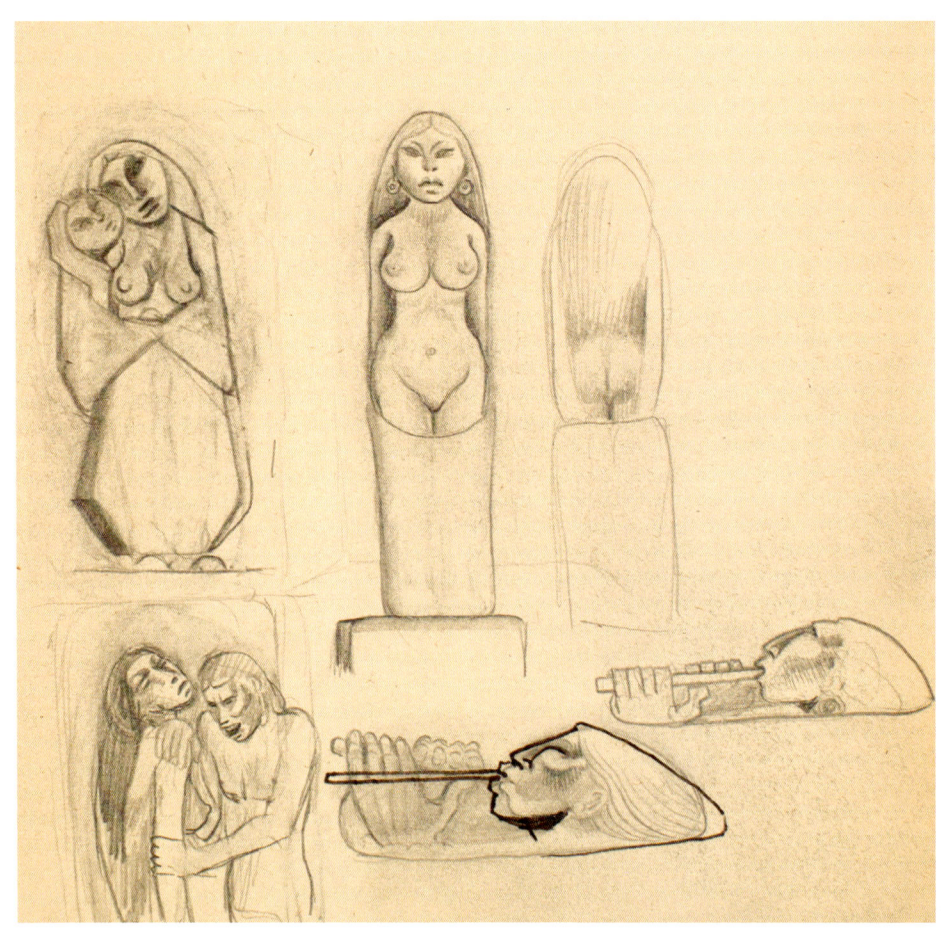

Plate 22
Nude Studies, Flute Players,
Man and Woman, c. 1965
Pencil, felt-tip pen, 8 15/16 × 11 15/16 in.
Chiinde, LLC.
HF1995.1-489F.D

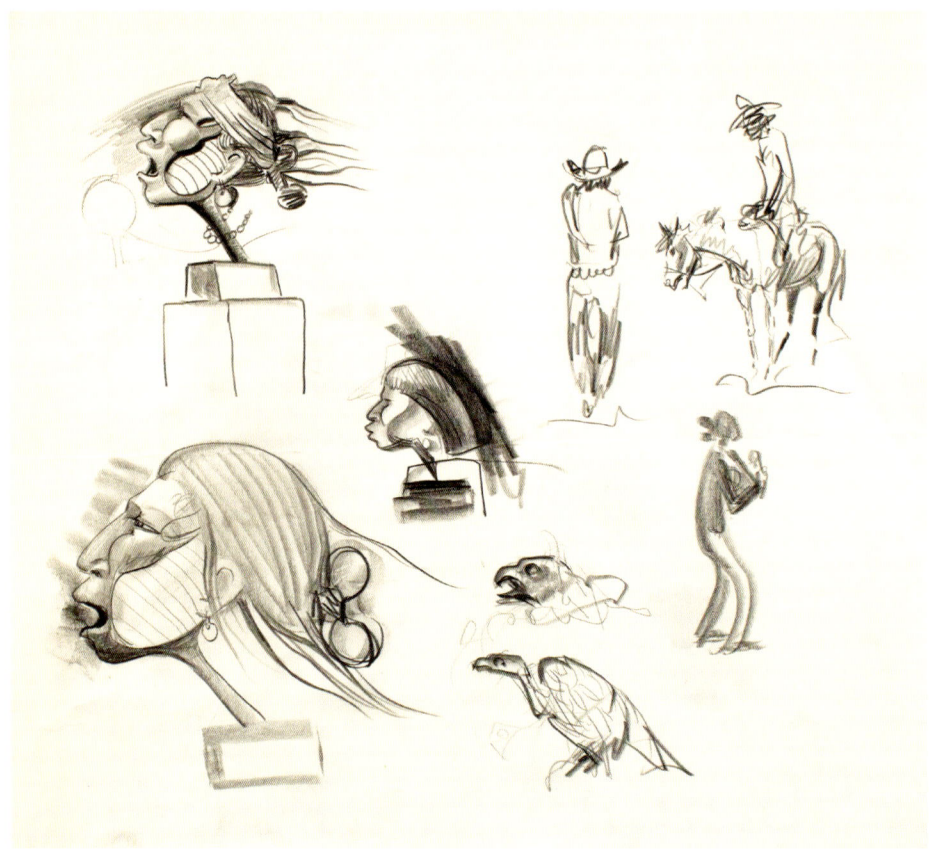

Plate 23
Various Figure Studies, c. 1965
Pencil, 12½ × 13⅛ in.
Chiinde, LLC
HF1995.1-276BD.D

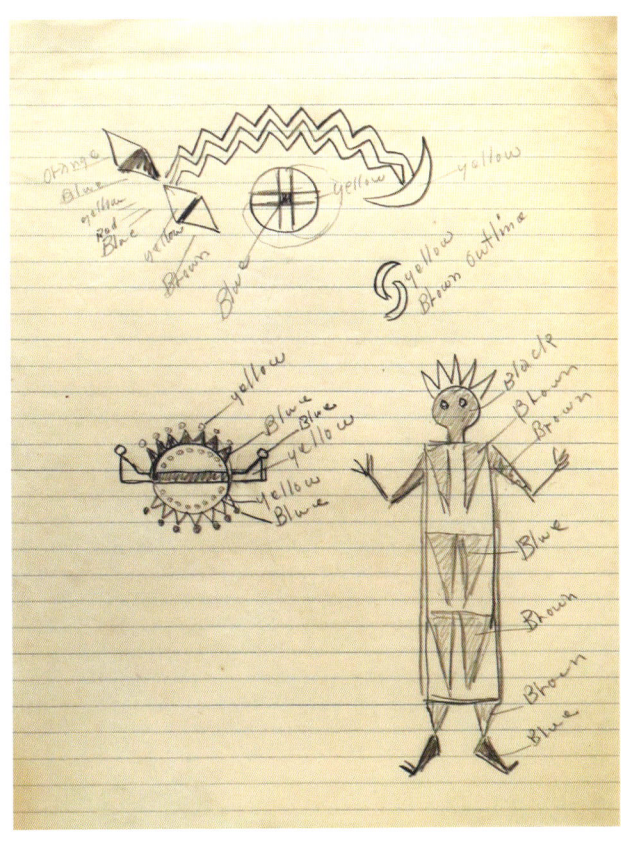

Plate 24
Page from a Sketchbook:
Apache Symbols, c. 1965
Pencil, 10½ × 8 in.
The Allan Houser Foundation
HF1995.1-406A-D

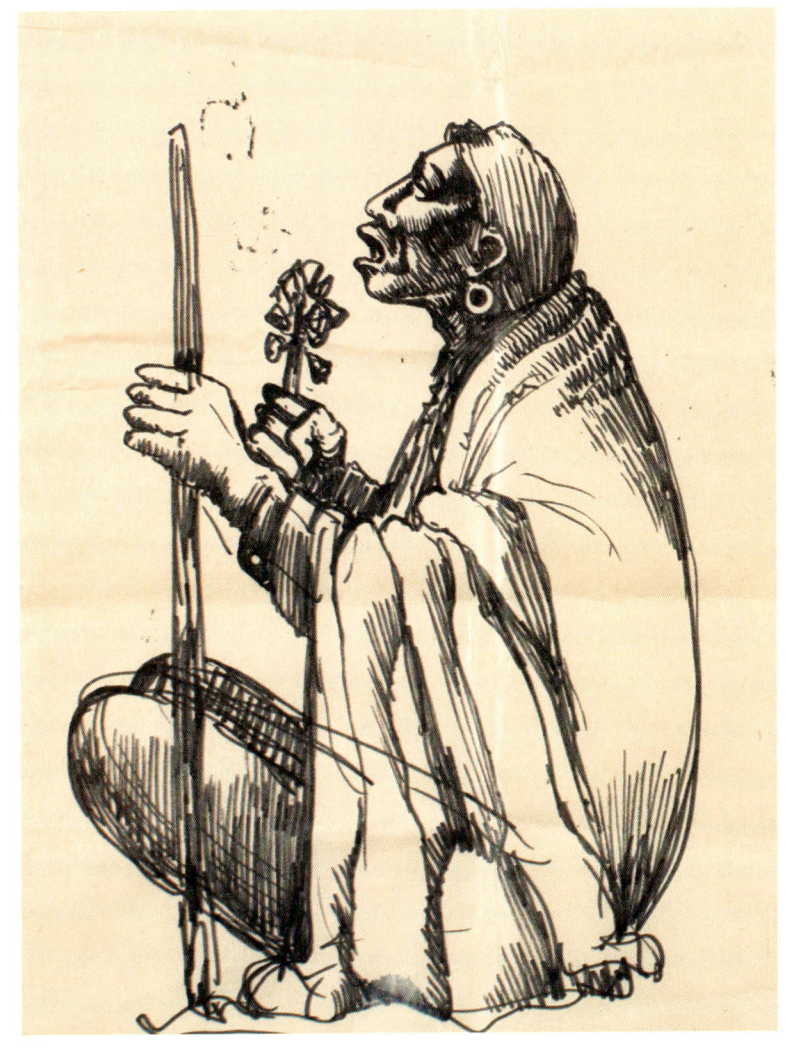

Plate 25
Man with Rattle and Stick
Singing, c. 1970
Felt-tip pen, 12 × 9 in.
The Allan Houser Foundation
HF1995.1-269AD.D

Sculpture —

I BELIEVE SCULPTURE IS THE ART WHICH PEOPLE RESPOND TO MOST NATURALLY — THEY CAN TAKE HOLD OF IT; THEY CAN ENJOY IT WITH THE SENCE OF TOUCH AS WELL AS THE SENCE OF SIGHT AND THEY CAN ENJOY IT FROM ALL SIDES.

LET US LOOK INTO ANOTHER DIRECTION. WHAT WOULD WE KNOW OF THE MAYAN THE AZTEC, THE INCA, THE TOLTEC CIVILIZATIONS IF SCULPTURE HAD NOT BEEN THE CHIEF ART OF THOSE PEOPLES?

TRY TO THINK SCULPTURALLY, THAT IS IN THREE DEMENSIONS; VISUALIZE THE THING IN YOUR MIND IN TERMS OF VOLUME, MASS, FORM.

YOU ASK WHAT ARE THE THREE DEMENTIONS? THEY ARE HIGHT WIDTH & DEPTH.

1. USE OAK IF RUGGED STRENGTH IS TO BE SHOWN OR THE GNARLED HAND OF THE AGED.

2. WALNUT IF A CERTAIN ANIMAL GRACE IS TO BE DEPICTED.

3. CHERRY IF THE COLOR IS TO PLAY A PART IN SHOWING THE GLOW OF HEALTH, THE INNER WORMTH.

THE KEY TO GOOD SCULPTURING IS SIMPLICITY.

THE BEST SOURCES OF IDEAS AND SUBJECT MATTER FOR AN AMERICAN INDIAN ARE IN HIS OWN BACKGROUND AND CULTURE.

ARE YOU GOING TO SHOW TIREDNESS, HUMBLENESS, IT MUST BE A SIMPLE STATEMENT.

IN YOUR SCULPTURE YOU ARE TALKING TO PEOPLE; SAYING SOMETHING TO THEM; YOUR SCULPTURE IS YOUR ALPHABET, YOUR GRAMMAR — ONE MIGHT CALL IT A HUMAN ALPHABET. YOUR BEST WAY OF SAYING ANYTHING, THE SUREST WAY TO BE UNDERSTOOD TO SPEAK AS SIMPLY AS YOU CAN. IN ANY ART FORM SPEAK SIMPLY SO THAT YOU MAY BE EASILY UNDERSTOOD.

Plates 26–28
Notes on Sculpture, c. 1970
Pencil, 8 × 10½ in.
The Allan Houser Foundation
HF1995.1-409A.D
HF1995.1-409B.D
HF1995.1-409C.D

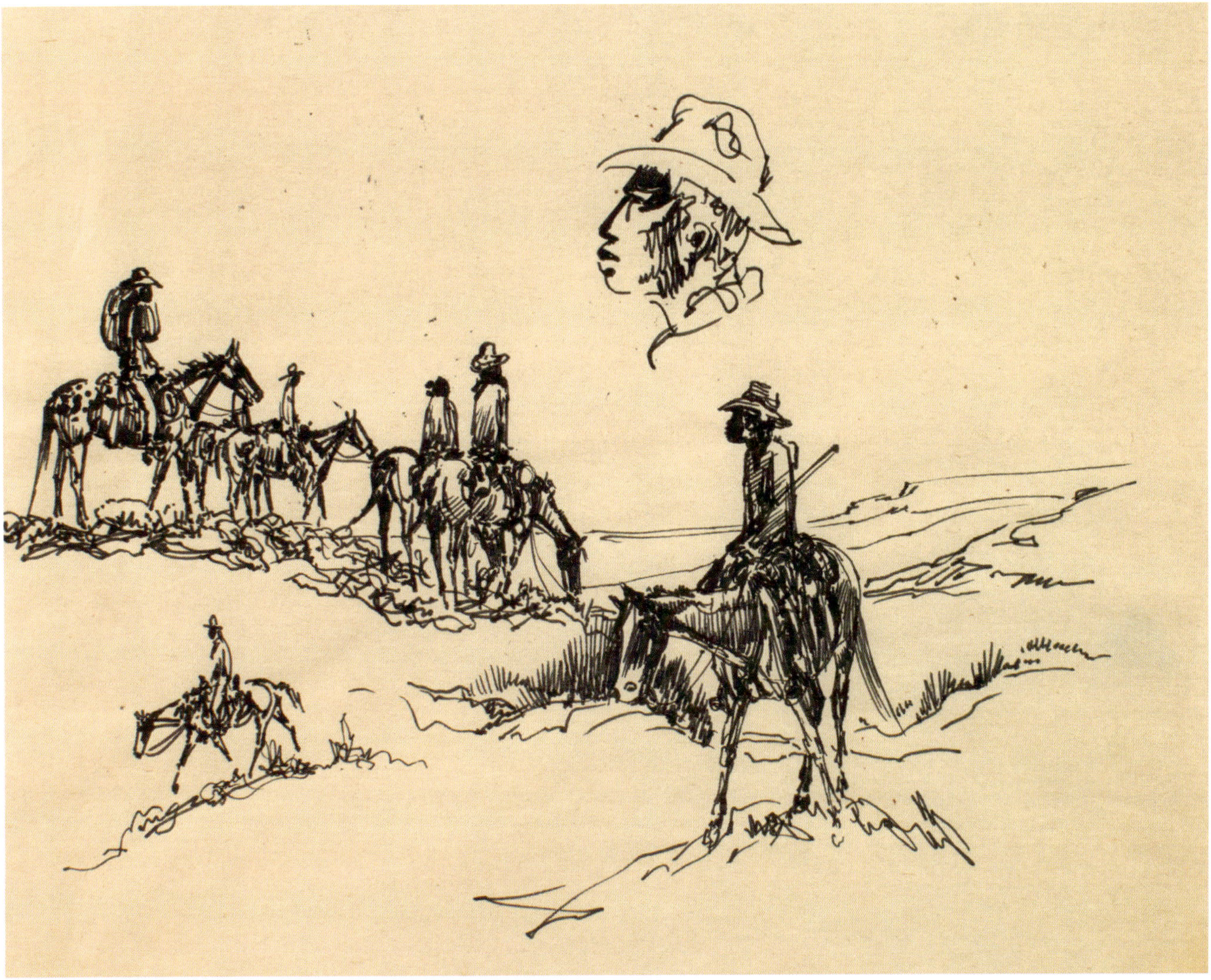

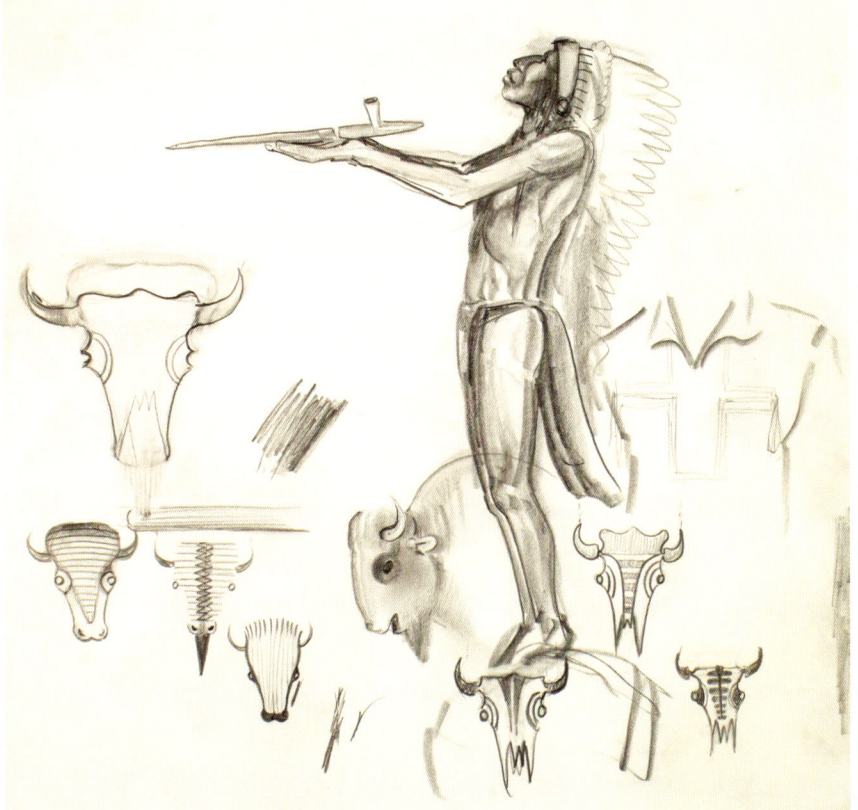

Plate 29
Horses and Riders in Landscape,
Male Profile, 1975
Felt-tip pen, 9 × 12 in.
Chiinde, LLC.
HF1995.1-269T.D

Plate 30
Offering the Pipe, Seven
Abstracted Buffalo Heads,
Buffalo, Shirt, 1975
Pencil, 12 7/16 × 13 1/16 in.
Chiinde, LLC.
HF1995.1-276P.D

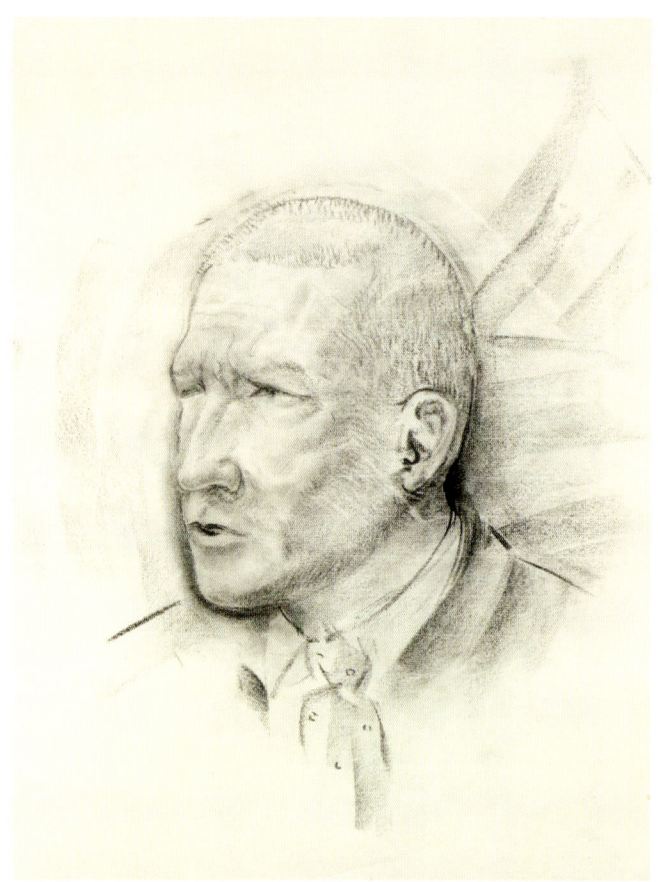

Plate 31
Study for Portrait of Stewart Udall, 1975
Charcoal, 23 ½ × 17 ⅞ in.
Allan Houser Inc.
HF1995.1-192

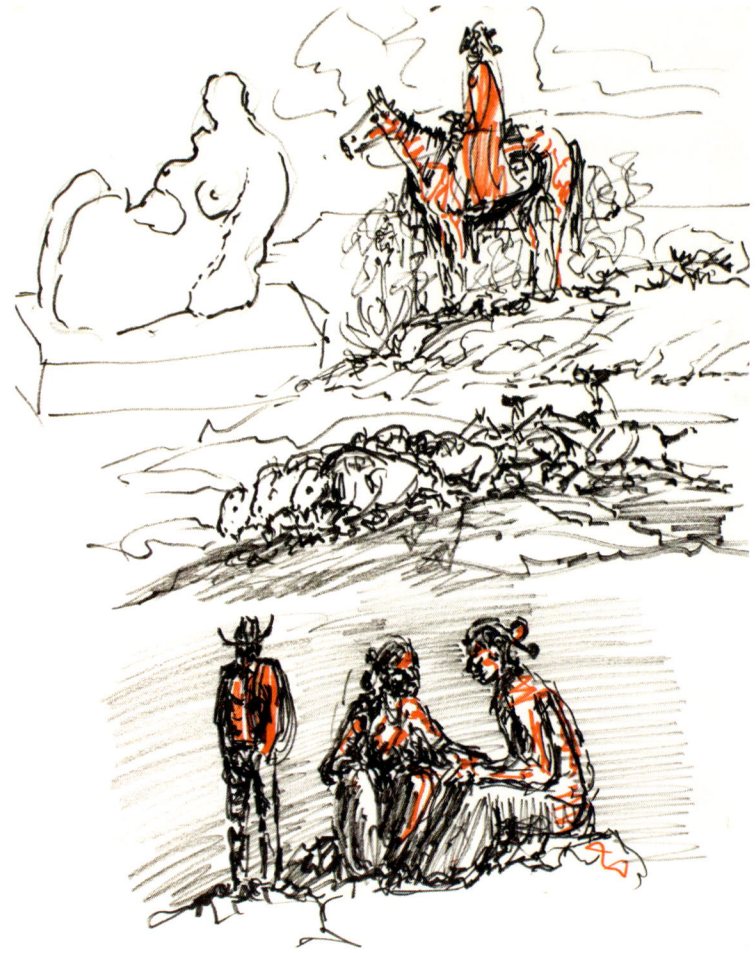

Plate 32
Four Figure Studies, c. 1975
Felt-tip pen, 11 × 13 ¹⁵⁄₁₆ in.
Chiinde, LLC.
HF1995.1-438.D

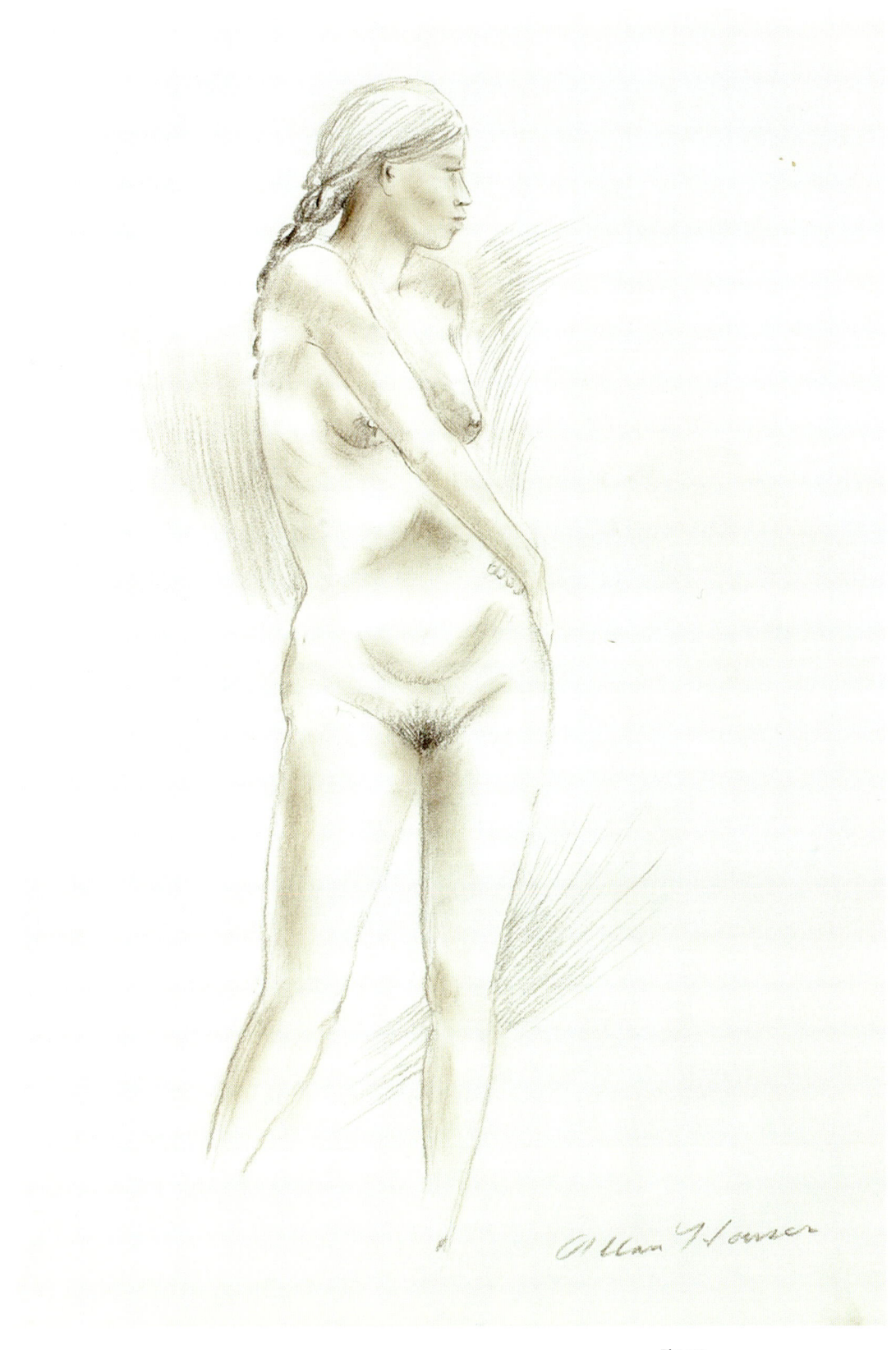

Plate 33
Nude Study, 1978
Conte pencil, 16 ¾ × 13 ¾ in.
Chiinde, LLC.
HF1995.1-264AG.D

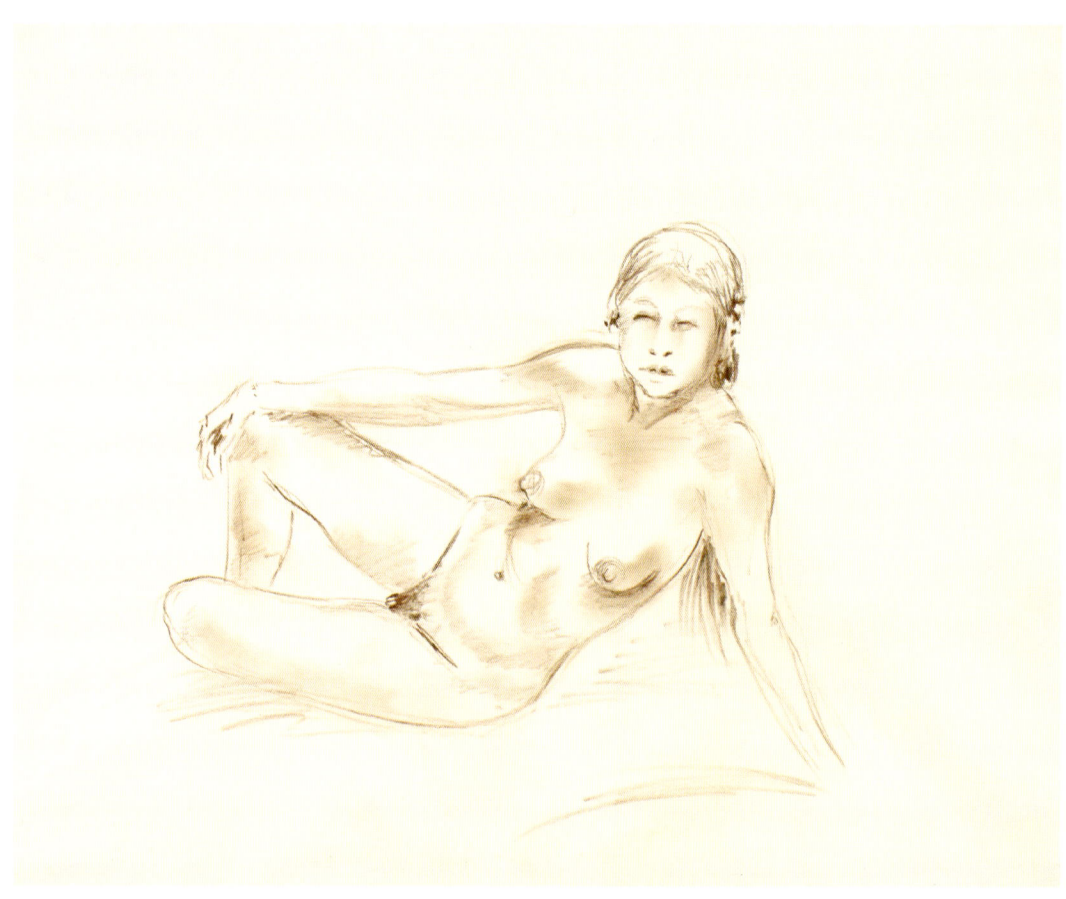

Plate 34
Nude Study, 1978
Pastel, 14 × 16 ¾ in.
Chiinde, LLC.
HF1995.1-308E.D

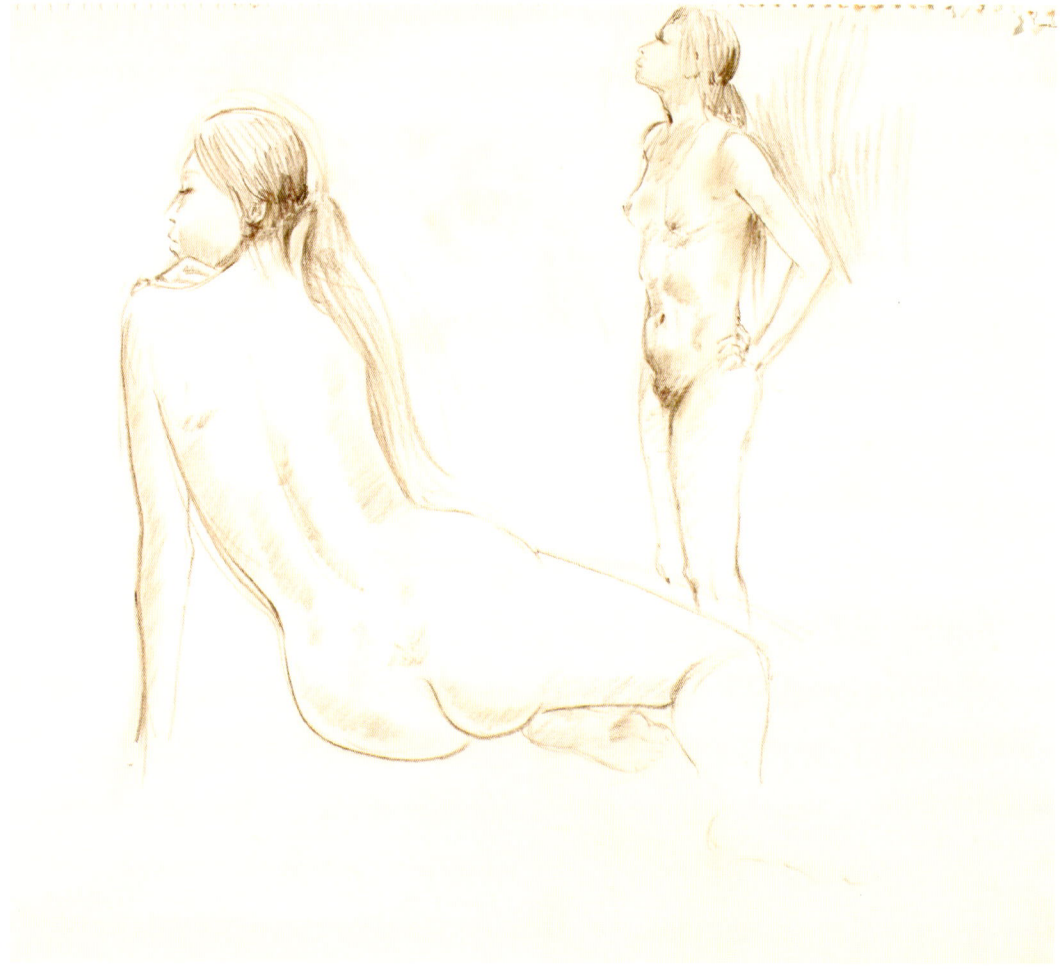

Plate 35
Two Nude Studies, 1978
Pastel, 14 × 16 ¾ in.
Chiinde, LLC.
HF1995.1-308I.D

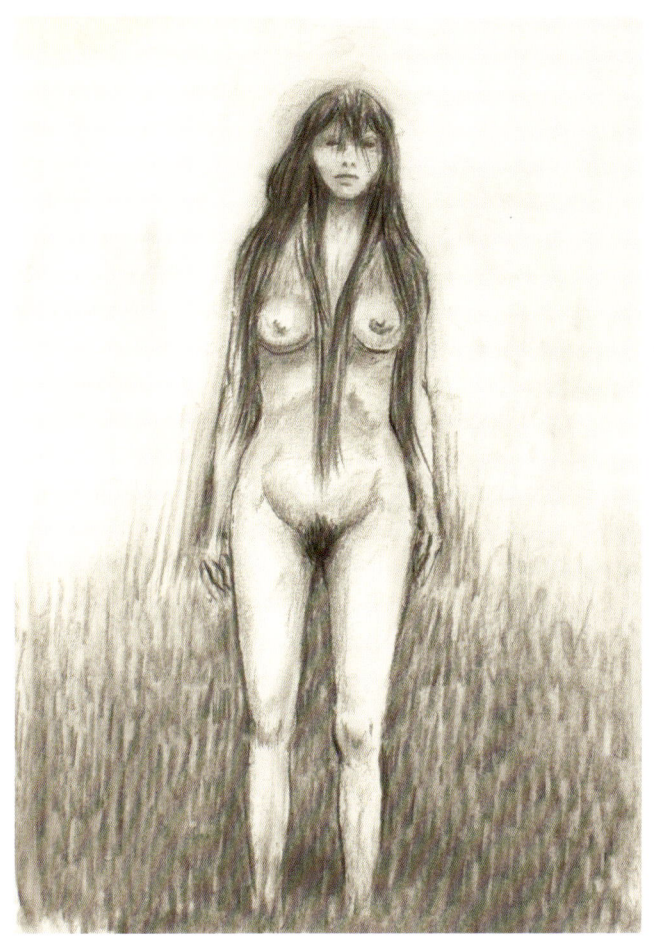

Plate 36
Nude Study, 1982
Charcoal, 17 × 14 in.
Chiinde, LLC.
HF1995.1-280.D

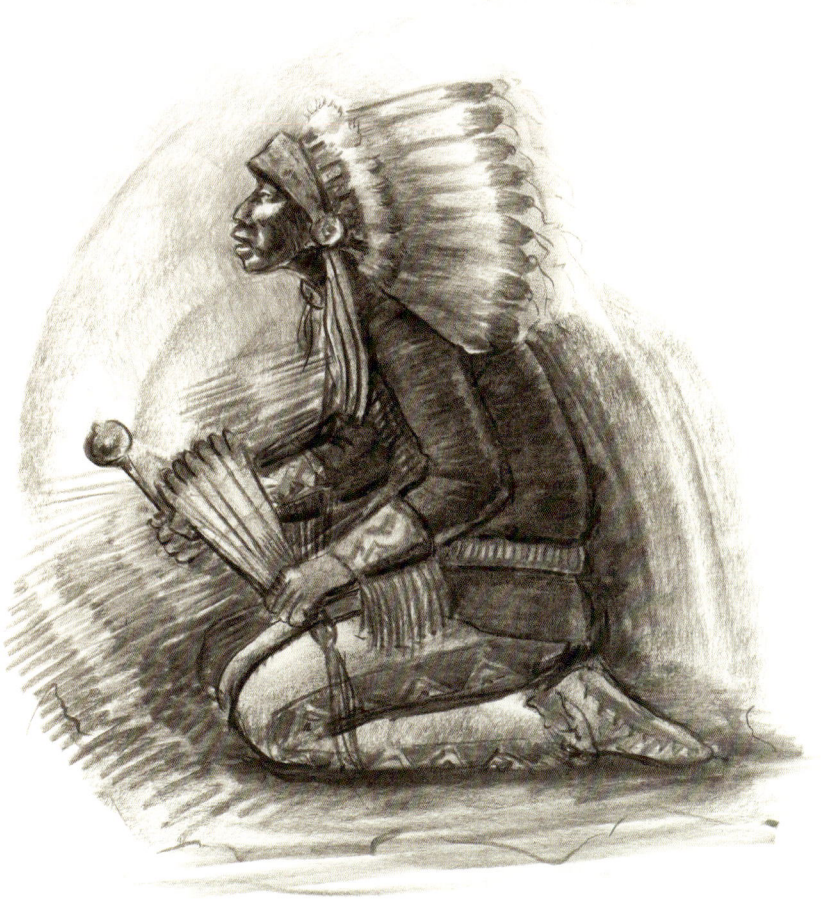

Plate 37
**Plains Warrior with Rattle
and Fan,** 1985
Charcoal, 24 × 17⅞ in.
Chiinde, LLC.
HF1995.1-302.D

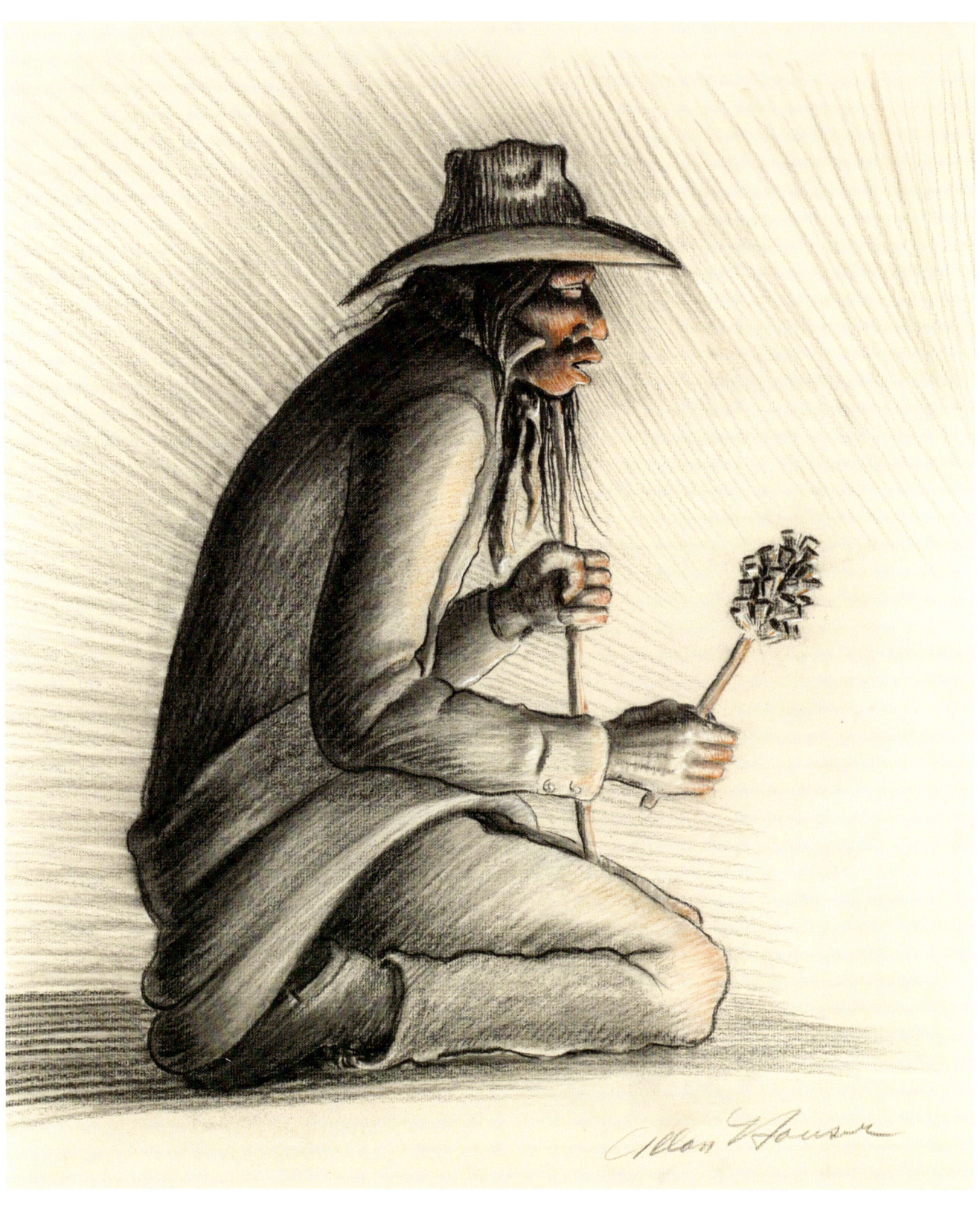

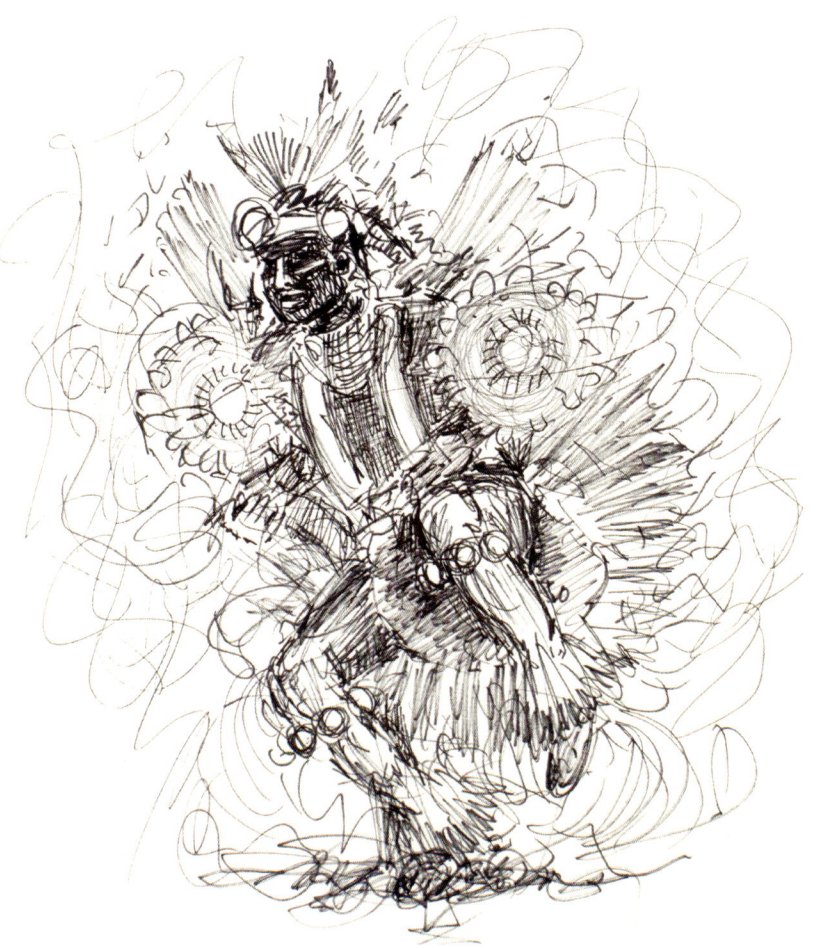

Plate 39
Fancy Dancer, c. 1985
Felt-tip pen, 8 15/16 × 11 15/16 in.
Chiinde, LLC.
HF1995.1-419D.D

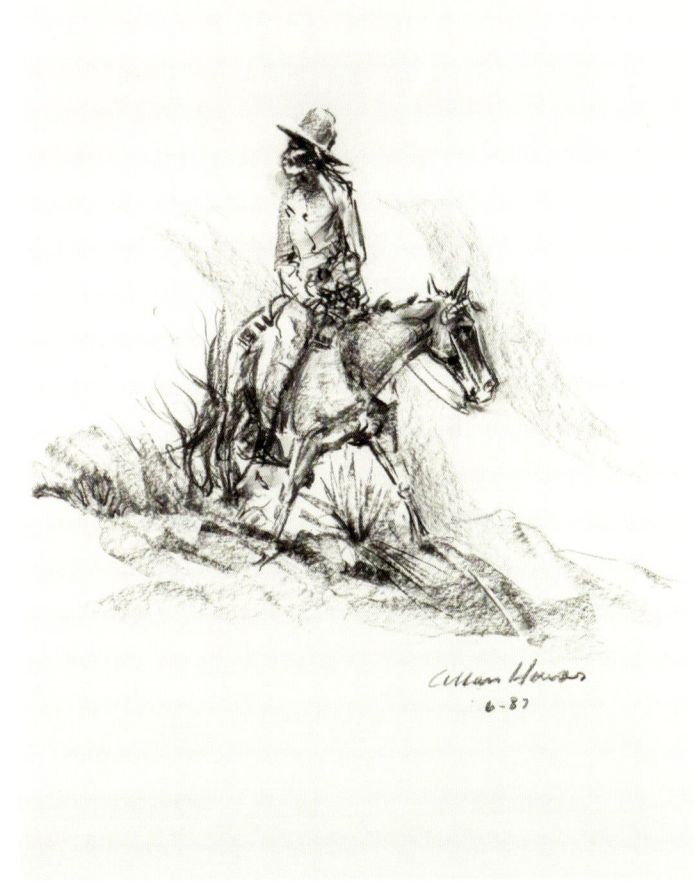

Plate 40
Horse and Rider, 1987
Charcoal, 24 × 18 in.
Chiinde, LLC.
HF1995.1-316.D

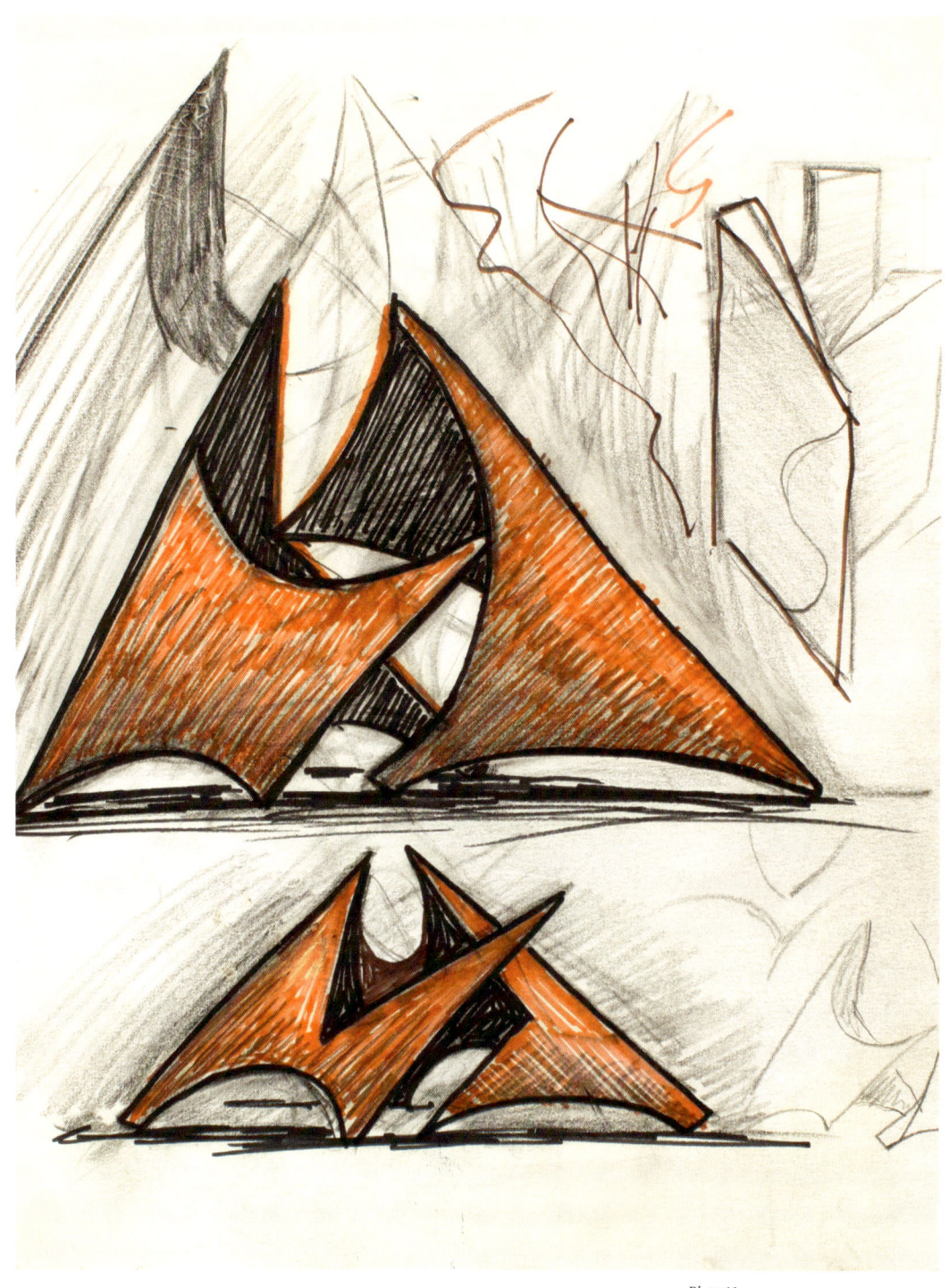

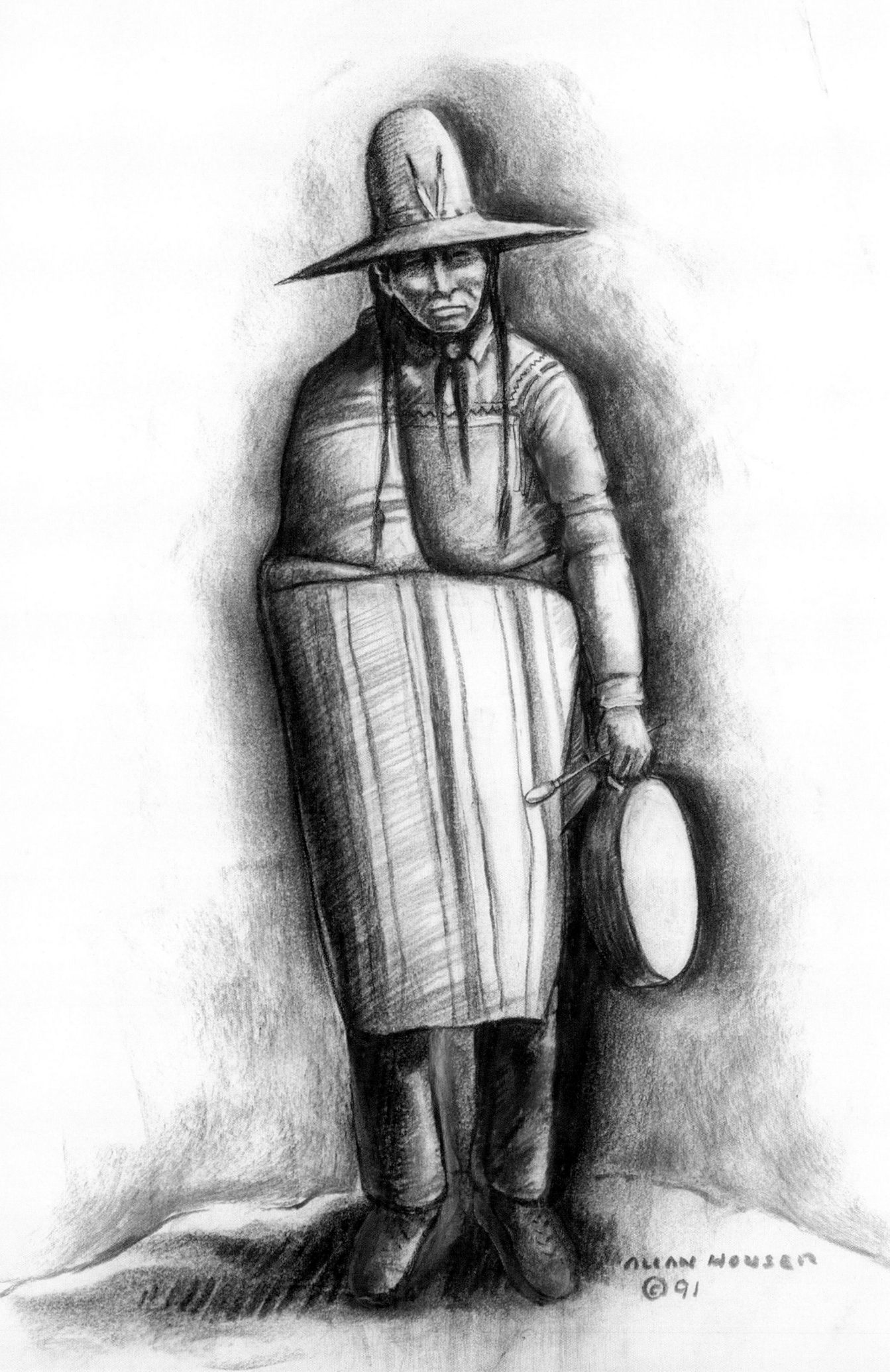

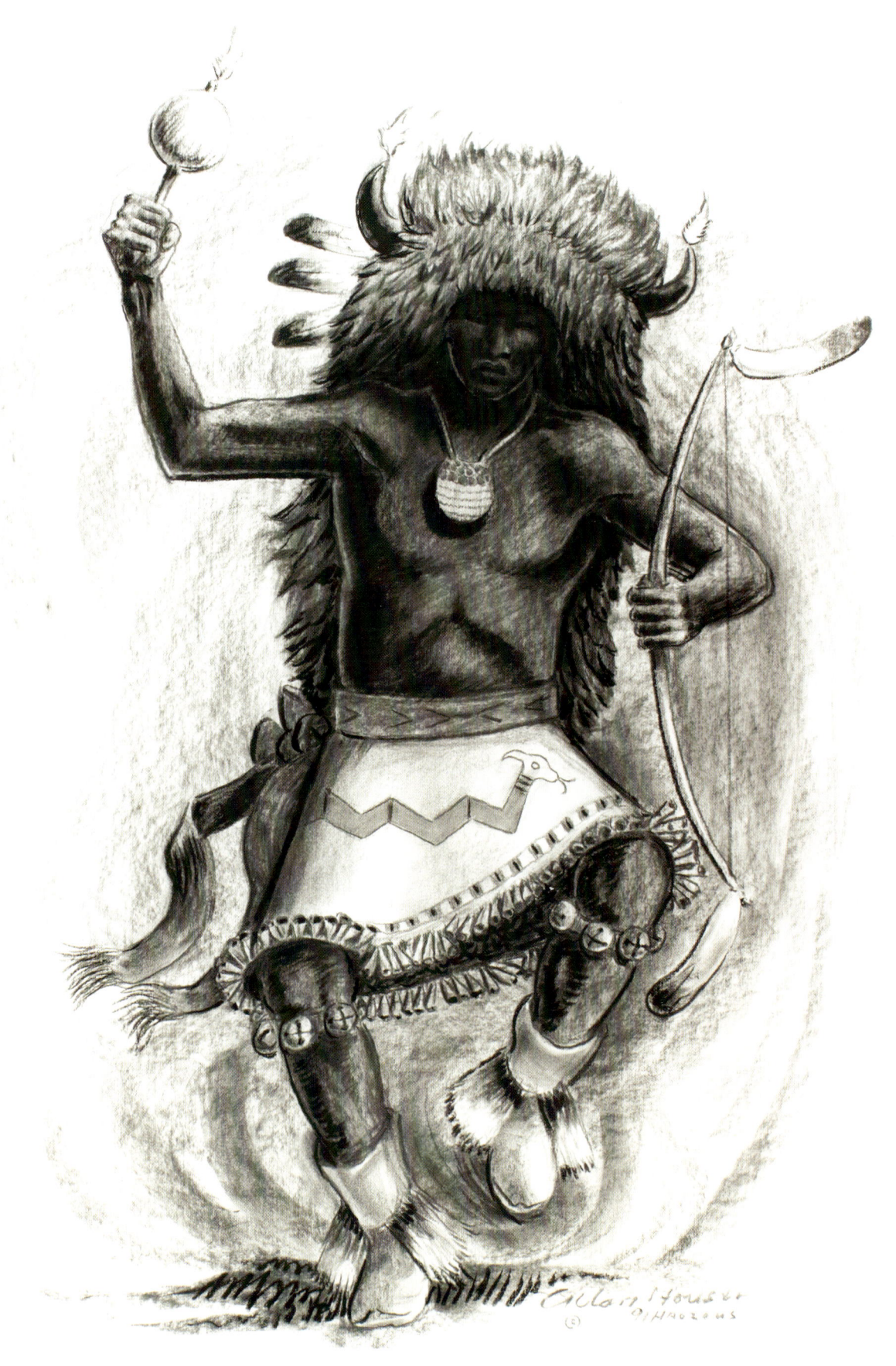

Plate 43
Pueblo Buffalo Dancer, 1991
Charcoal, 43 × 30 ½ in.
Houser / Haozous Family Limited Partnership
HF1995.1-252.a.D

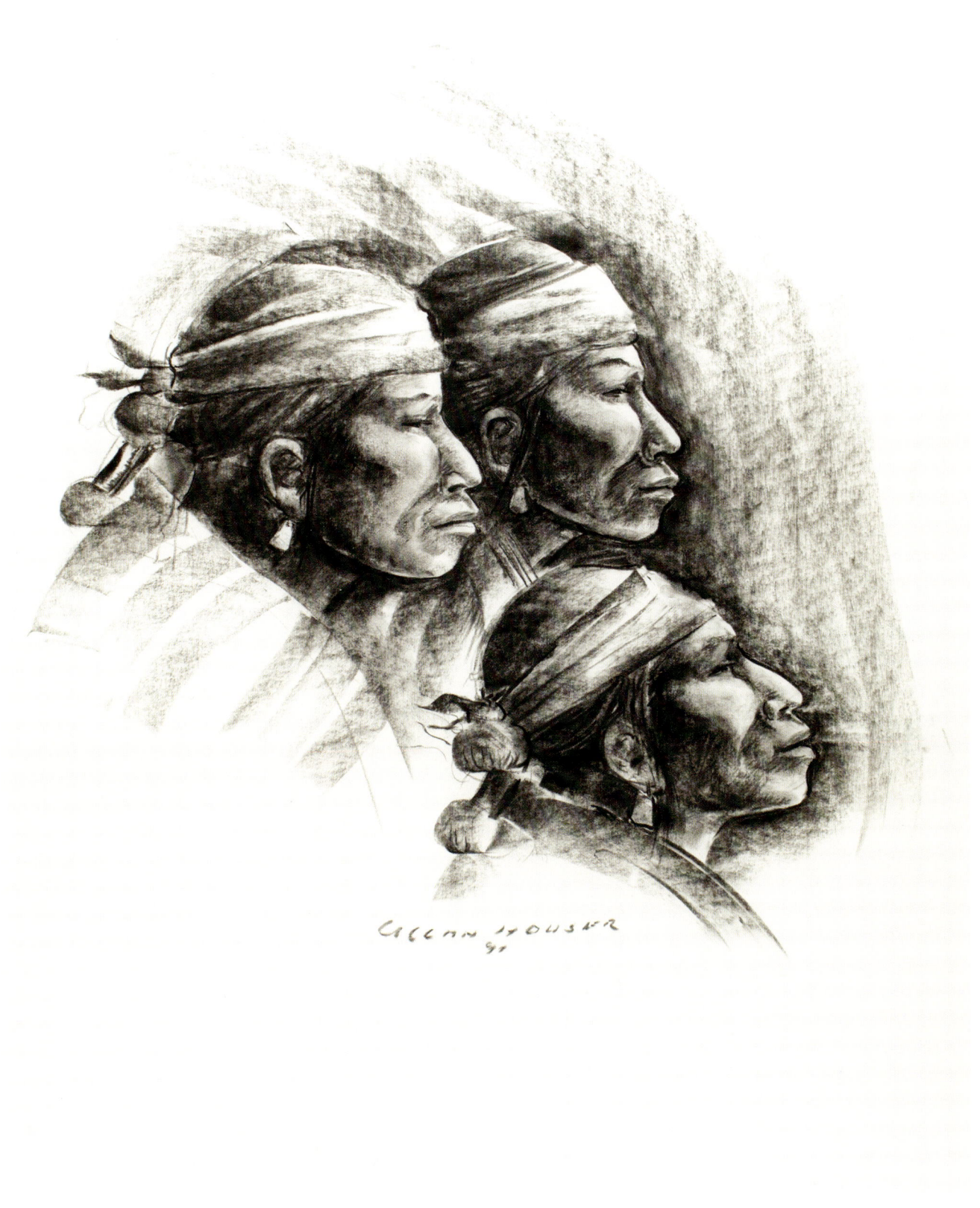

Plate 44
Three Navajo Men, 1991
Charcoal, 40½ × 29¼ in.
Allan Houser Inc.
HF1995.1-742.D

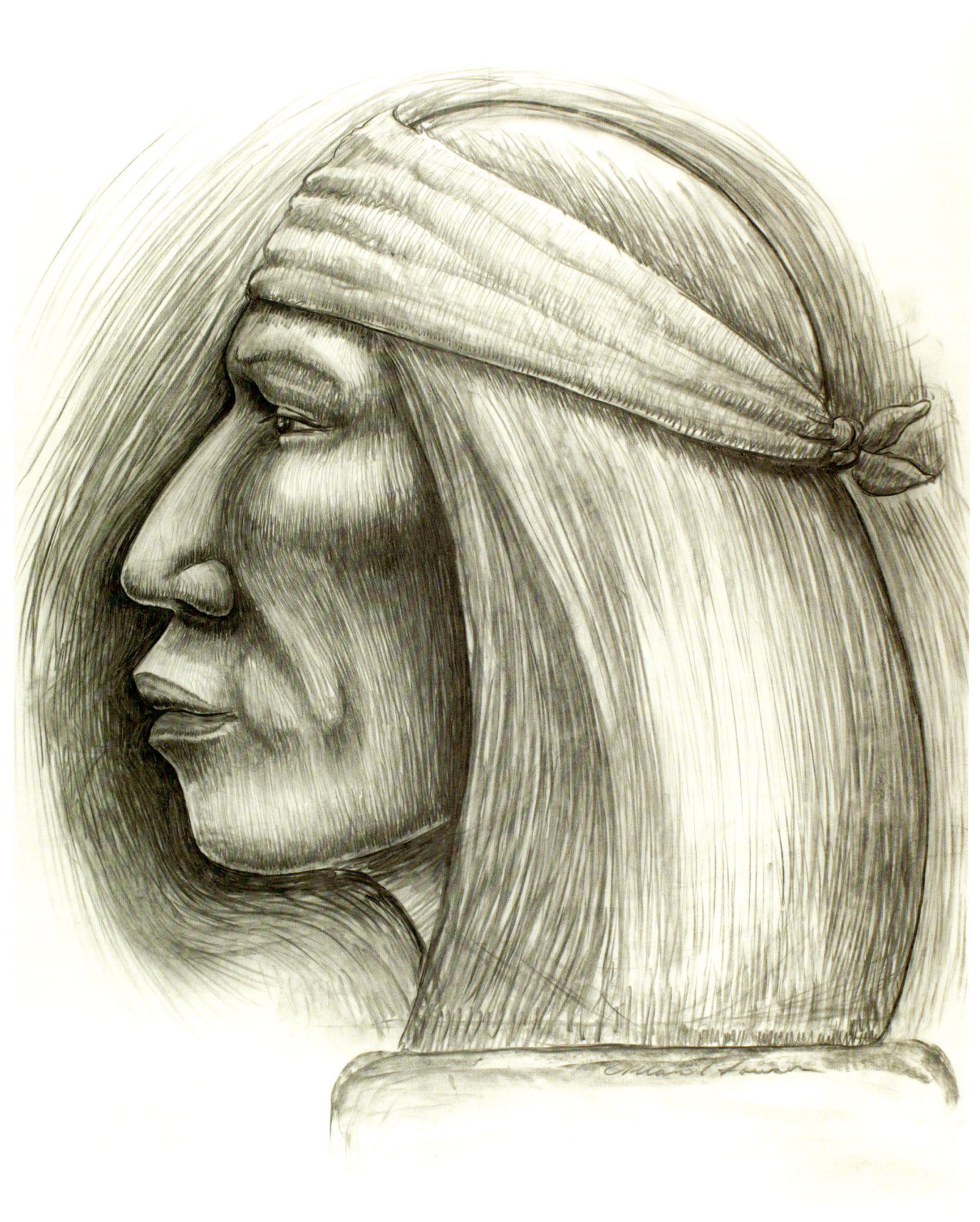

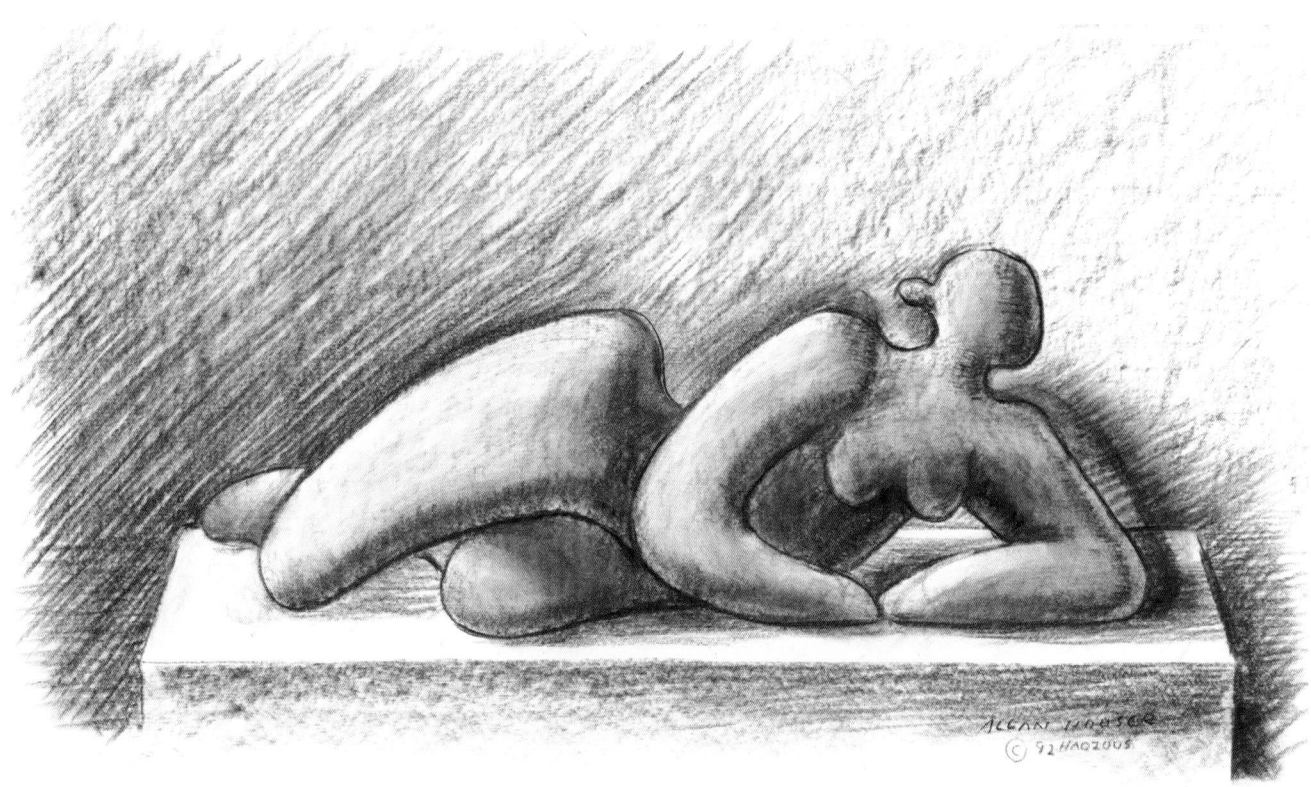

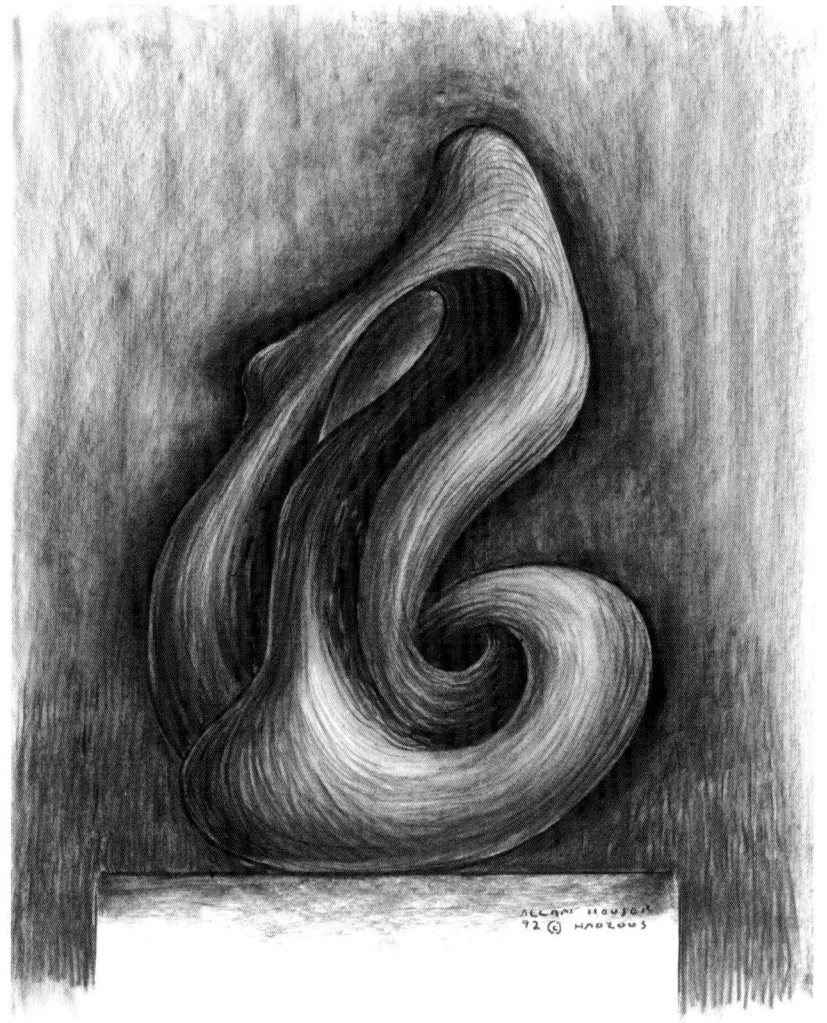

Plate 46
Study for Reclining Figure, 1992
Charcoal, 22 ¼ × 30 ⅛ in.
Houser / Haozous Family Limited Partnership
HF1995.1-017.a.D

Plate 47
Non-objective Form, 1992
Charcoal, 30 × 22 in.
Allan Houser Inc.
HF1995.1-36.D

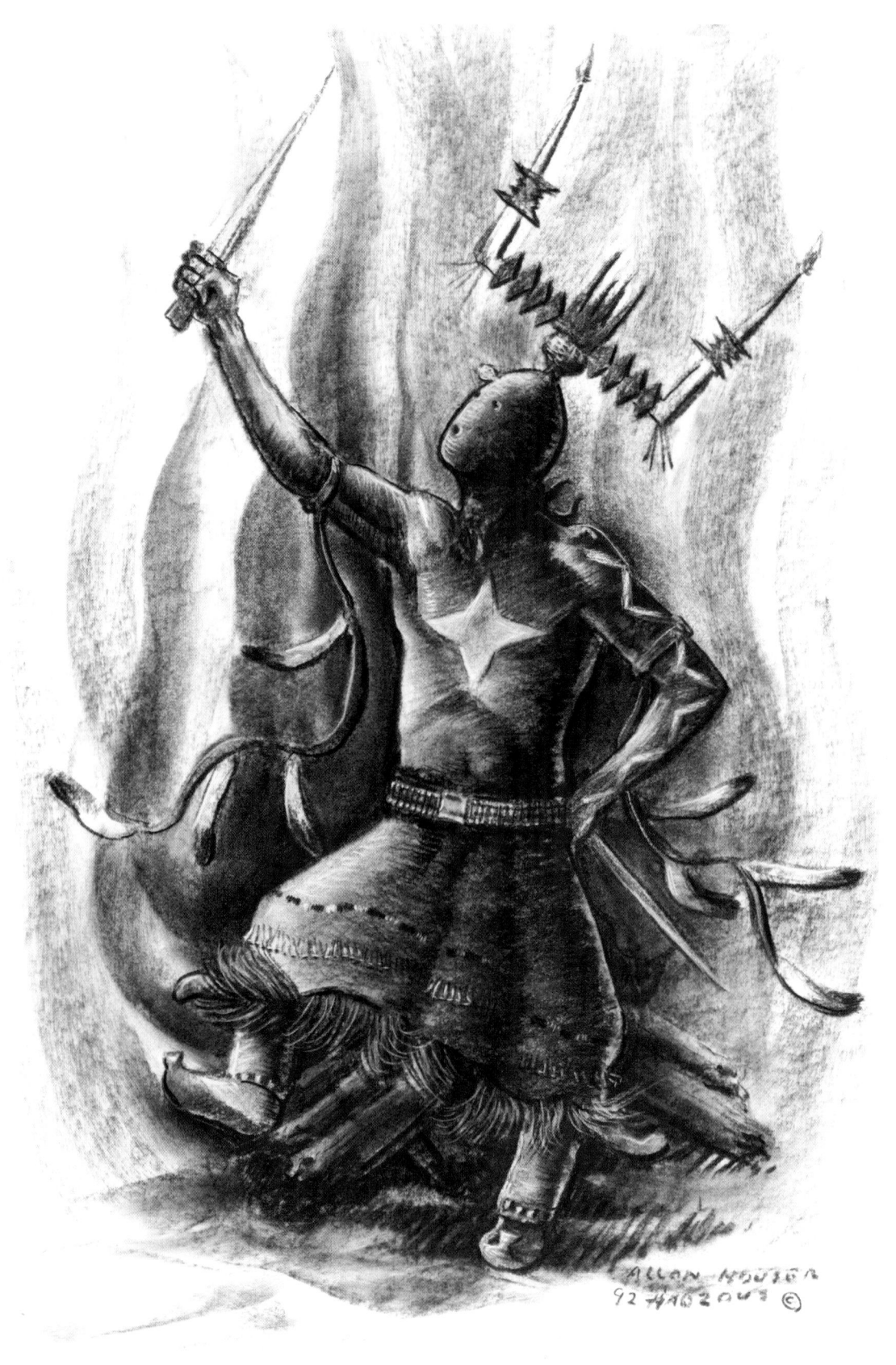

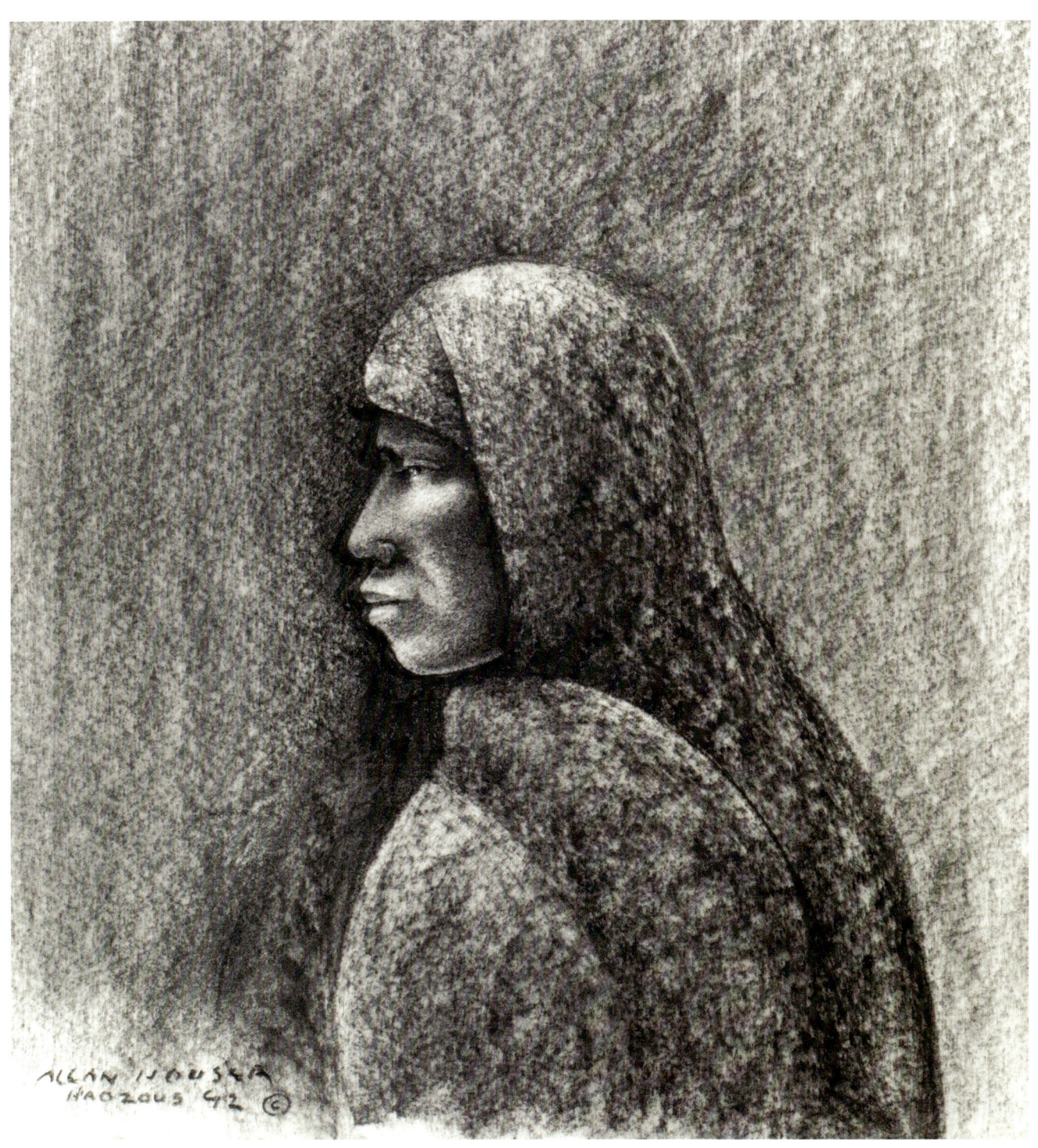

Plate 49
Female Profile, 1992
Charcoal, 21 × 19½ in.
Allan Houser Inc.
HF1995.1-122.D

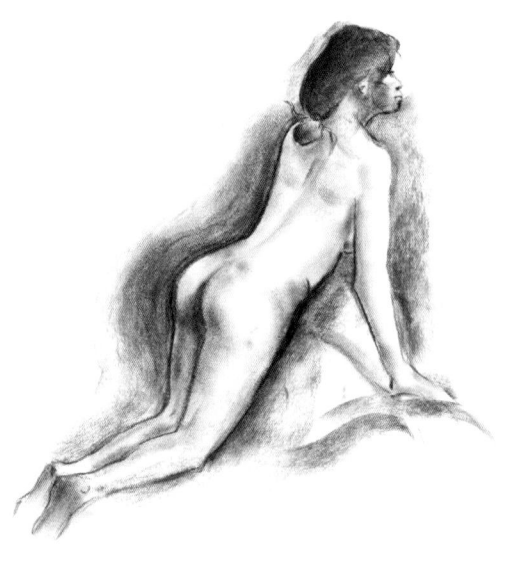

Plate 50
Nude Study, 1992
Charcoal, 30 × 22 ¼ in.
Chiinde, LLC.
HF1995.1-228.D

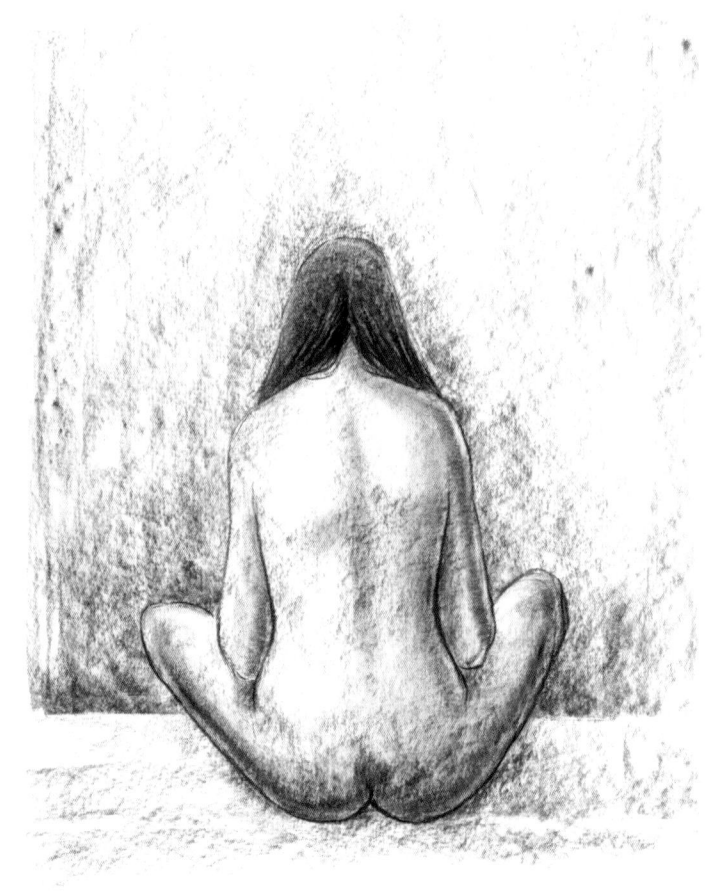

Plate 51
Nude Study, 1992
Charcoal, 30 × 22 ¼ in.
Allan Houser Inc.
HF1995.1-233.D

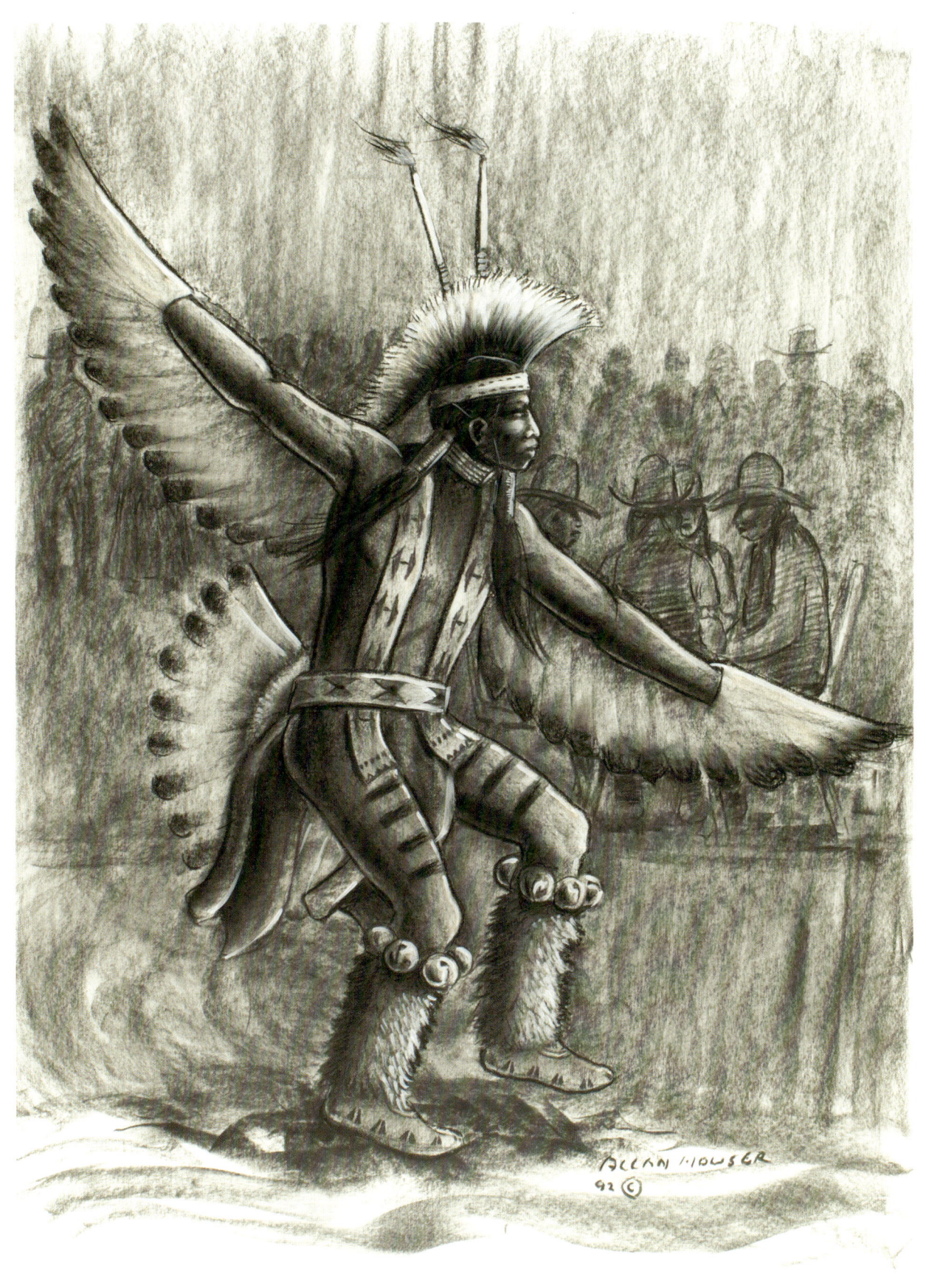

Plate 52
Eagle Dancer, 1992
Charcoal, 44 ½ × 30 ½ in.
Allan Houser Inc.
HF1995.1-253.D

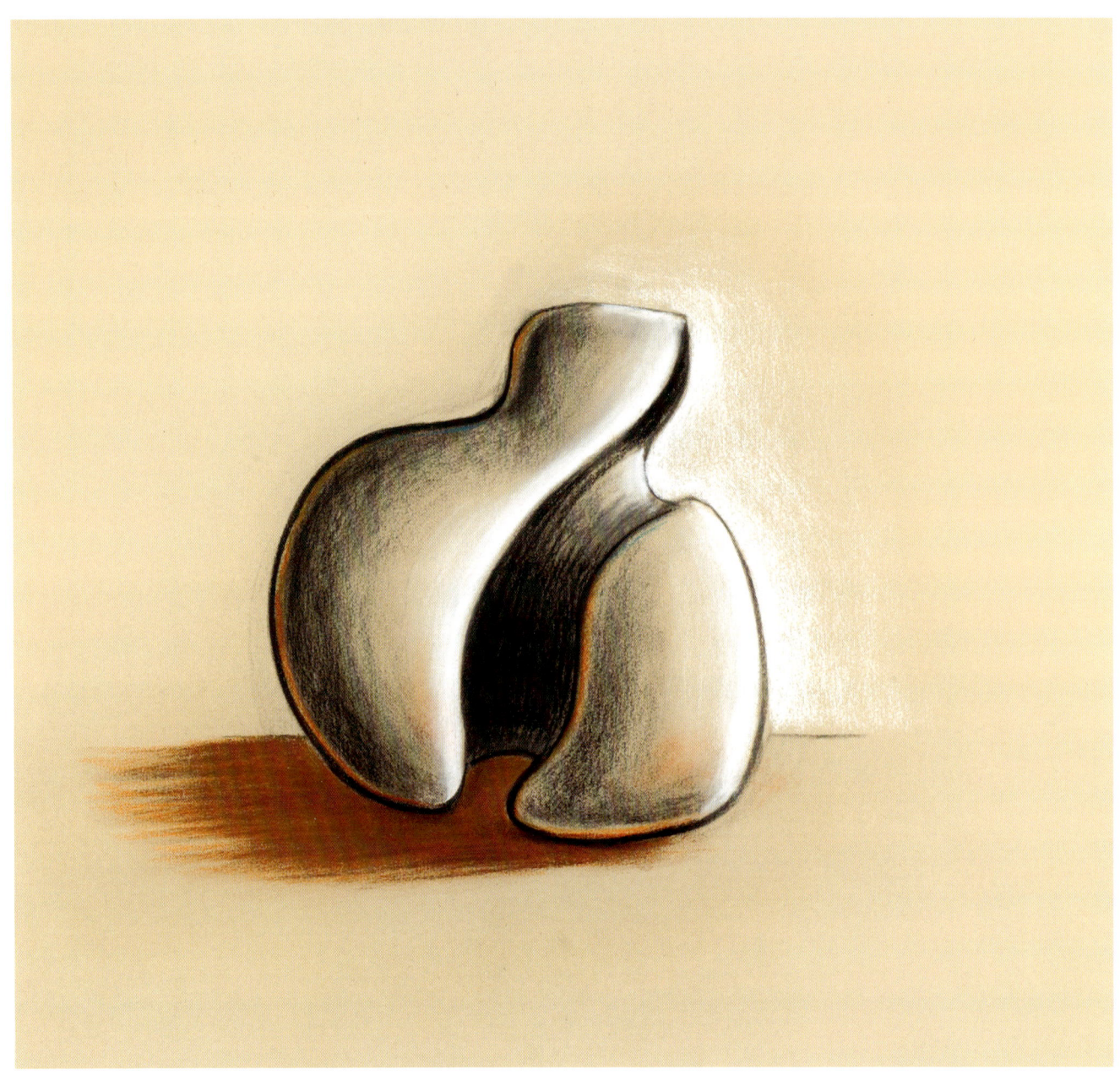

Plate 53
Non-objective Form, c. 1992
Pastel, 21 × 22 in.
Allan Houser Inc.
HF1995.1-3.D

Plate 54
Abstract Female Figure, c. 1992
Pastel, 29 × 19 in.
Allan Houser Inc.
HF1995.1-1.D

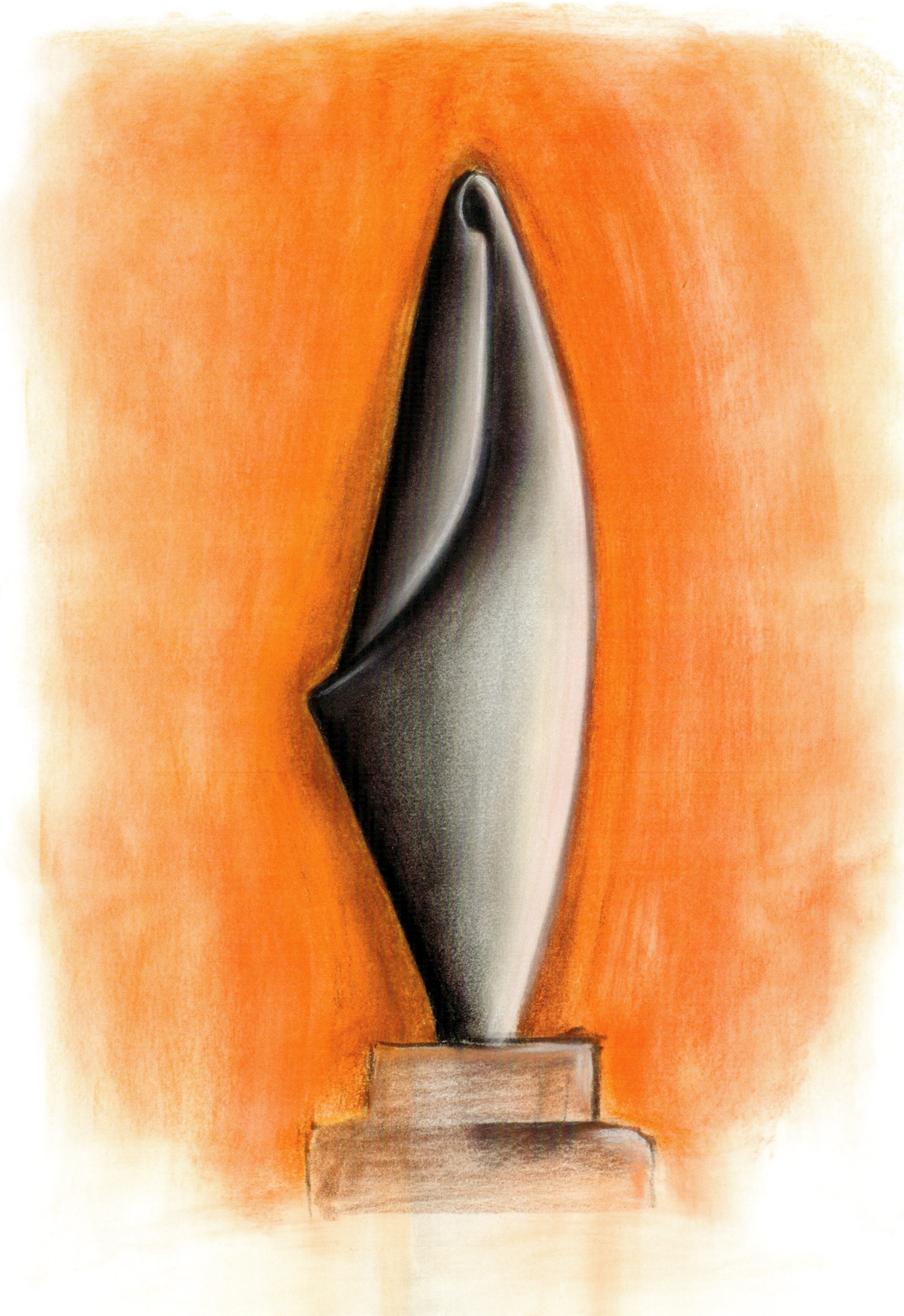

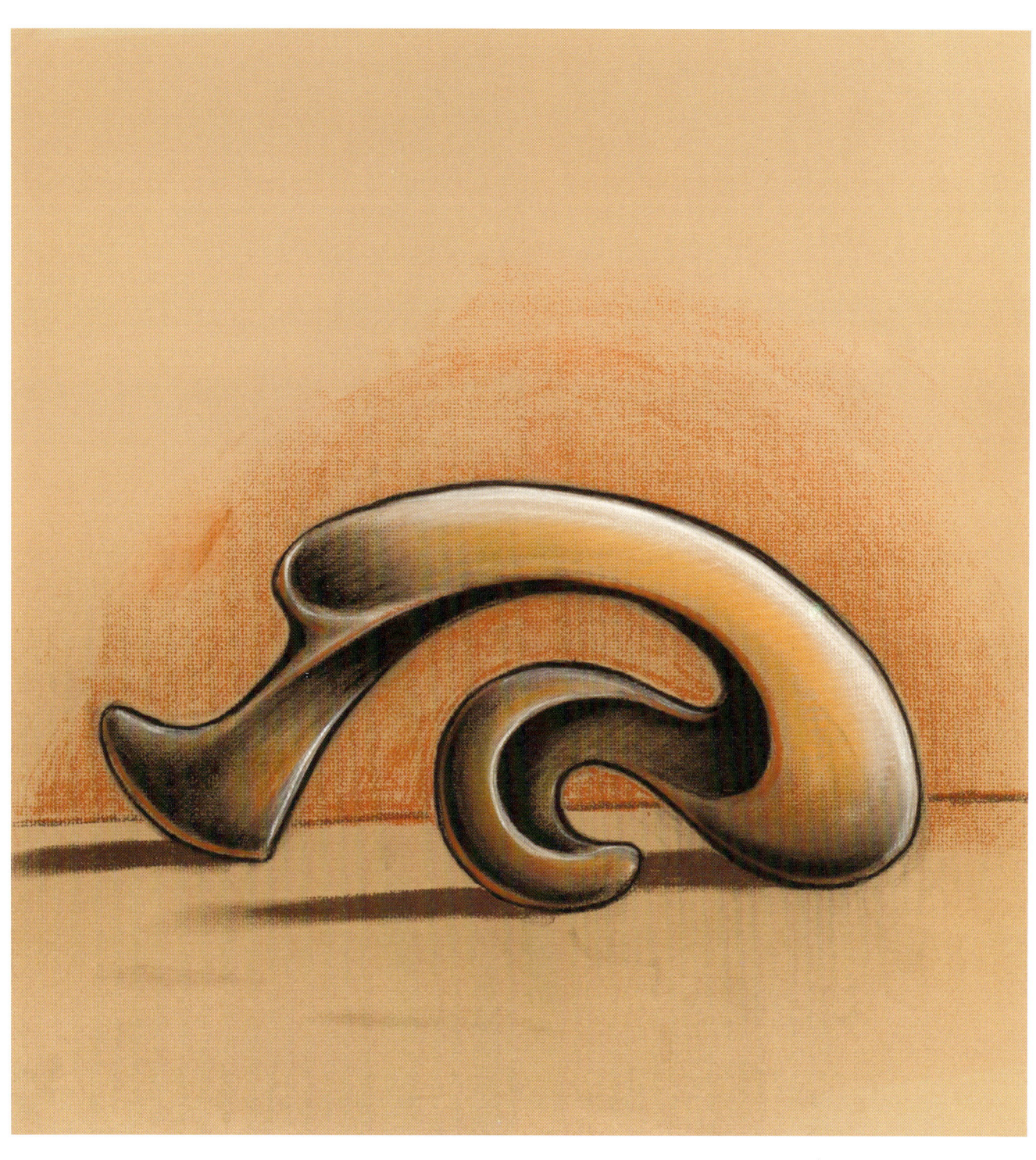

Plate 55
Non-objective Form, c. 1992
Pastel, 23 ½ × 22 in.
Allan Houser Inc.
HF1995.1-10.D

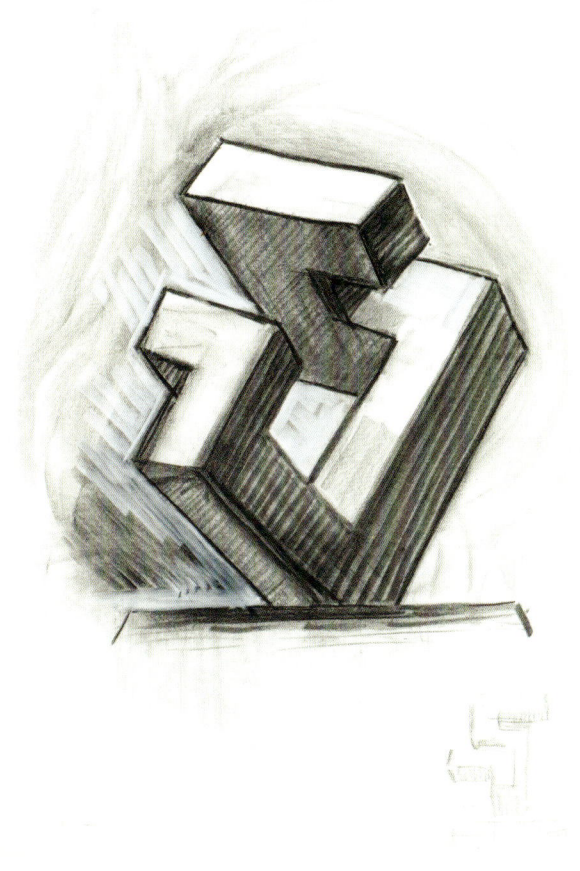

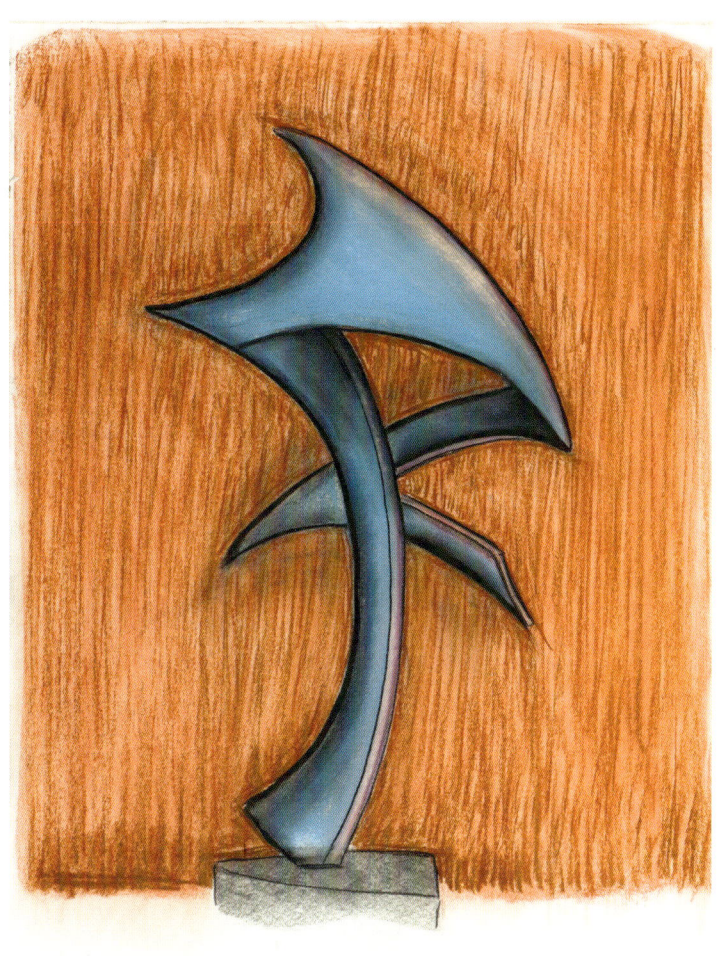

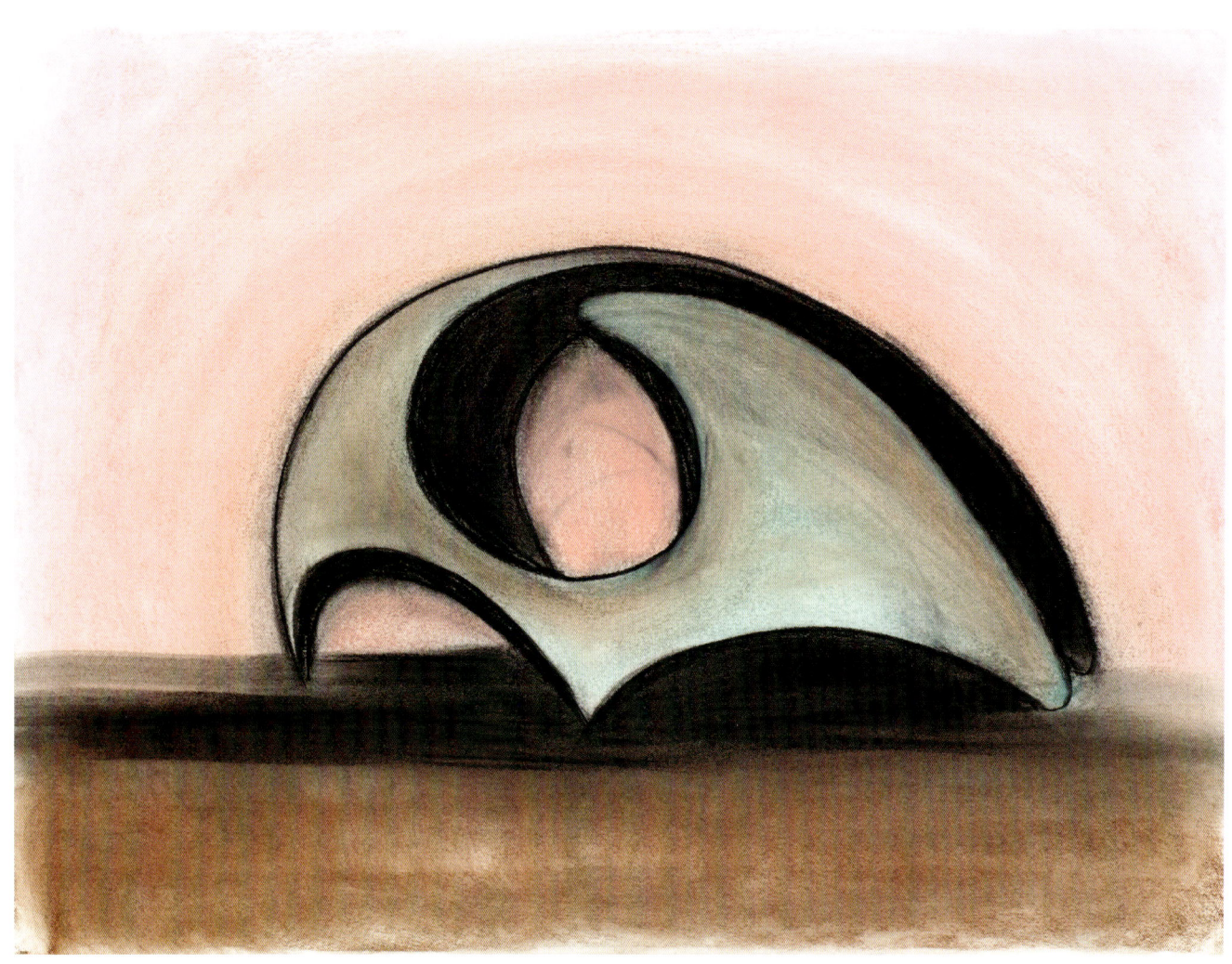

Plate 58
Non-objective Form, c. 1992
Pastel, 22 ¼ × 30 in.
Allan Houser Inc.
HF1995.1-26.D

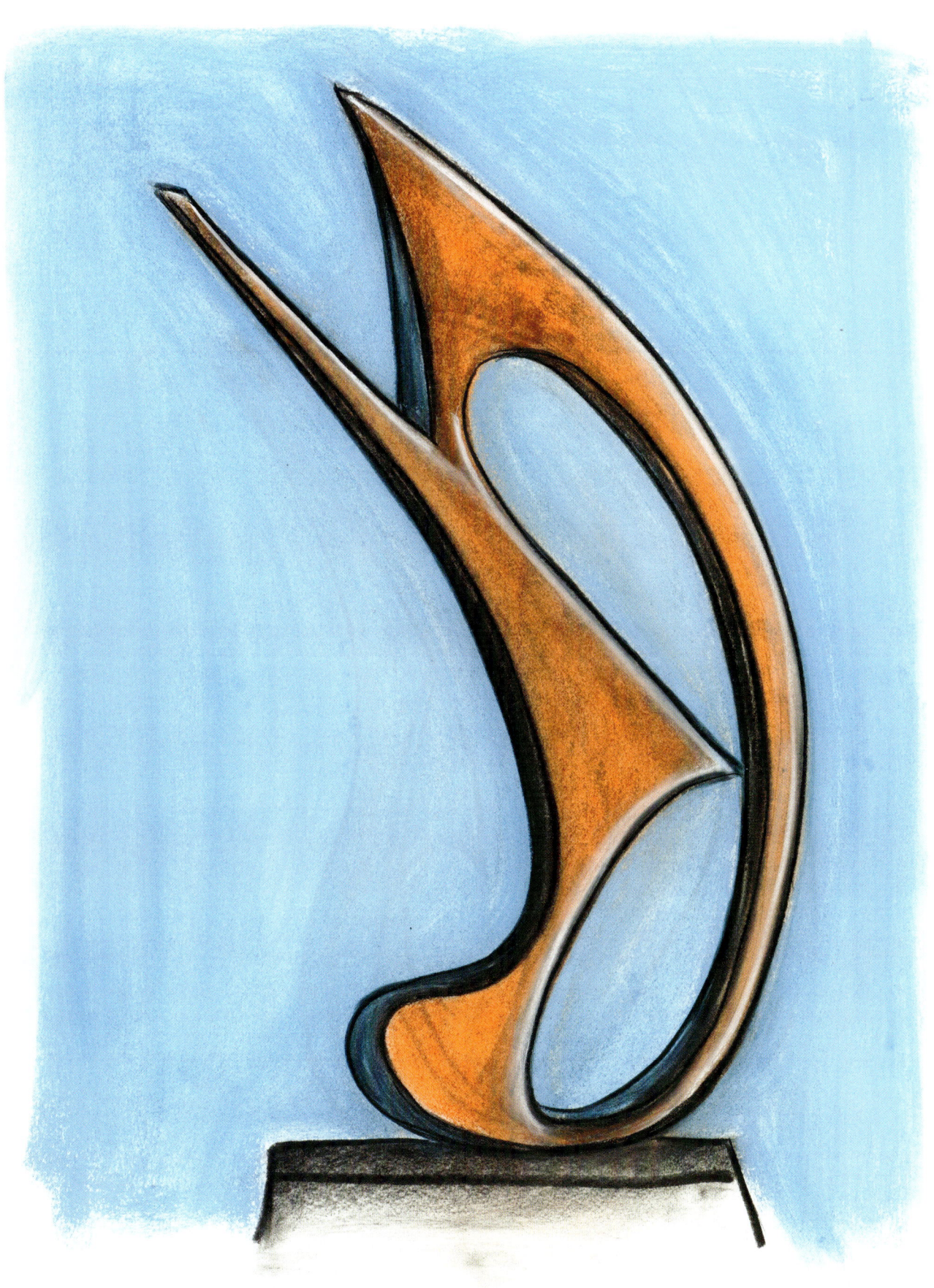

Plate 59
Non-objective Form, c. 1992
Pastel, 30 × 22 ¼ in.
Allan Houser Inc.
HF1995.1-27.D

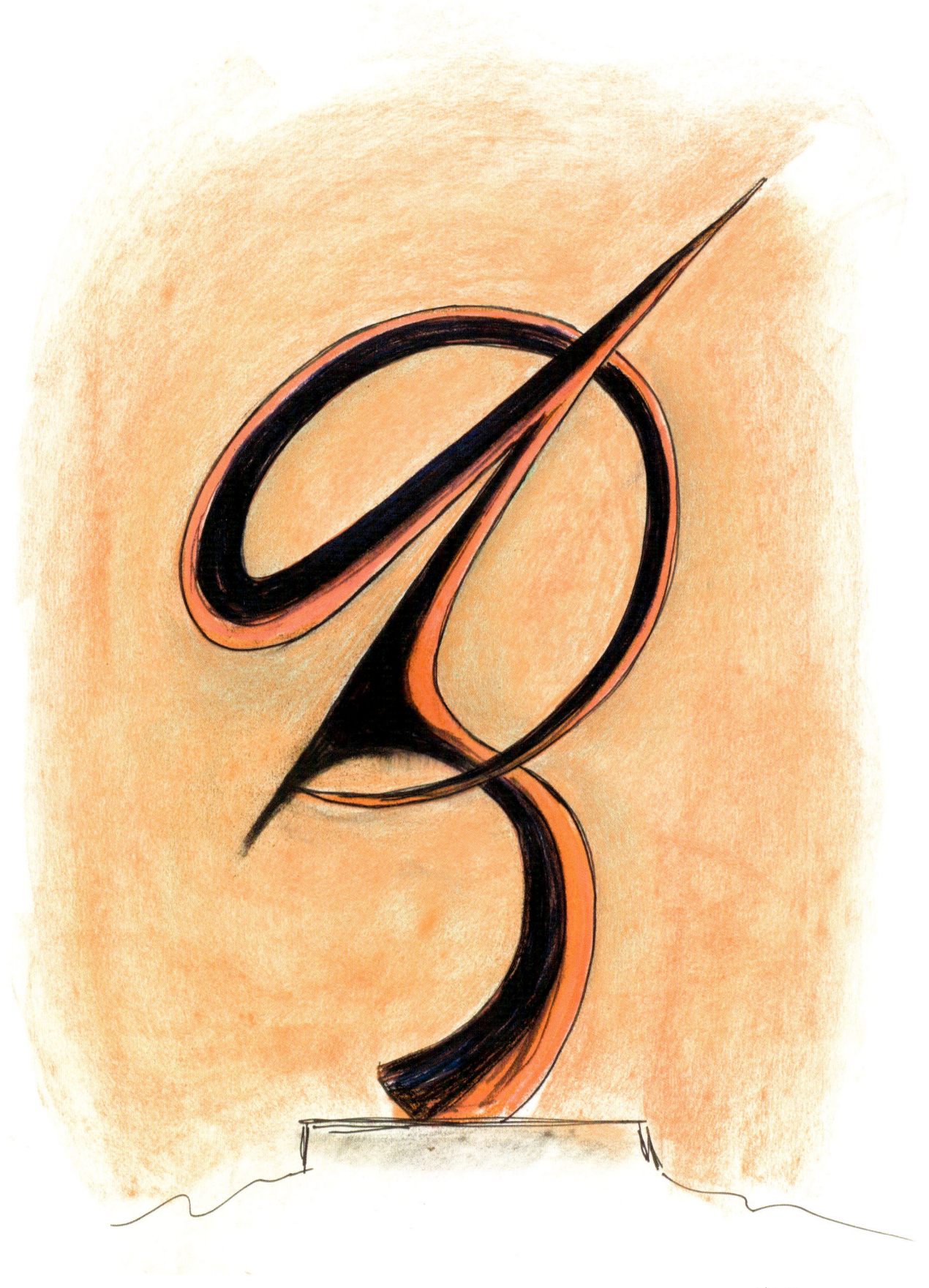

Plate 60
Non-objective Form, c. 1992
Pastel, 30 × 22 ¼ in.
Allan Houser Inc.
HF1995.1-28.D

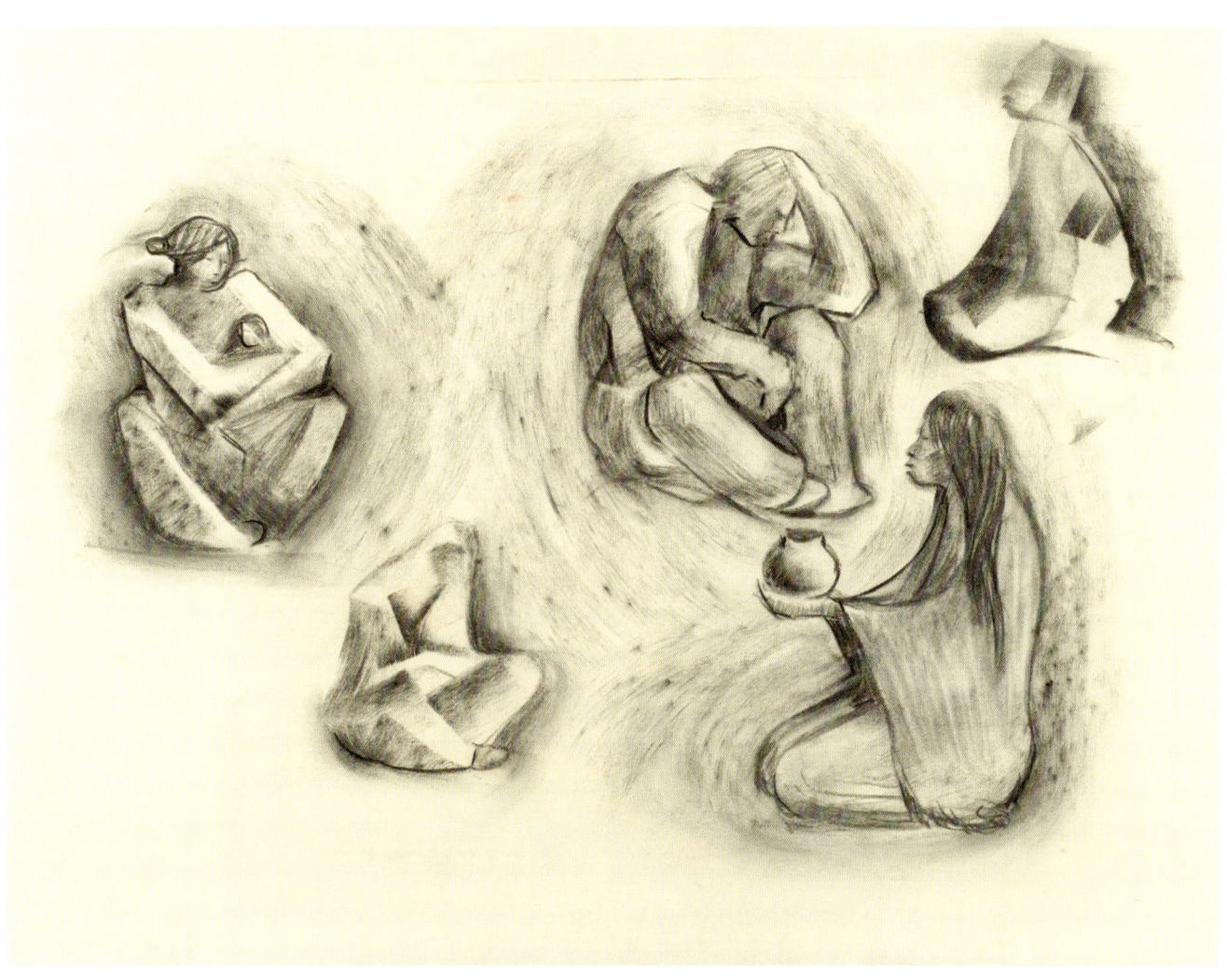

Plate 61
Five Abstracted Figure Studies,
c. 1992
Charcoal, 22 × 30 in.
Houser / Haozous Family Limited Partnership
HF1995.1-031.a.D

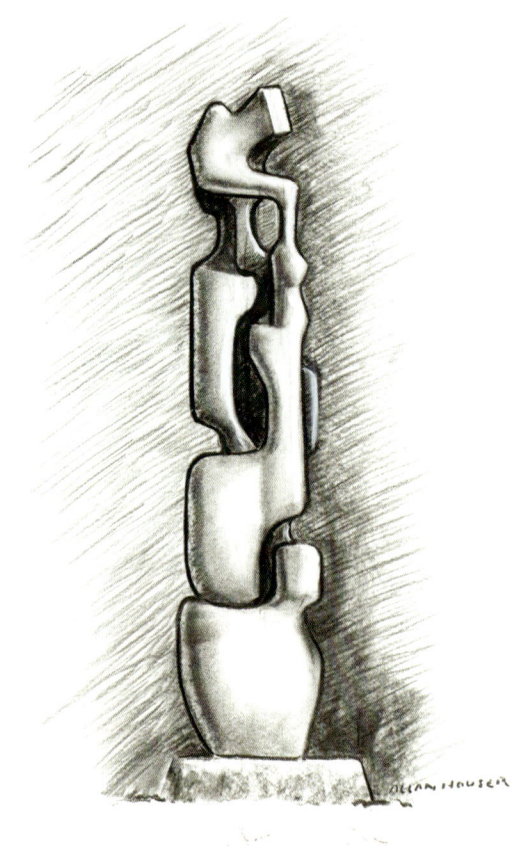

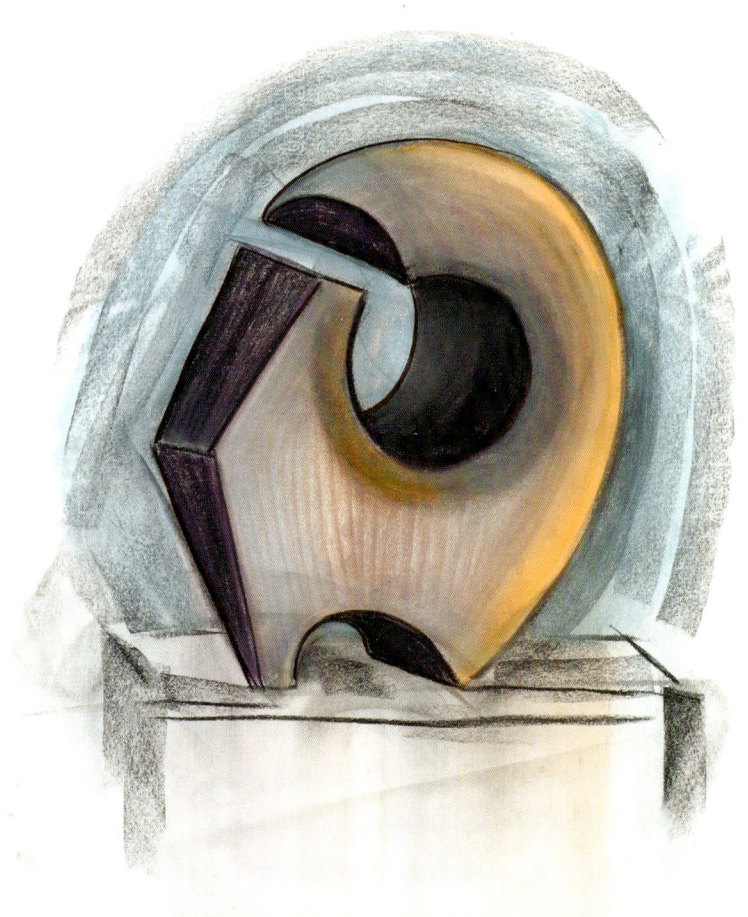

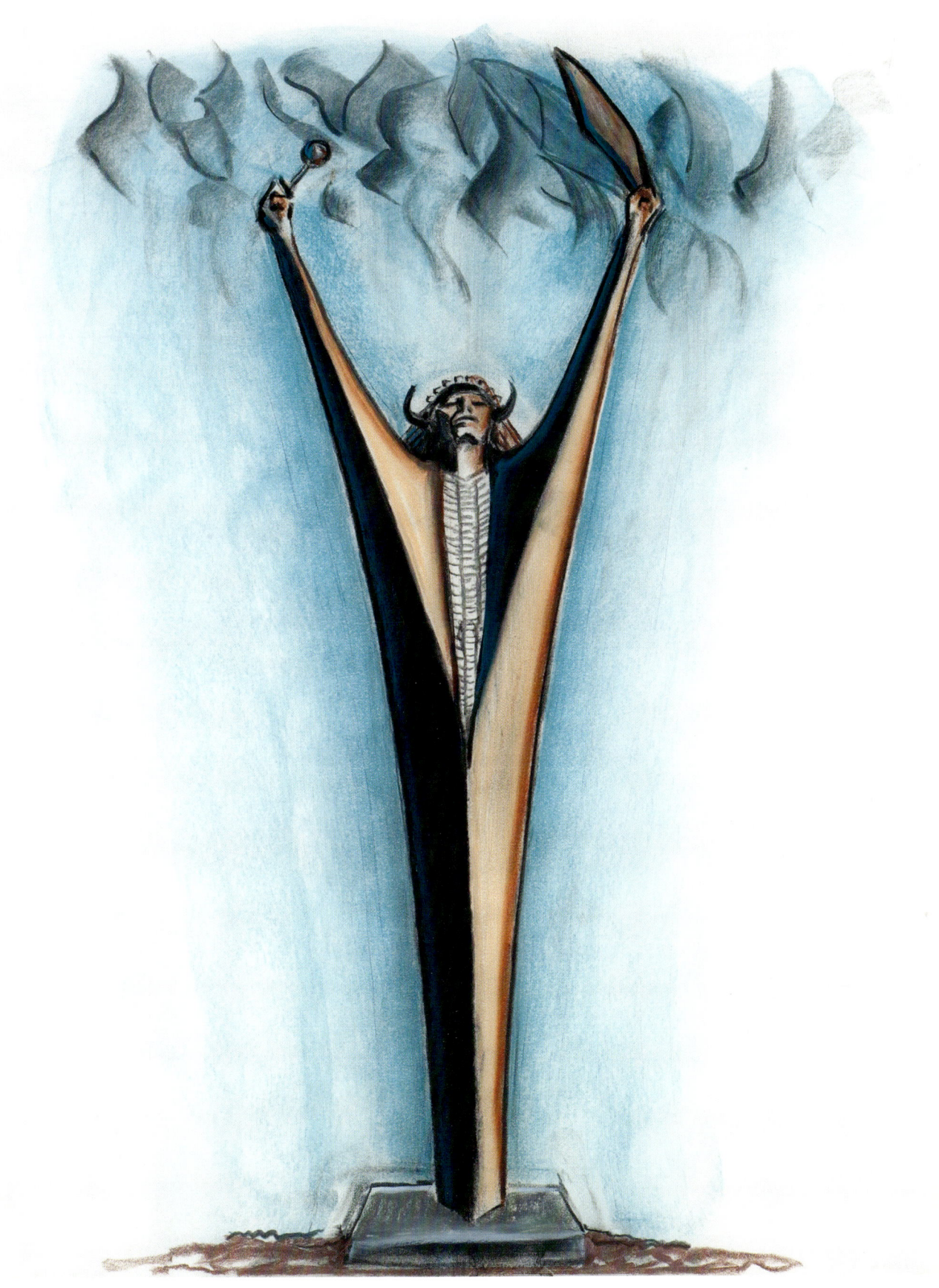

Plate 64
Offering to the Great Spirit,
c. 1992
Pastel, 24 × 19 in.
Allan Houser Inc.
HF1995.1-42.D

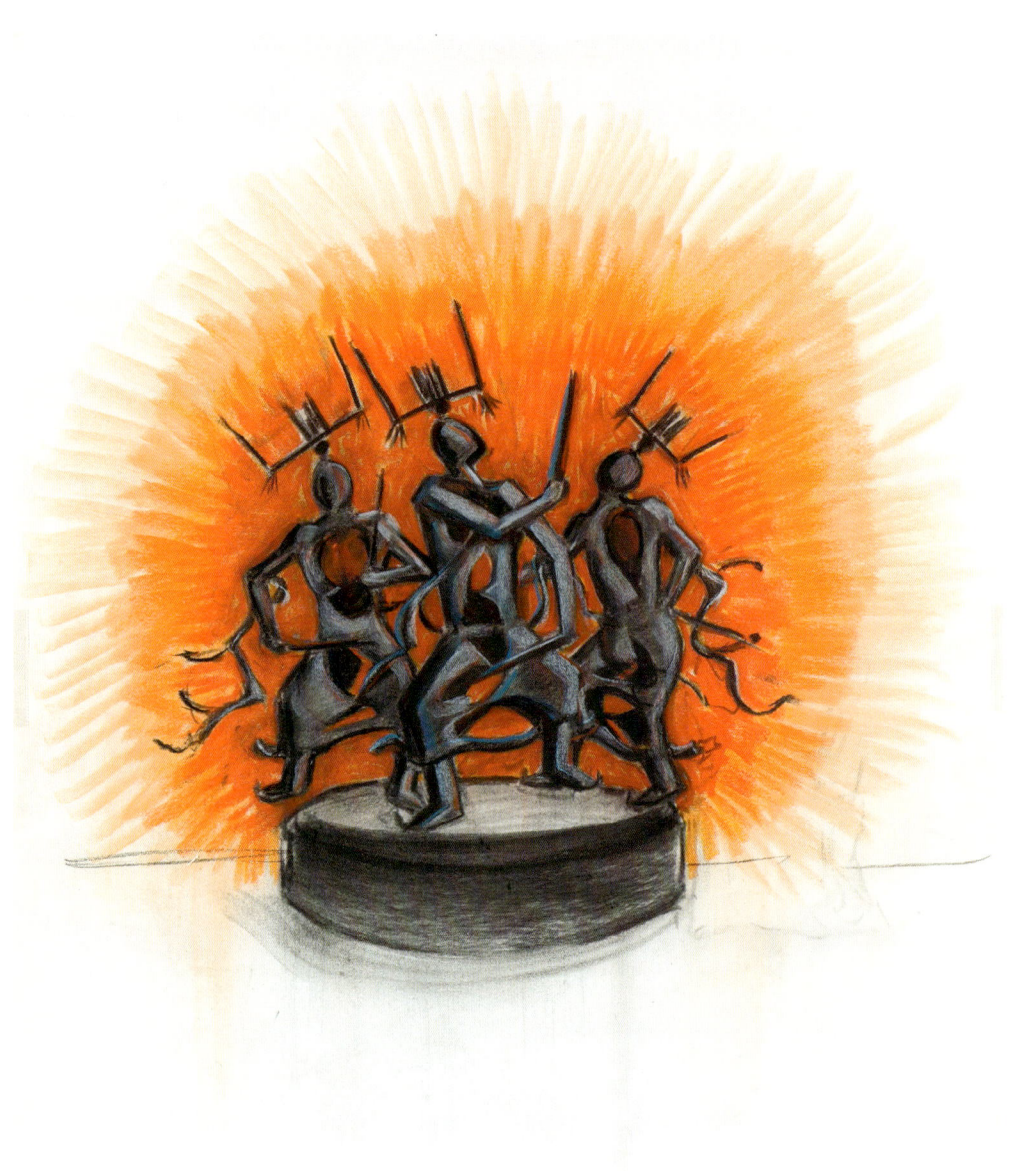

Plate 65
Three Ga'an Dancers, c. 1992
Pastel, 24 × 19 in.
Allan Houser Inc.
HF1995.1-47.D

Plate 66
Two Apache Warriors in Chains,
c. 1992
Charcoal, 30 × 22 ¼ in.
Allan Houser Inc.
HF1995.1-54.D

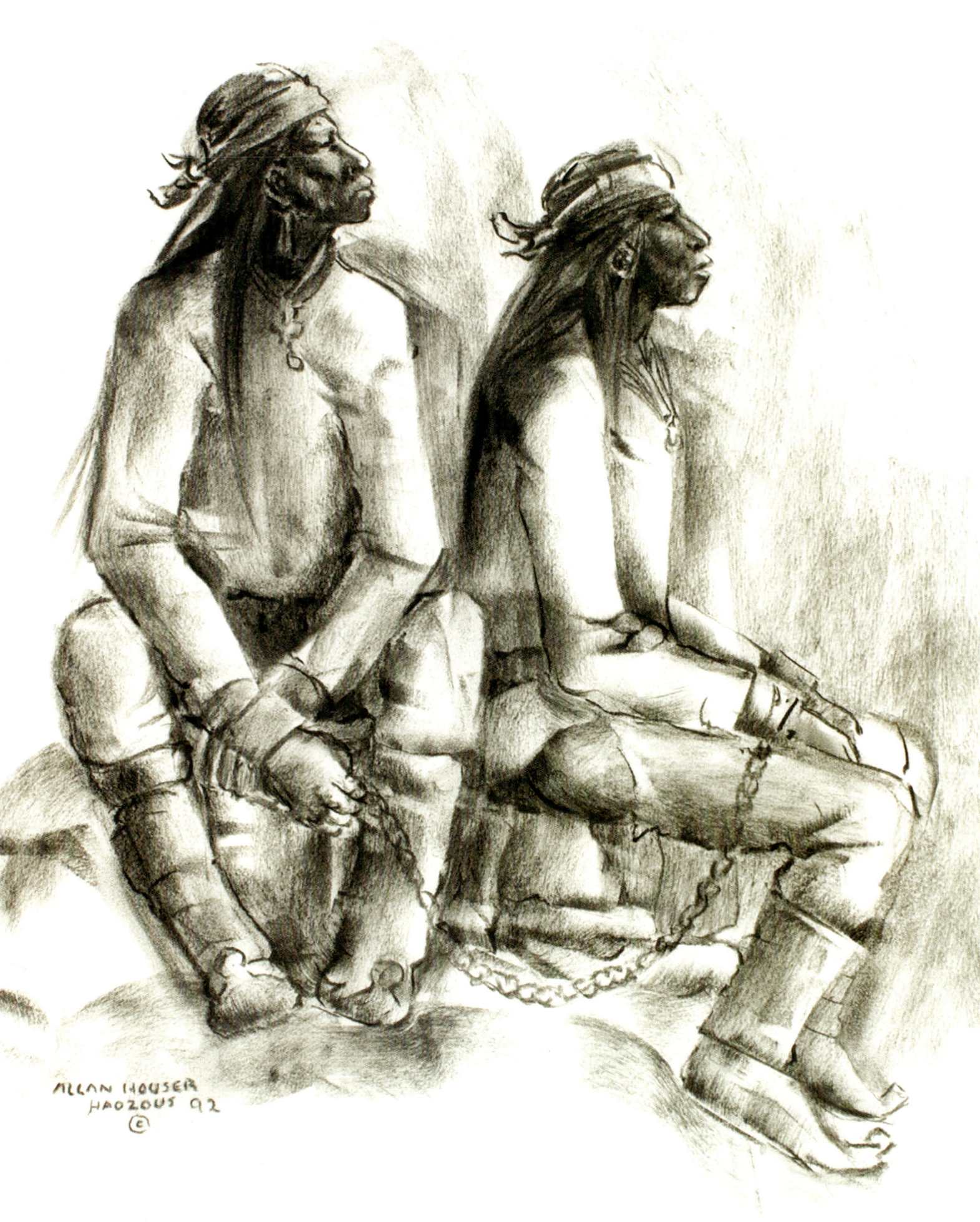

ALLAN HOUSER
HAOZOUS 92
©

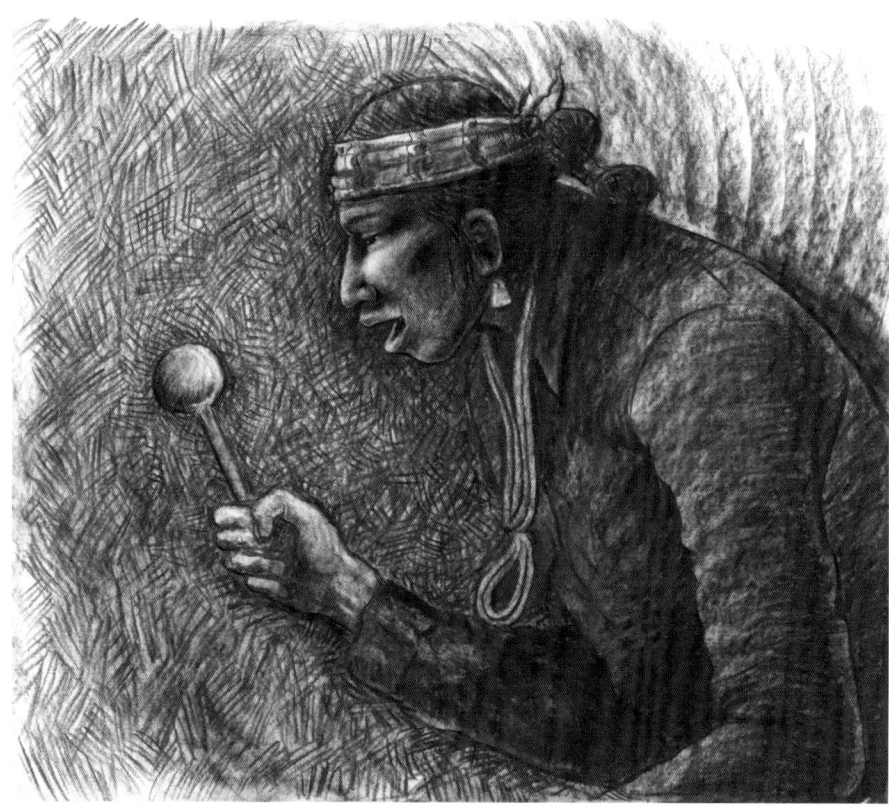

Plate 67
Navajo Singer with a Rattle, c. 1992
Charcoal, 25 ½ × 22 in.
Allan Houser Inc.
HF1995.1-61.D

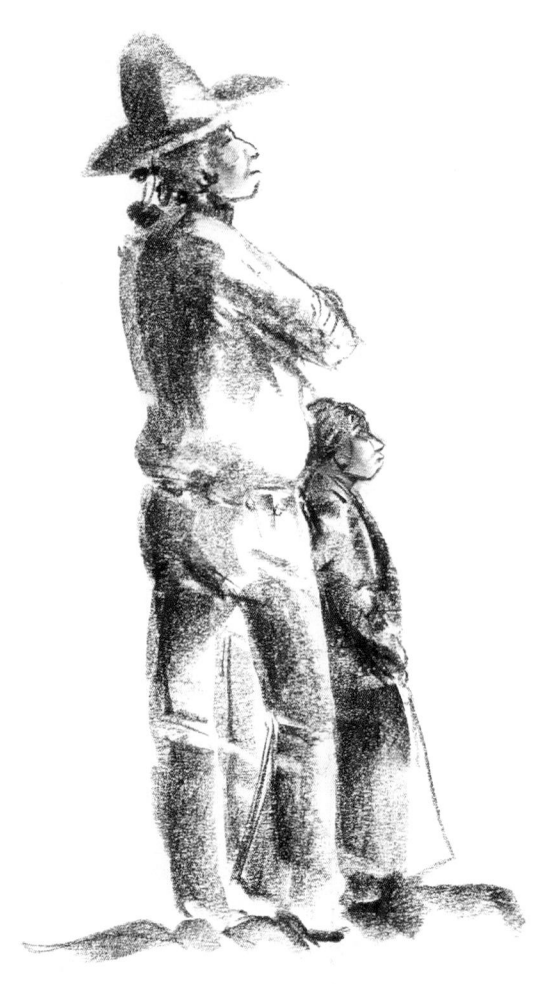

Plate 68
Man and Girl Standing, c. 1992
Charcoal, 17 × 14 in.
Allan Houser Inc.
HF1995.1-70.D

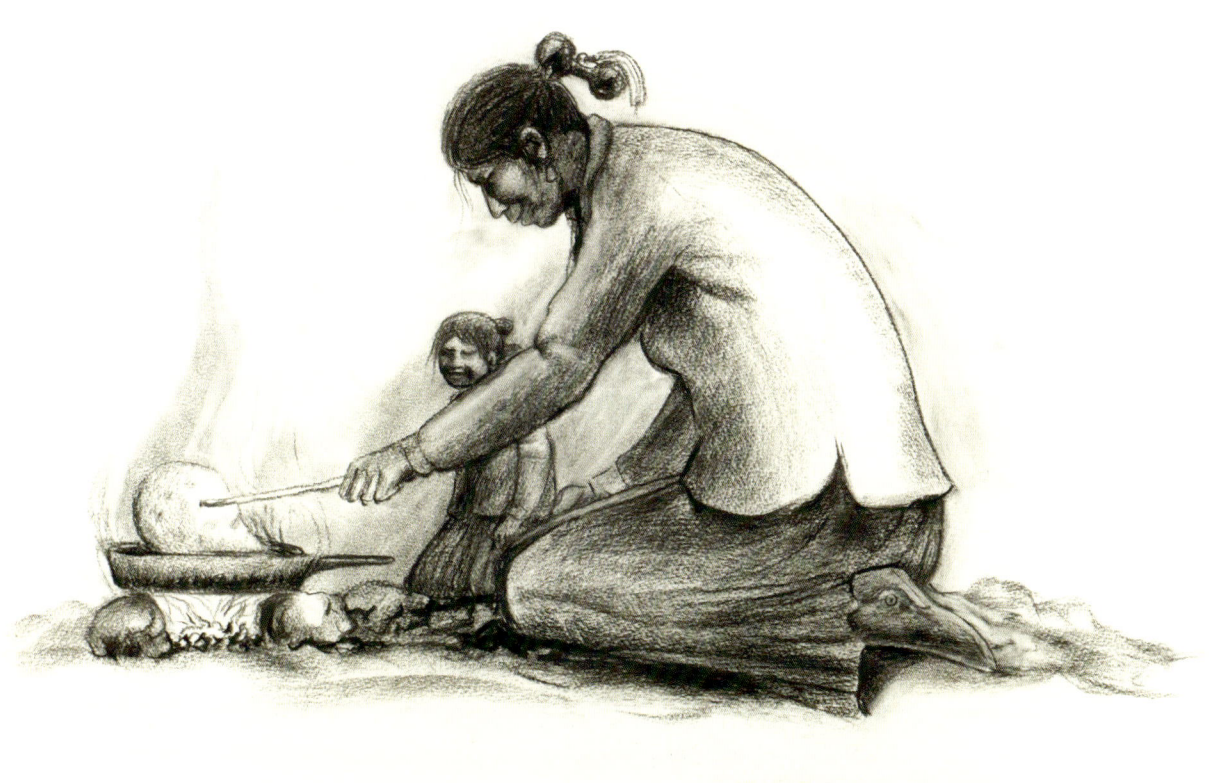

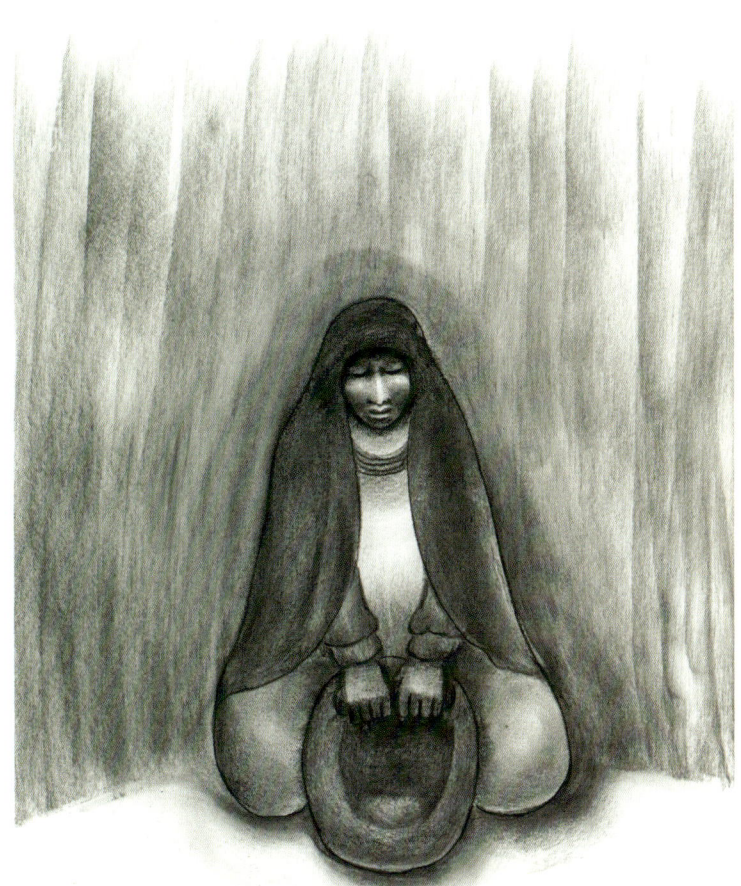

Plate 69
Woman and Child Cooking,
c. 1992
Charcoal, 22 × 30 in.
Allan Houser Inc.
HF1995.1-73.D

Plate 70
Woman at Metate, c. 1992
Charcoal, 30 × 22 in.
Allan Houser Inc.
HF1995.1-86.D

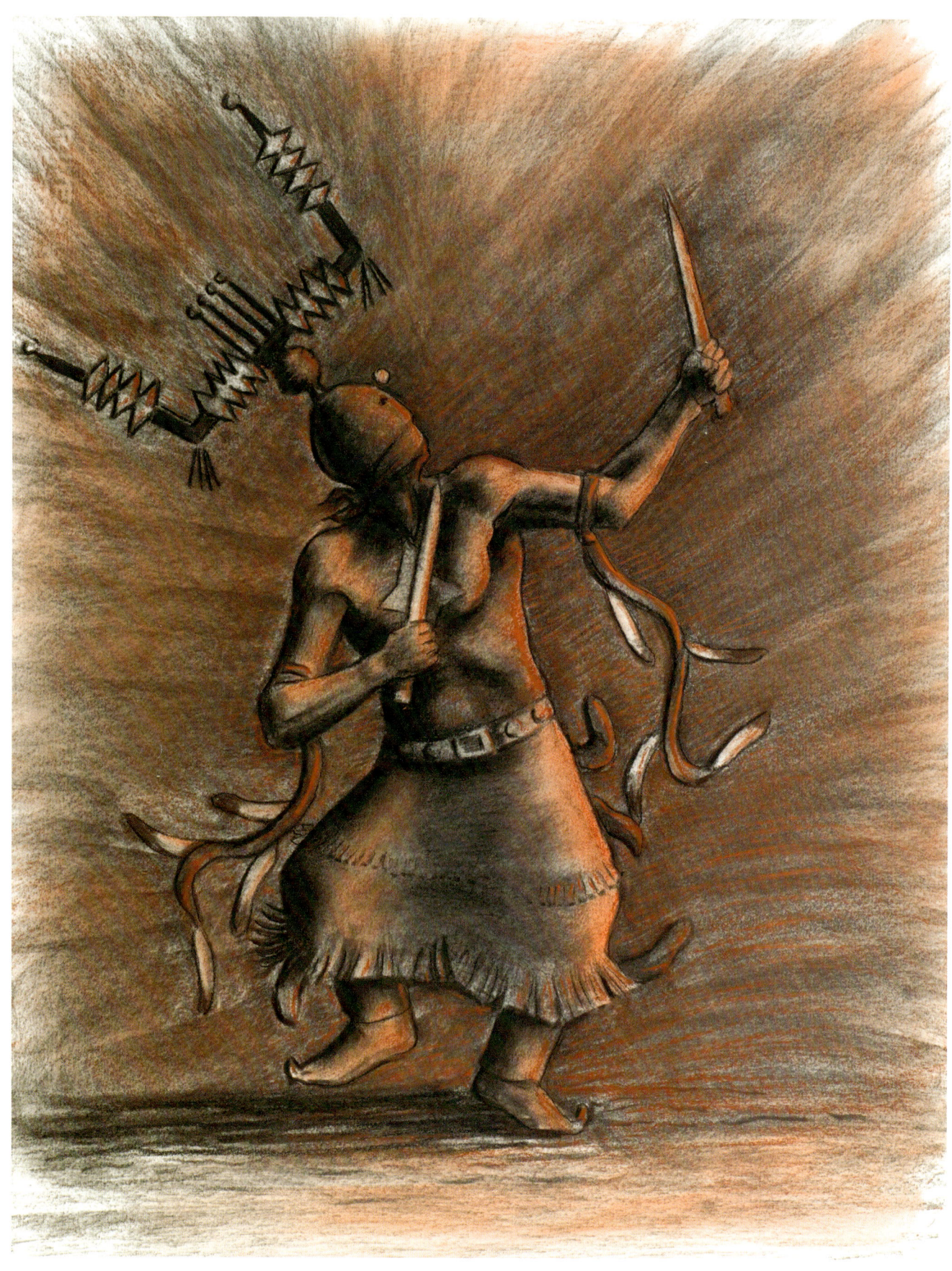

Plate 71
Ga'an Dancer, c. 1992
Charcoal and pastel, 30 × 22 in.
Allan Houser Inc.
HF1995.1-99.D

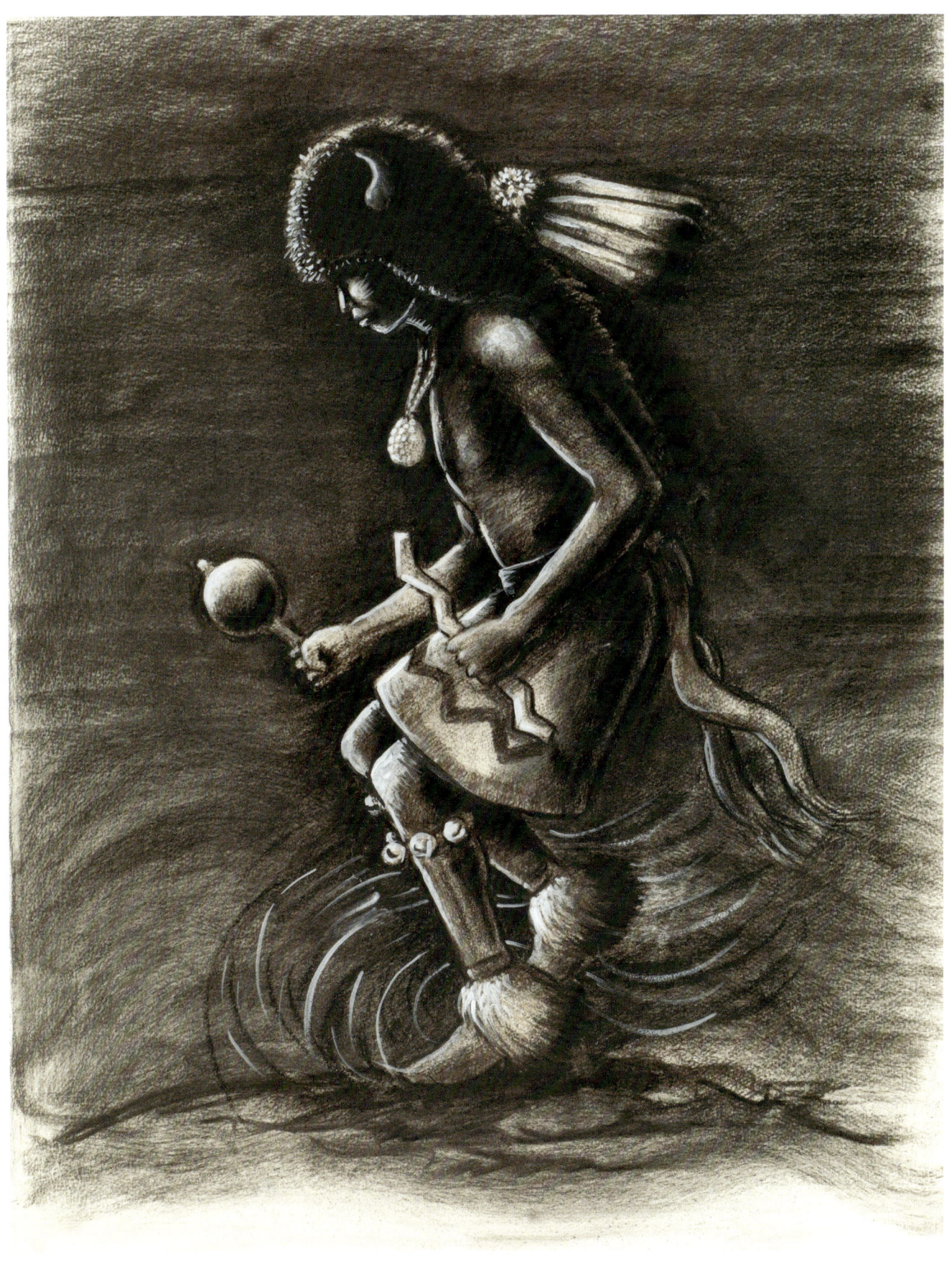

Plate 72
Pueblo Buffalo Dancer, c. 1992
Charcoal, 30 × 22 in.
Allan Houser Inc.
HF1995.1-116.D

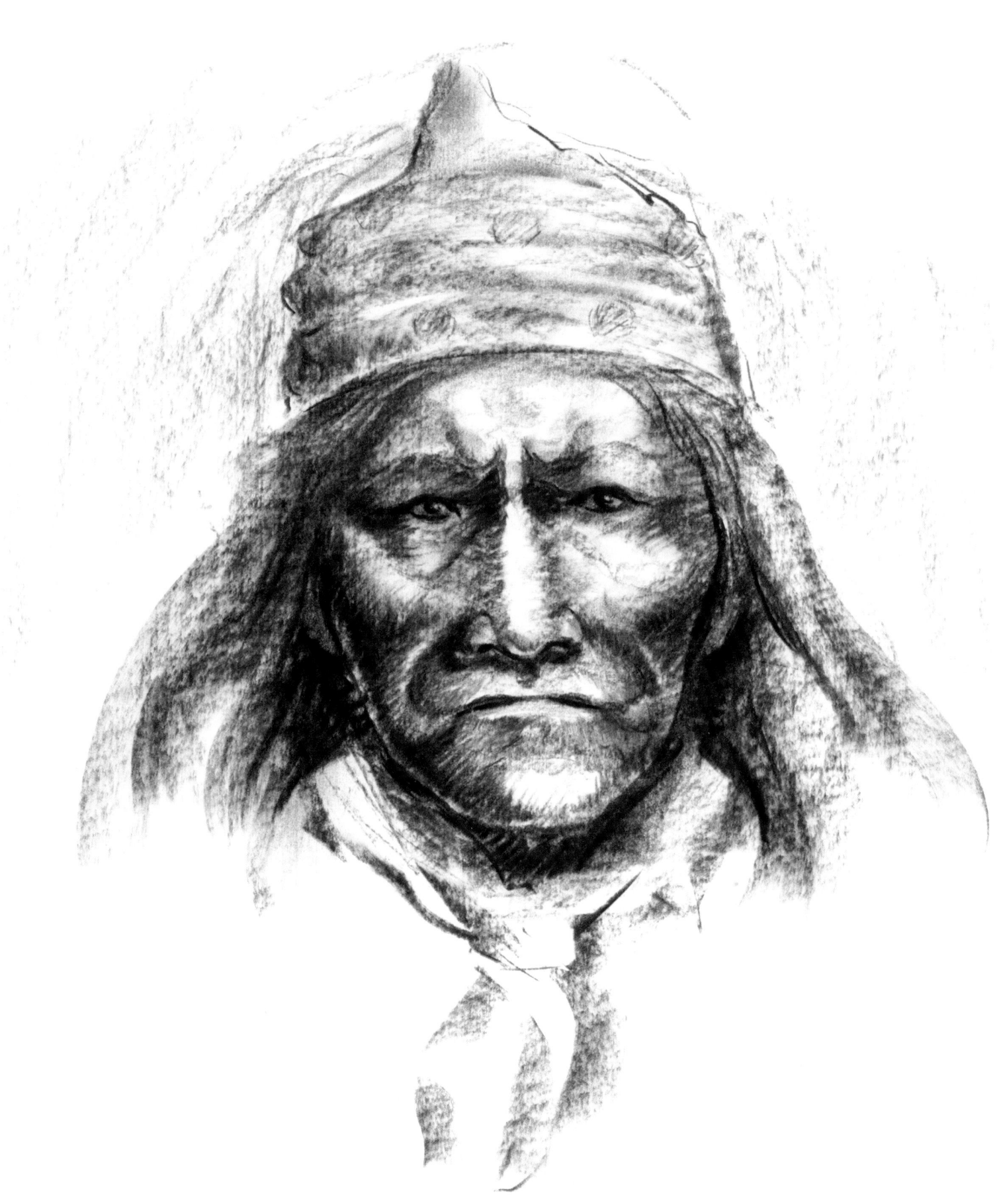

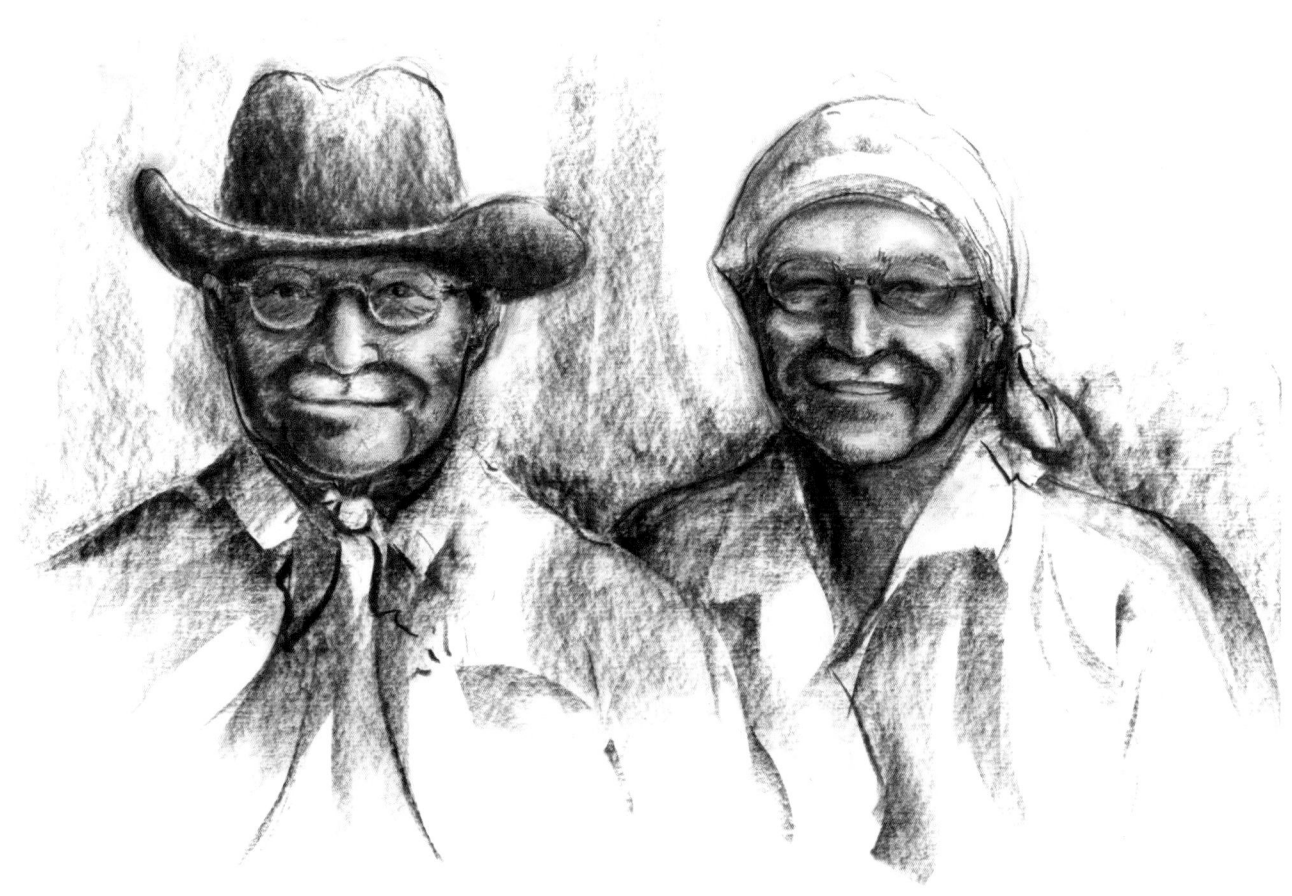

Plate 74
**Portrait of Sam and Blossom
Haozous,** c. 1992
Charcoal, 22 × 30 in.
Allan Houser Inc.
HF1995.1-136.D

Plate 73
Bust of Geronimo, c. 1992
Charcoal, 30 × 22 in.
Allan Houser Inc.
HF1995.1-132.D

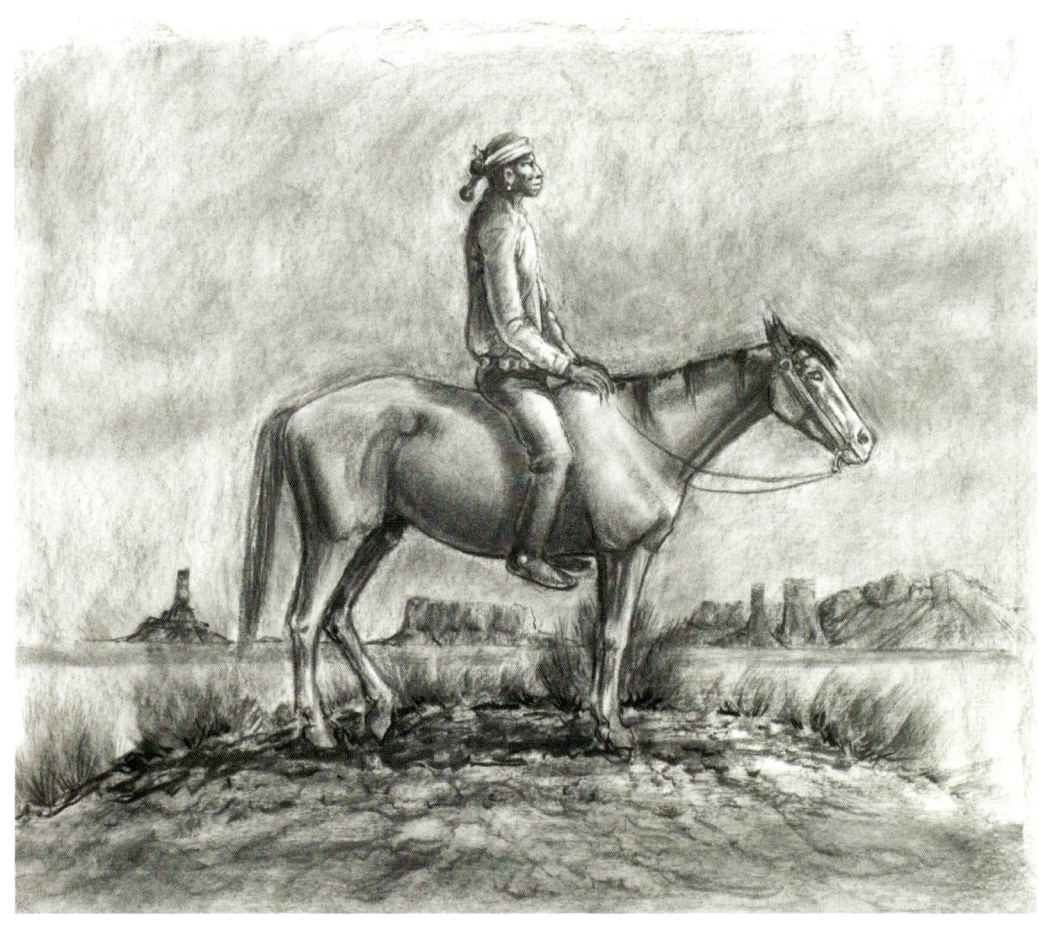

Plate 75
Navajo Man on Horseback,
c. 1992
Charcoal, 20 × 23 in.
Allan Houser Inc.
HF1995.1-148.a.D

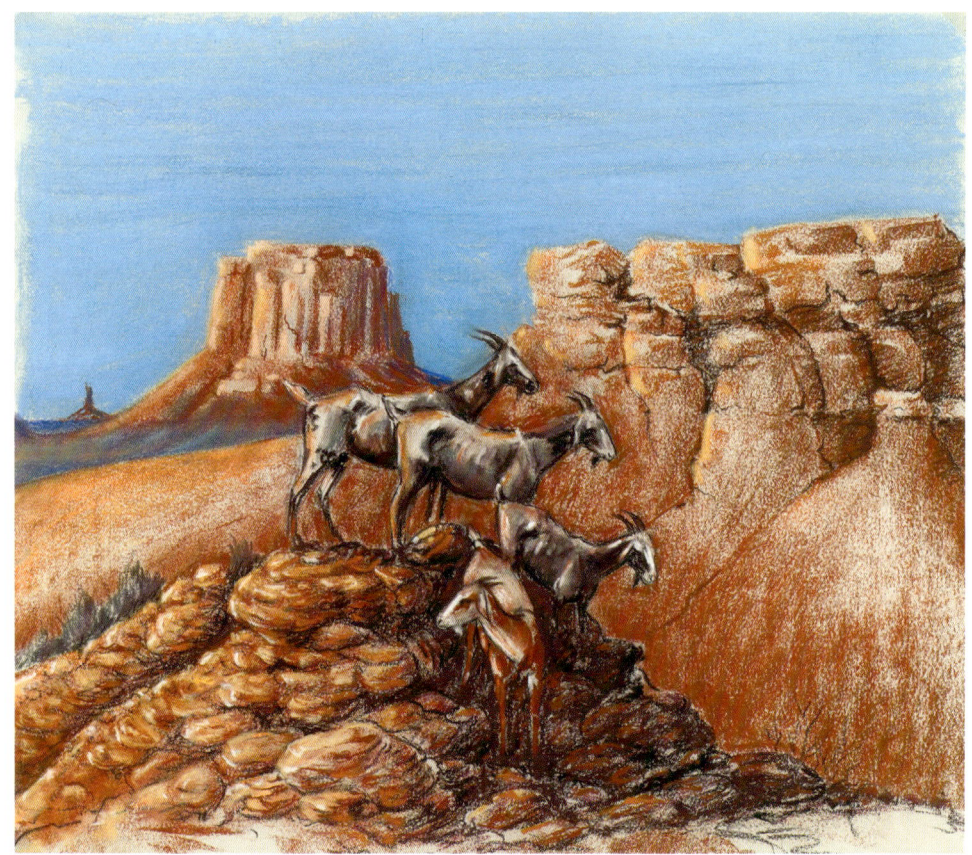

Plate 76
Four Goats in Landscape,
c. 1992
Pastel, 19 × 22 in.
Allan Houser Inc.
HF1995.1-156.D

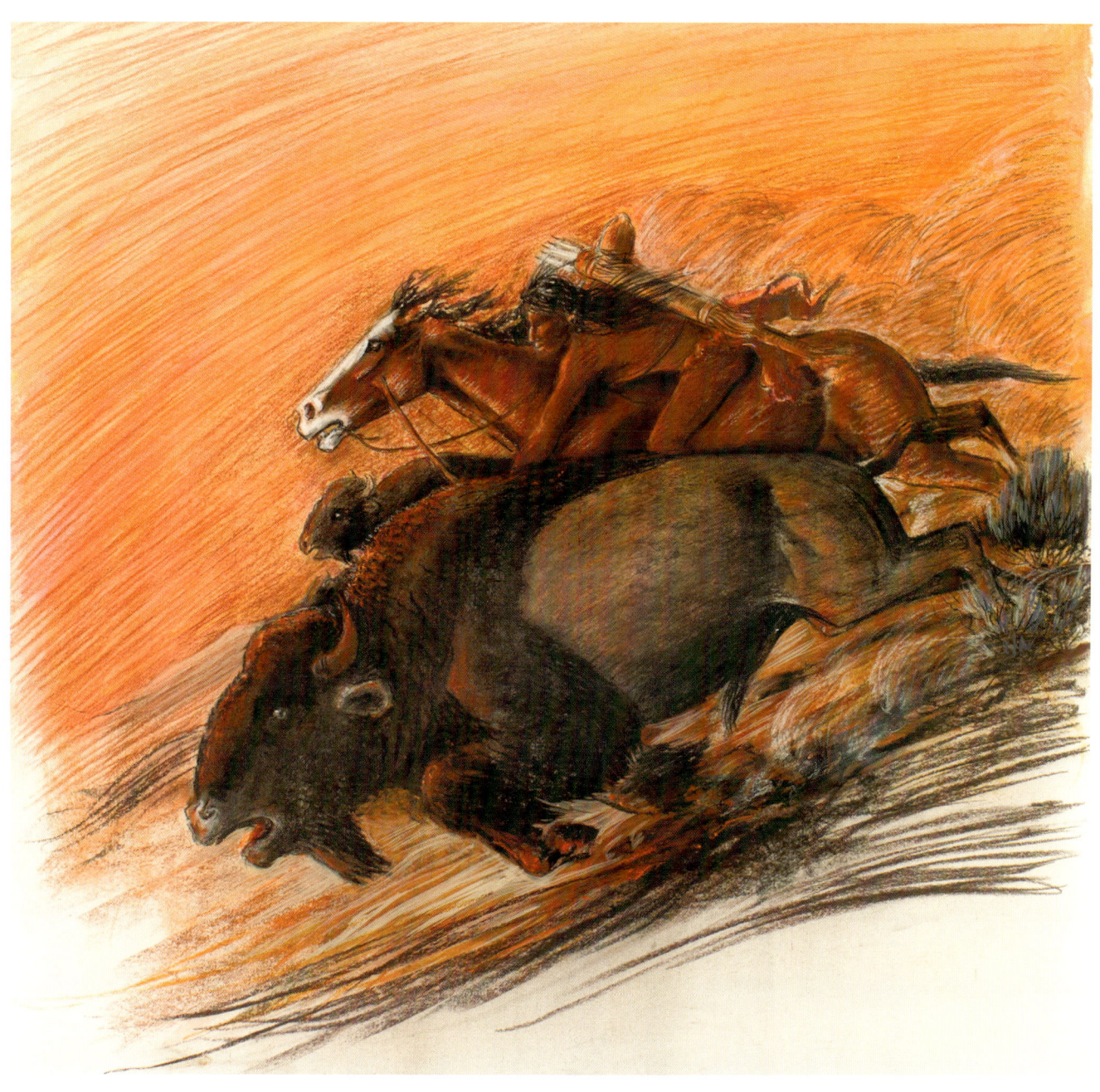

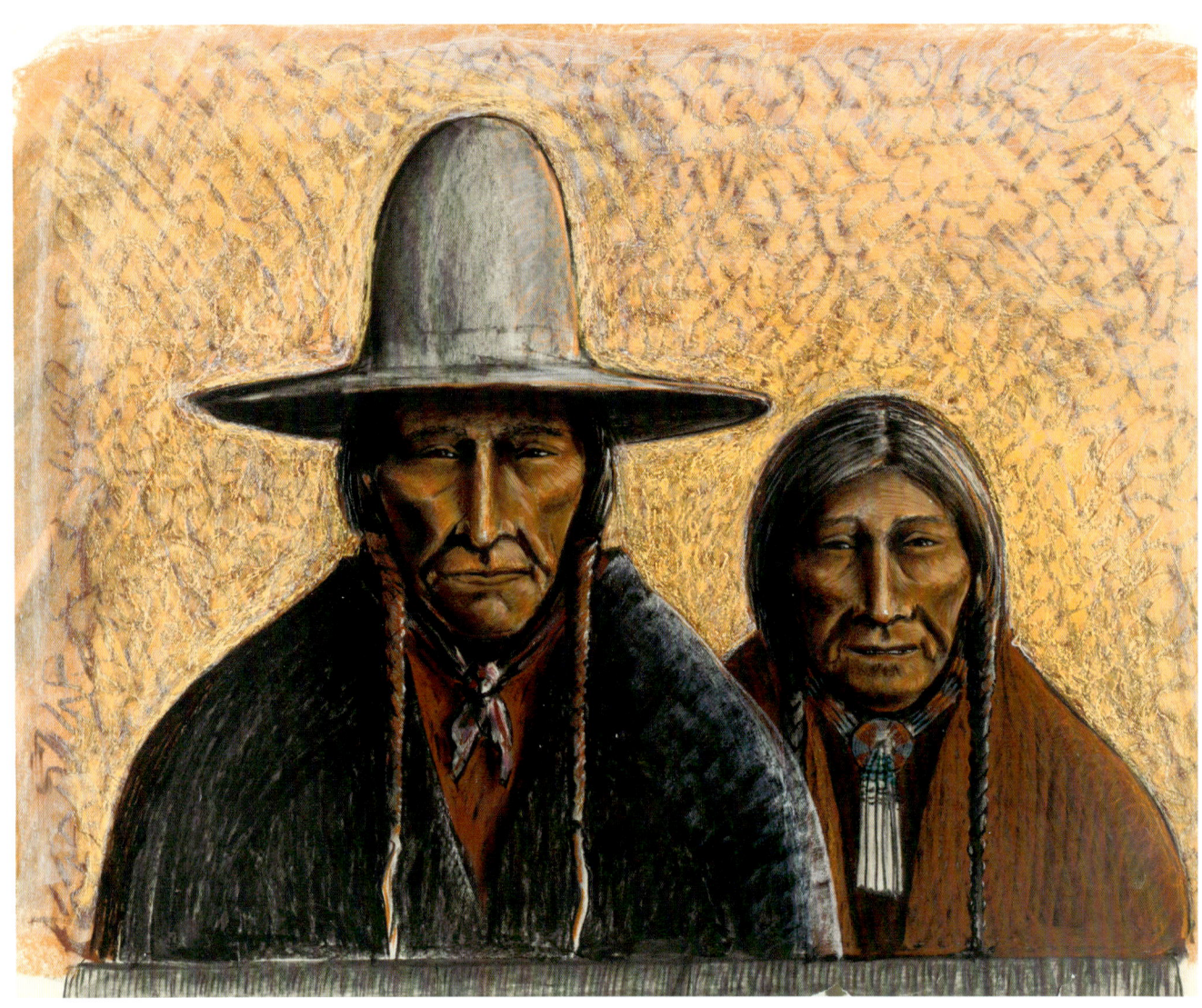

Plate 78
Portrait of a Man and a Woman,
c. 1992
Pastel and acrylic, 24 ½ × 31 ¼ in.
Allan Houser Inc.
HF1995.1-166.D

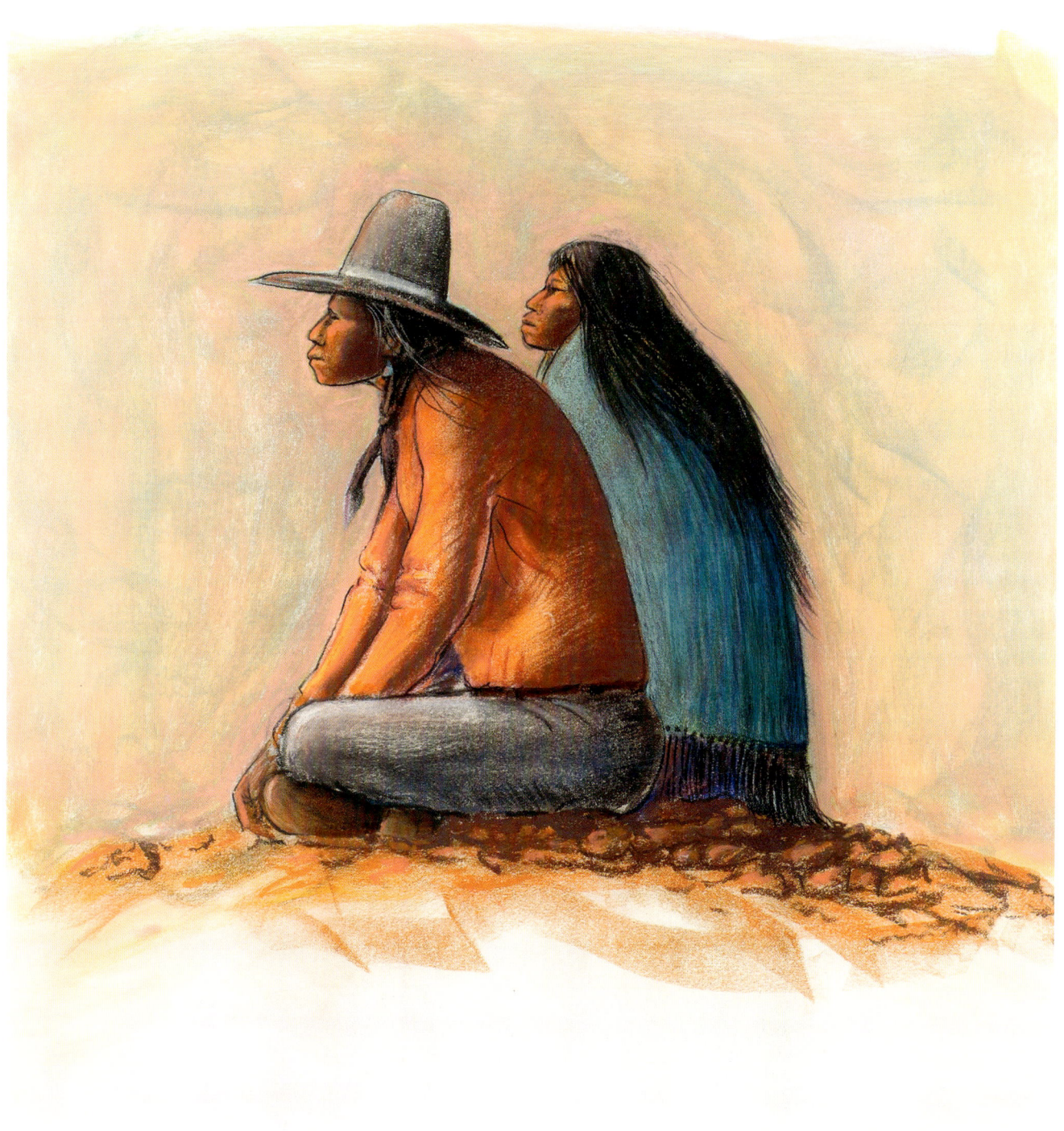

Plate 79
Seated Apache Couple, c. 1992
Pastel, 24 × 19 in.
Allan Houser Inc.
HF1995.1-170.D

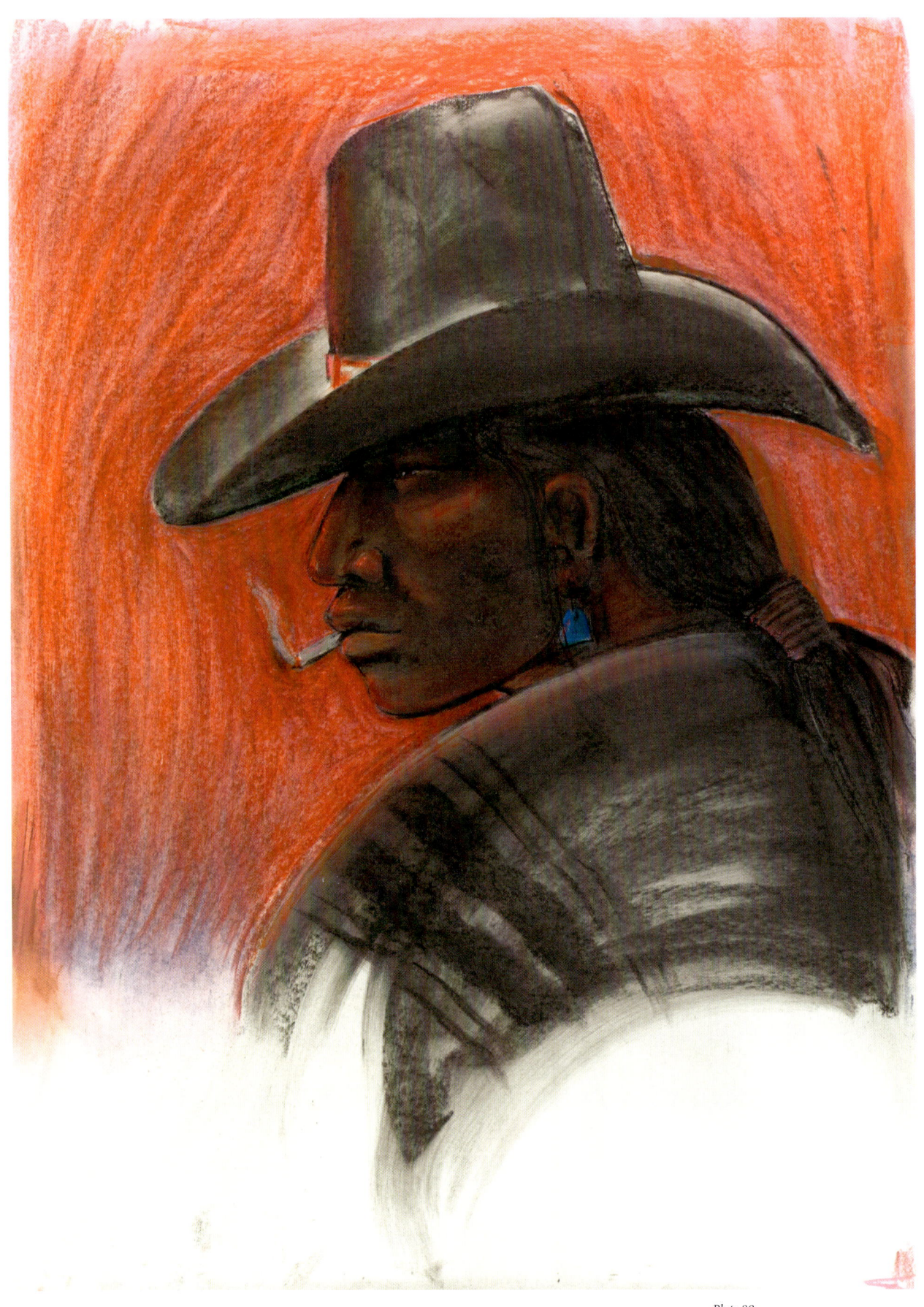

Plate 80
**Portrait of a Man in Hat
Smoking,** c. 1992
Pastel, 30 × 22 in.
Allan Houser Inc.
HF1995.1-179.D

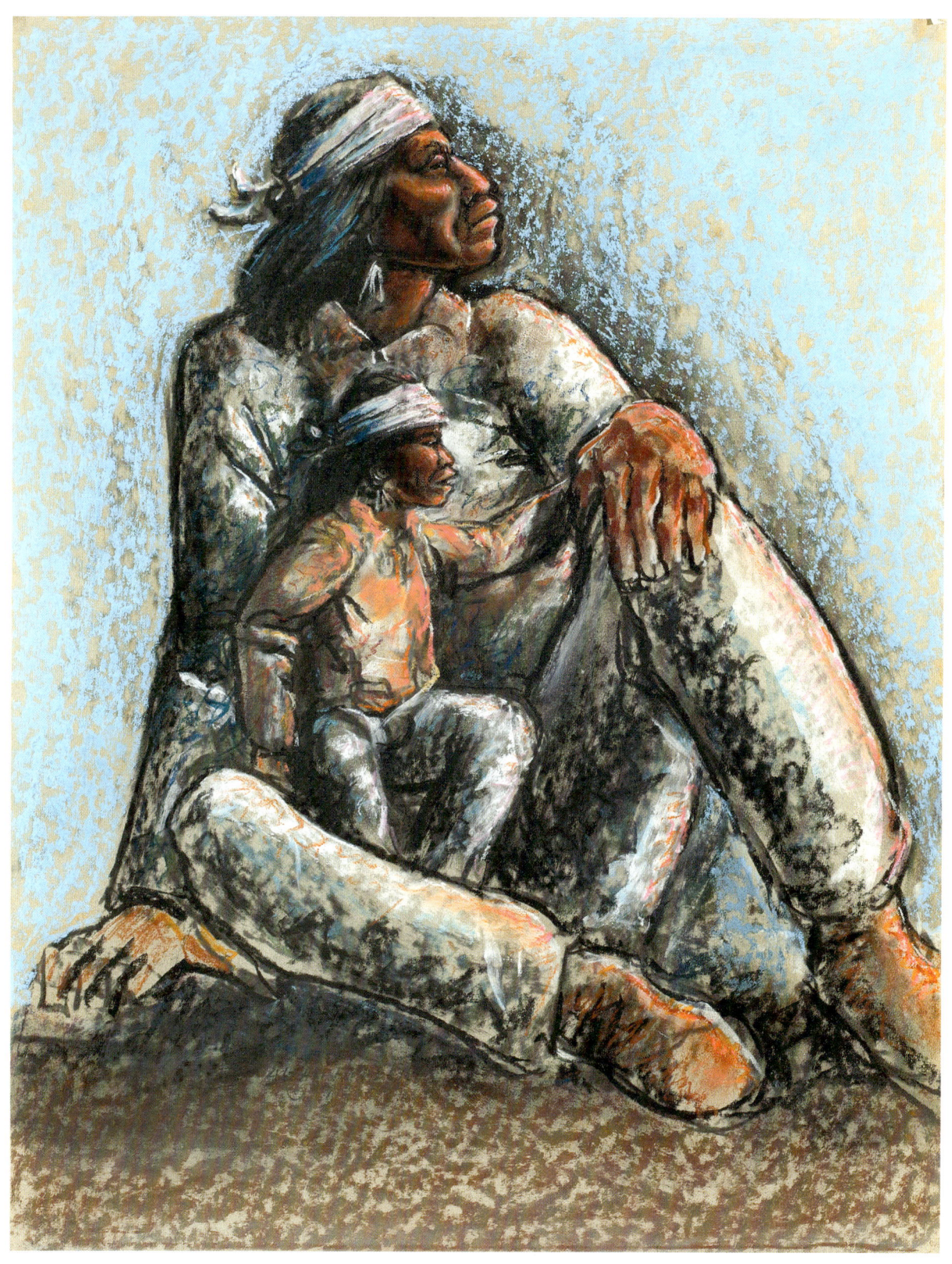

Plate 81

Apache Father and Son, c. 1992

Oil stick, 23 ¾ × 18 in.

Allan Houser Inc.

HF1995.1-182.D

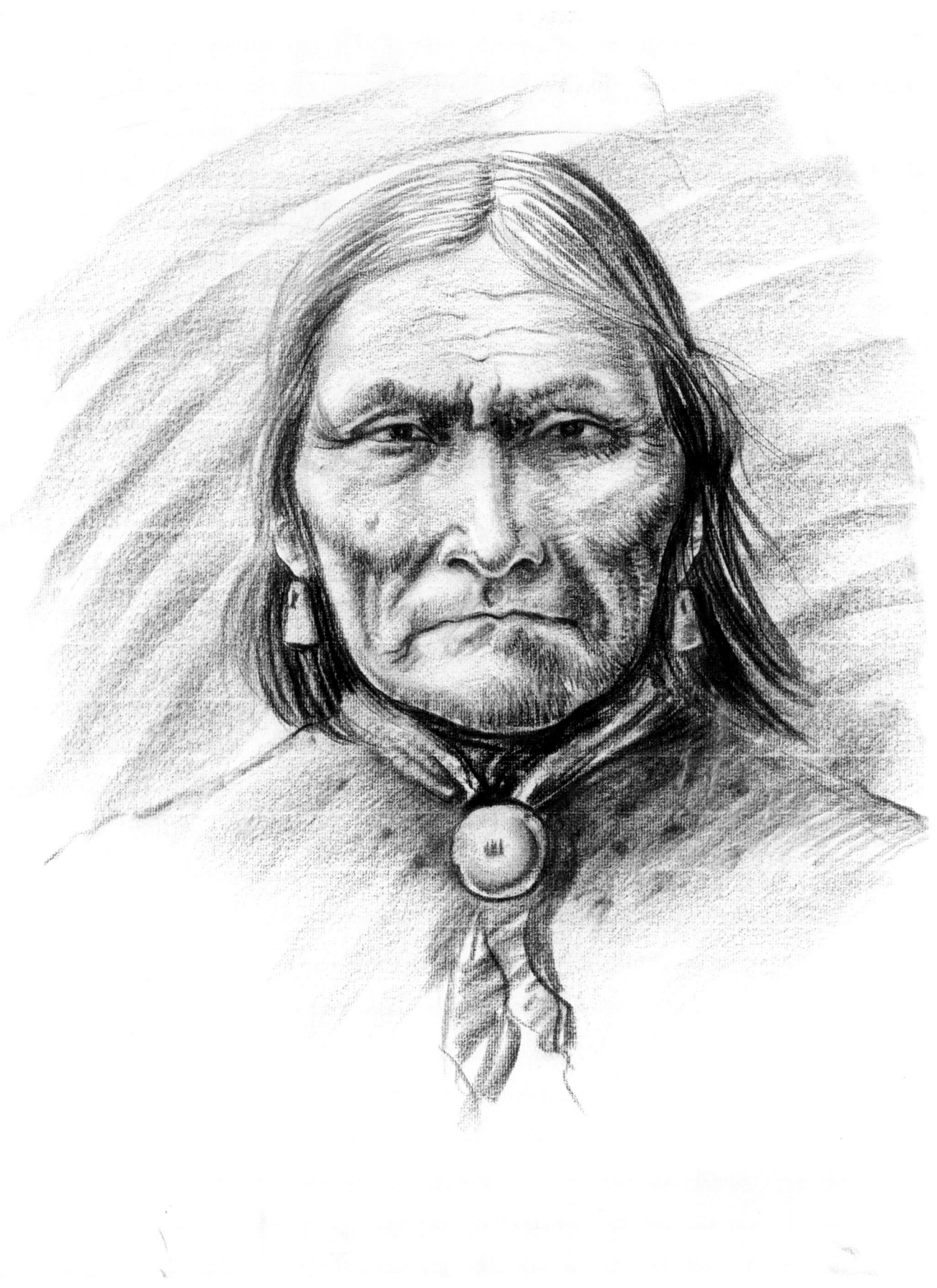

Plate 82
Bust of Geronimo, c. 1992
Charcoal, 23 ½ × 17 ⅞ in.
Allan Houser Inc.
HF1995.1-193.D

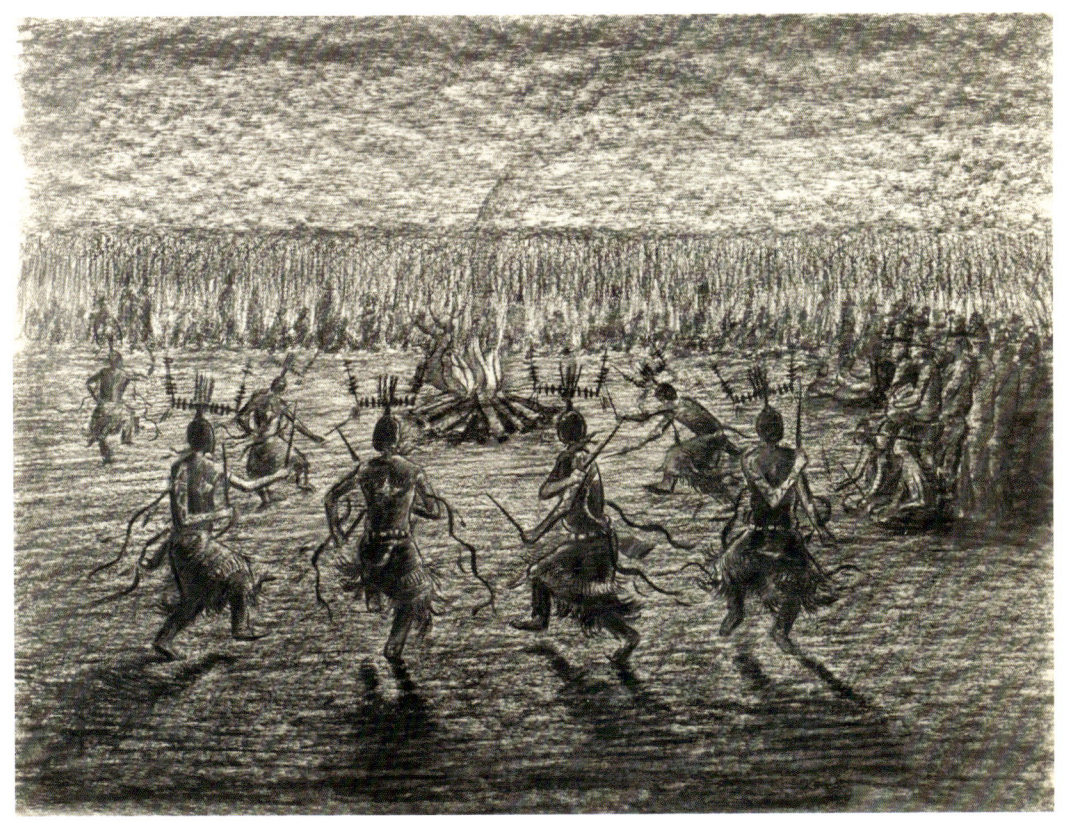

Plate 83
Seven Ga'an Dancers,
c. 1992
Charcoal, 22 × 30 in.
Allan Houser Inc.
F1995.1-203.D

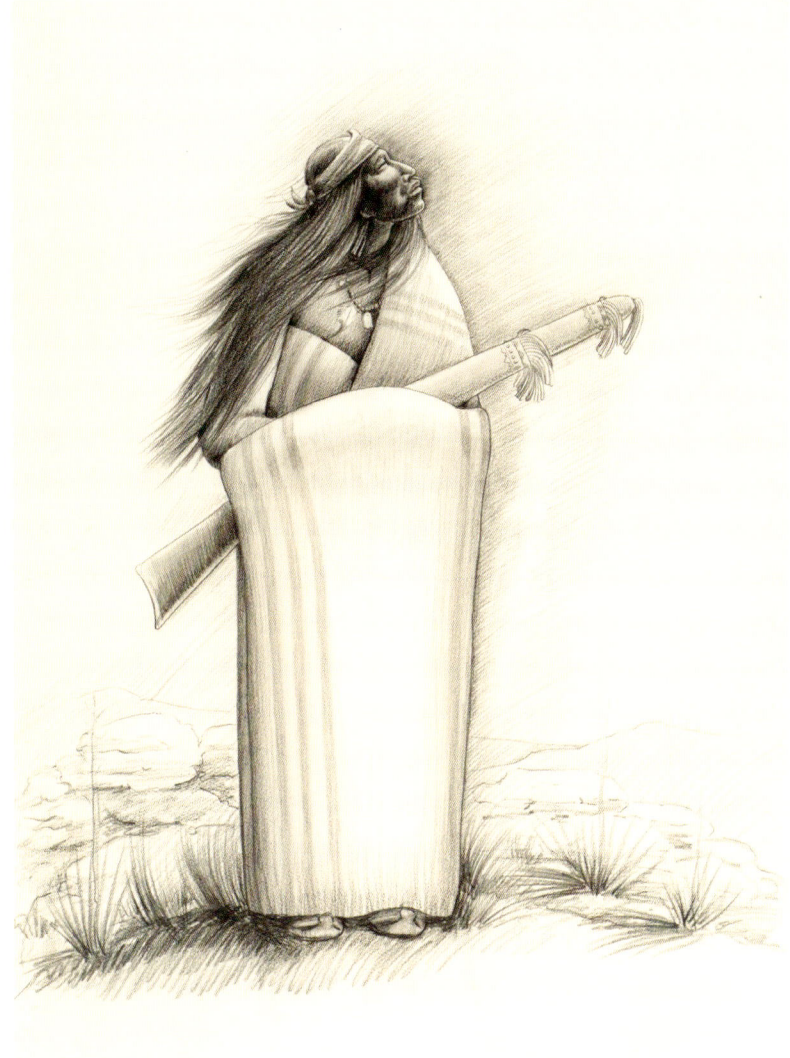

Plate 84
**Warrior in a Blanket
with a Rifle,** c. 1992
Charcoal, 30 × 22 in.
Allan Houser Inc.
HF1995.1-206.D

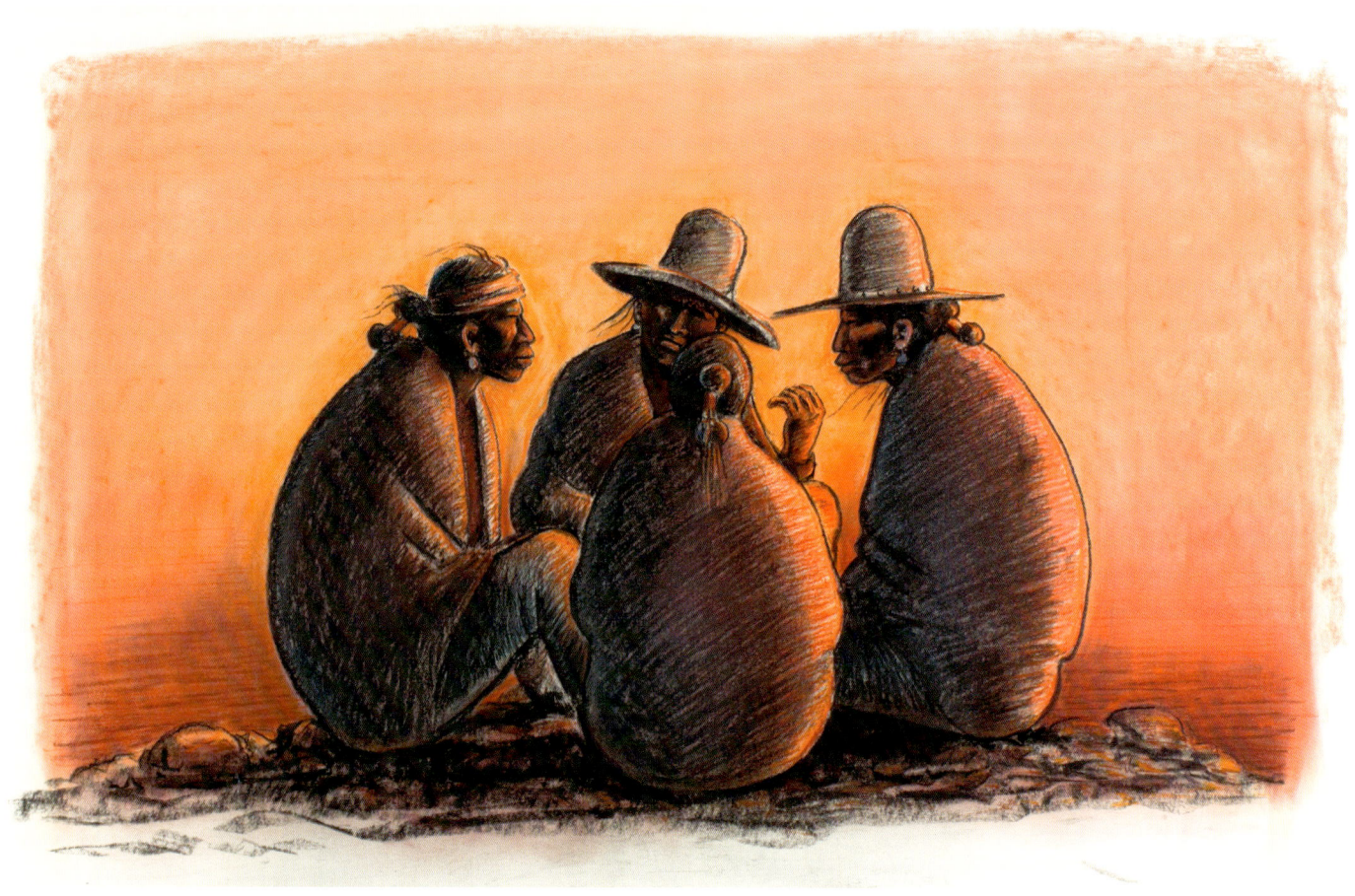

Plate 85
**Three Navajo Men and a
Woman in a Circle (Talking),**
c. 1992
Pastel, 29 ⅛ × 42 ⅞ in.
Allan Houser Inc.
HF1995.1-249.D

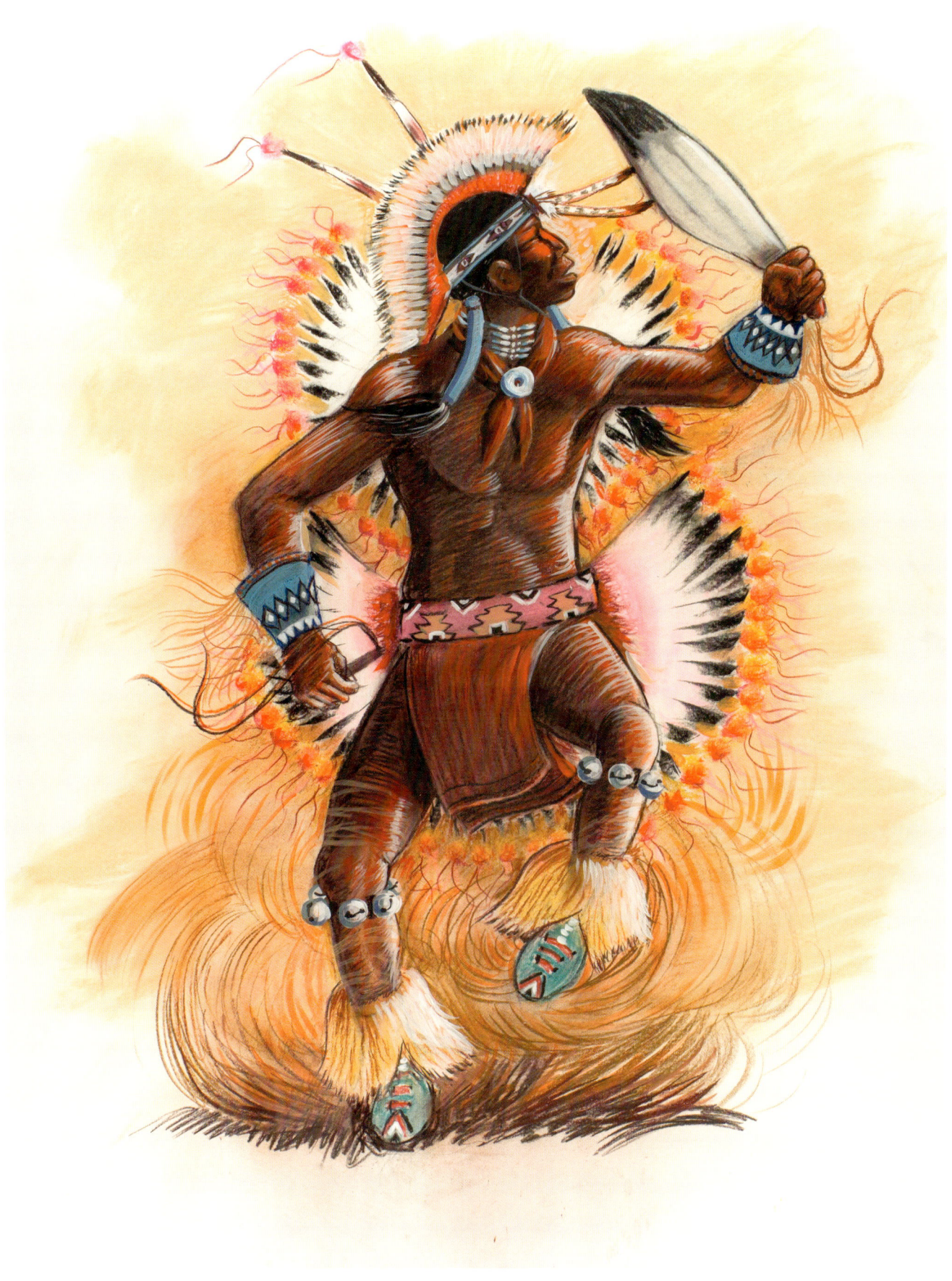

Plate 86
Plains Fancy Dancer, c. 1992
Pastel, 50 × 38 ¼ in.
Allan Houser Inc.
HF1995.1-761.D

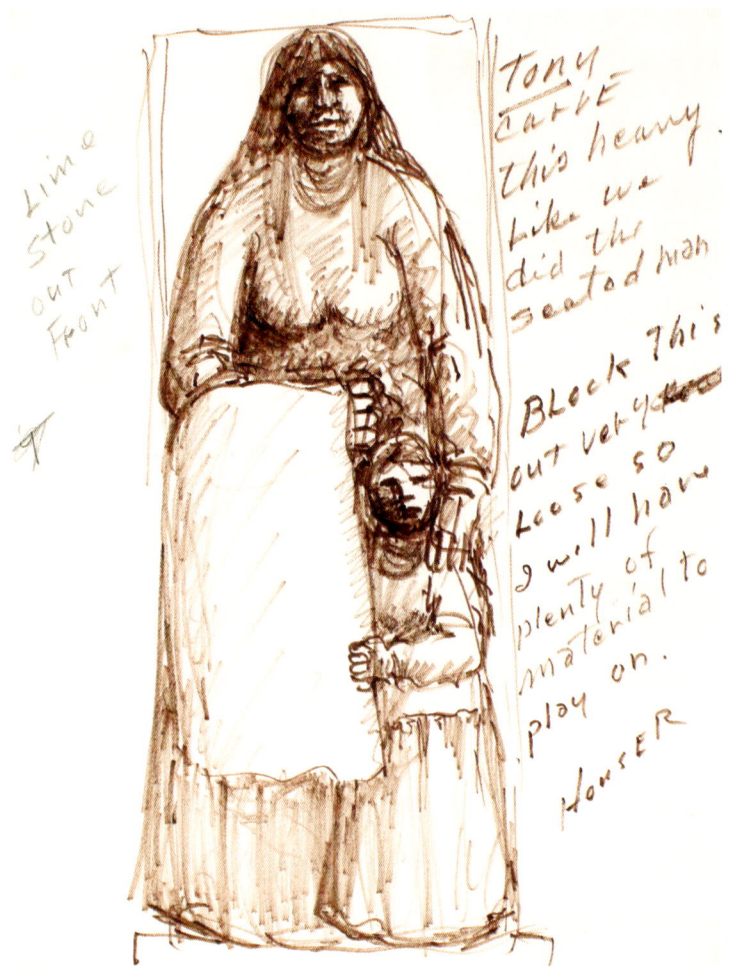

Plate 87
Study for "Mother and Child,"
c. 1992
Pencil, brown felt-tip pen,
17 × 14 in.
Chiinde, LLC.
HF1995.1-284.D

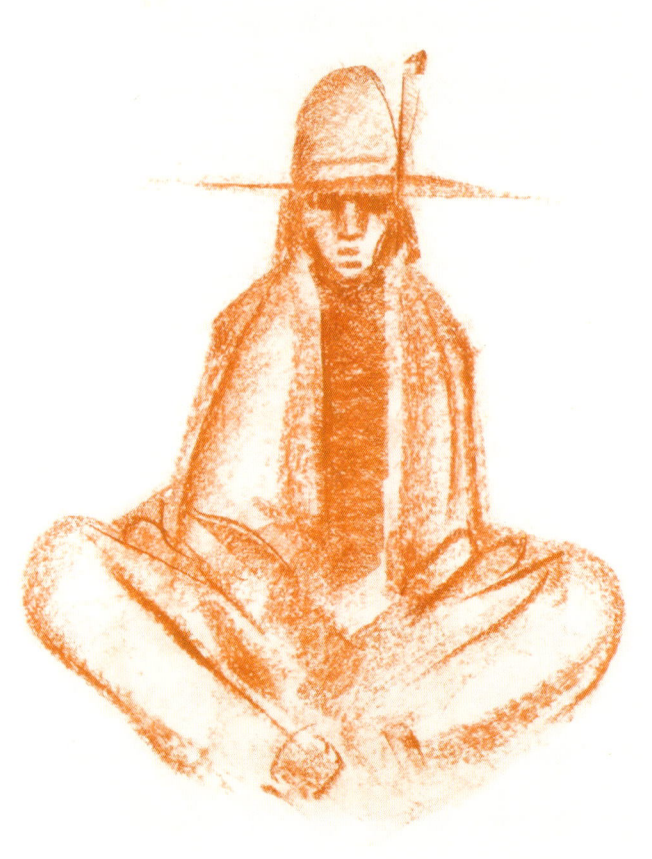

Plate 88
Male Figure, c. 1992
Pastel, 24 × 18 in.
Chiinde, LLC.
HF1995.1-287.D

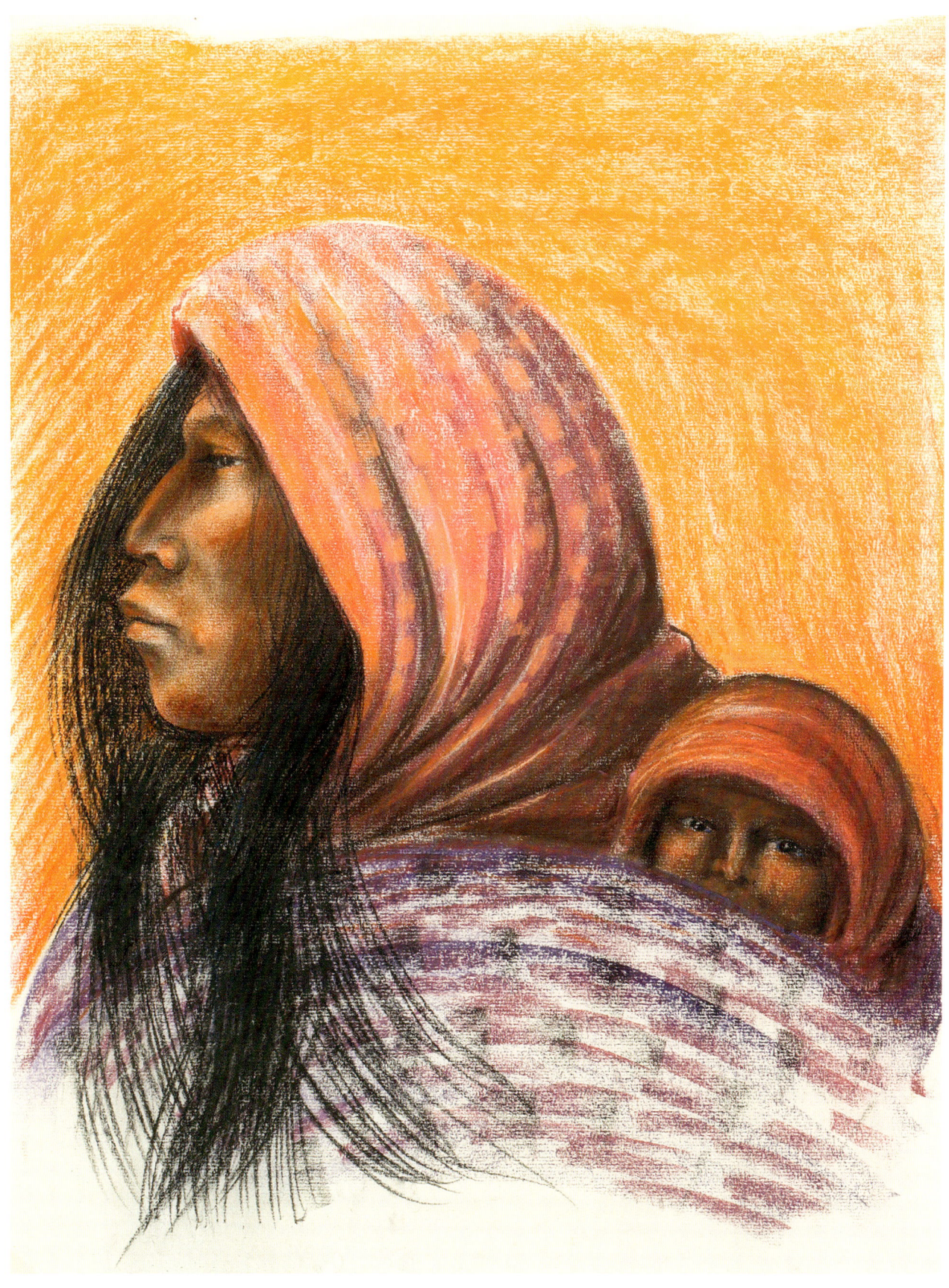

Plate 89
Mother and Child, c. 1992
Pastel, 24 × 18 in.
Chiinde, LLC.
HF1995.1-292.D

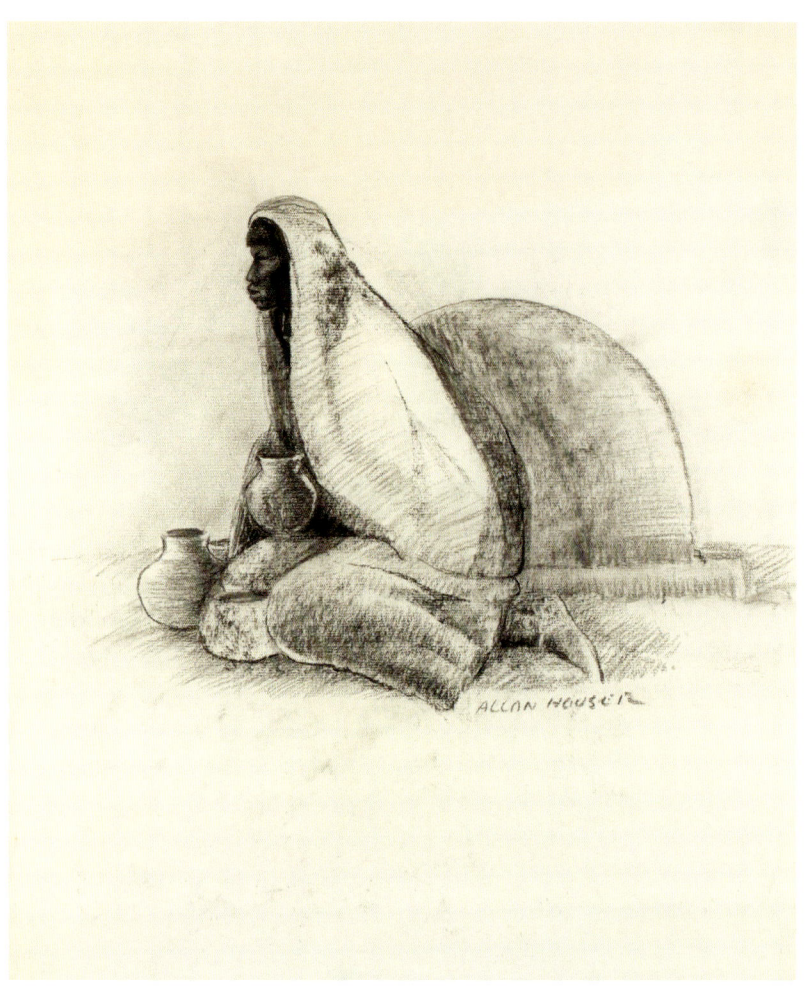

Plate 90
**Woman with Pots Sitting by
Horno Oven,** c. 1992
Charcoal, 24 × 18 in.
Chiinde, LLC.
HF1995.1-297.D

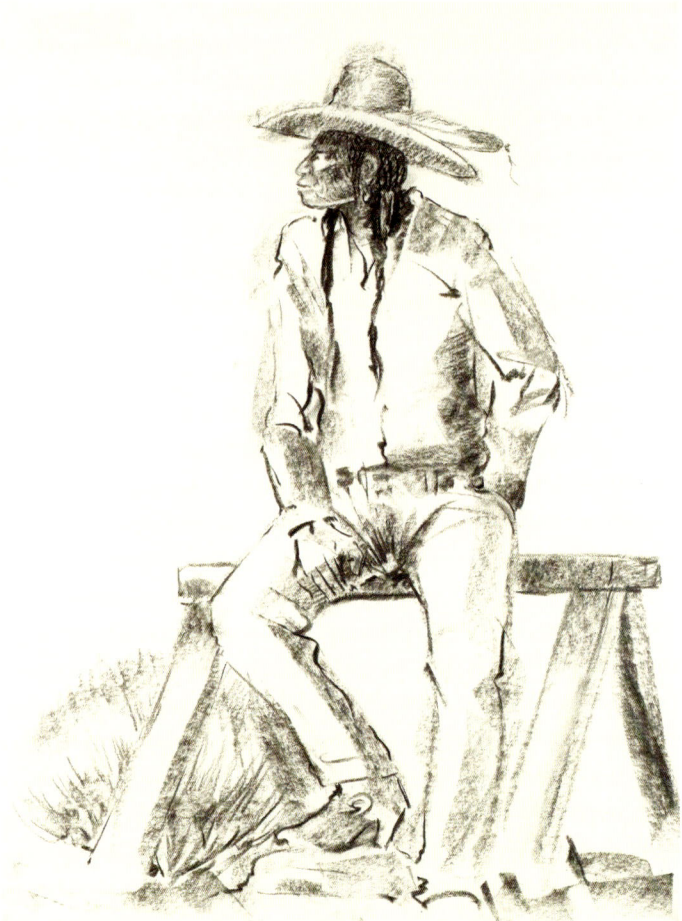

Plate 91
Man on a Sawhorse, c. 1992
Charcoal, 24 × 17⅞ in.
Chiinde, LLC.
HF1995.1-304.D

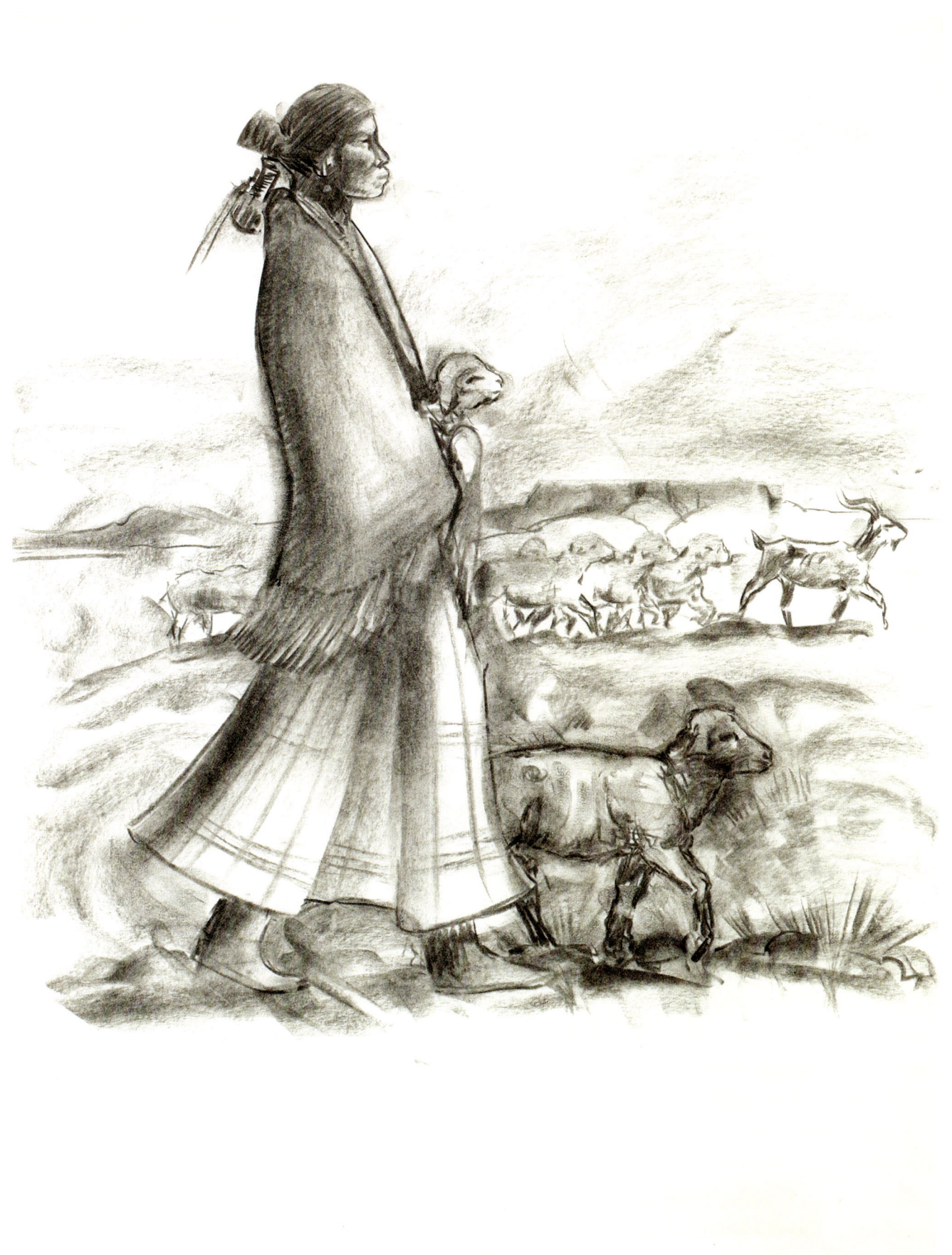

Plate 92
Navajo Shepherdess, c. 1992
Charcoal, 24 × 18 in.
Chiinde, LLC.
HF1995.1-312.D

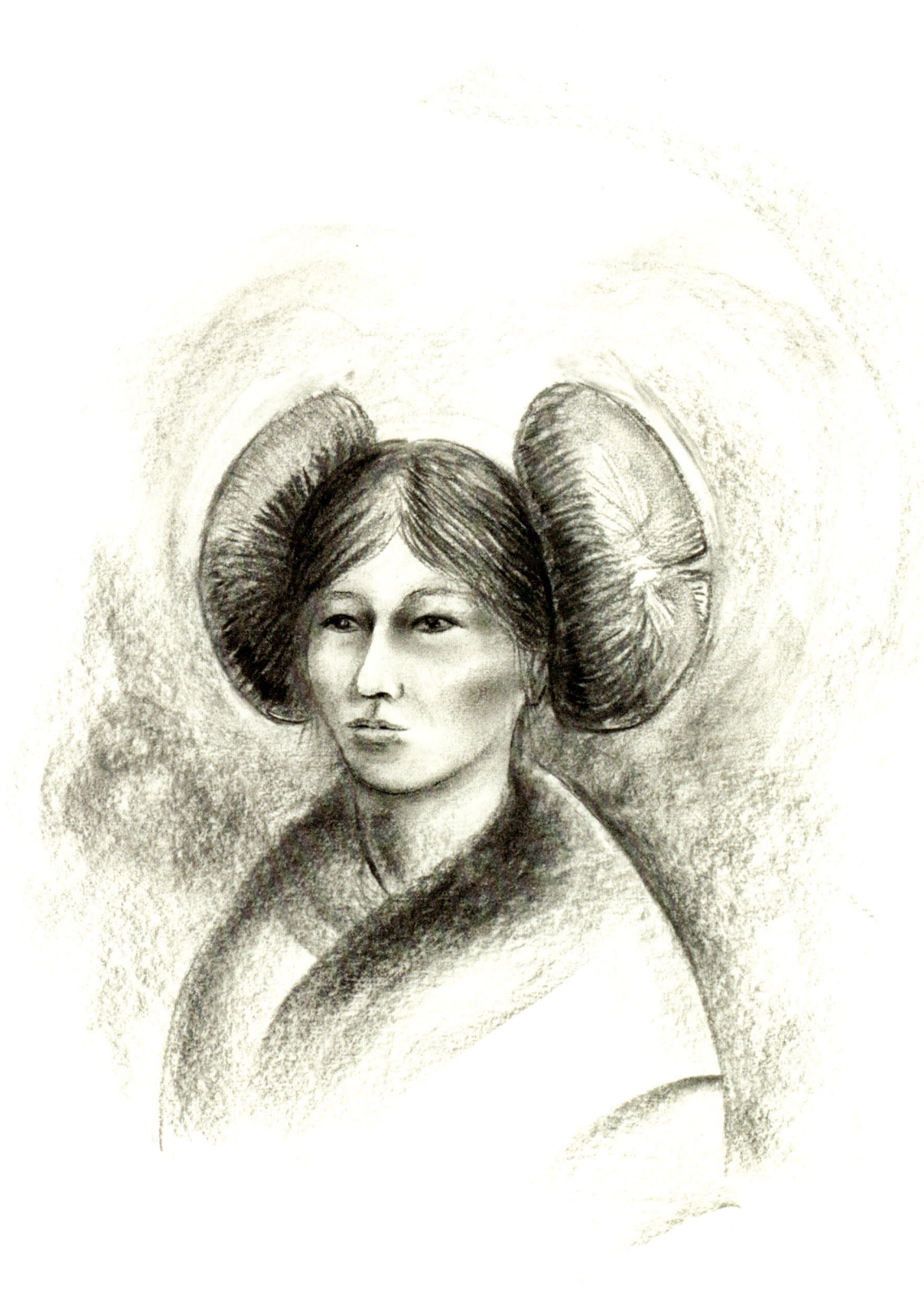

Plate 93
Hopi Maiden, c. 1992
Charcoal, 18 × 24 in.
Chiinde, LLC.
HF1995.1-336.D

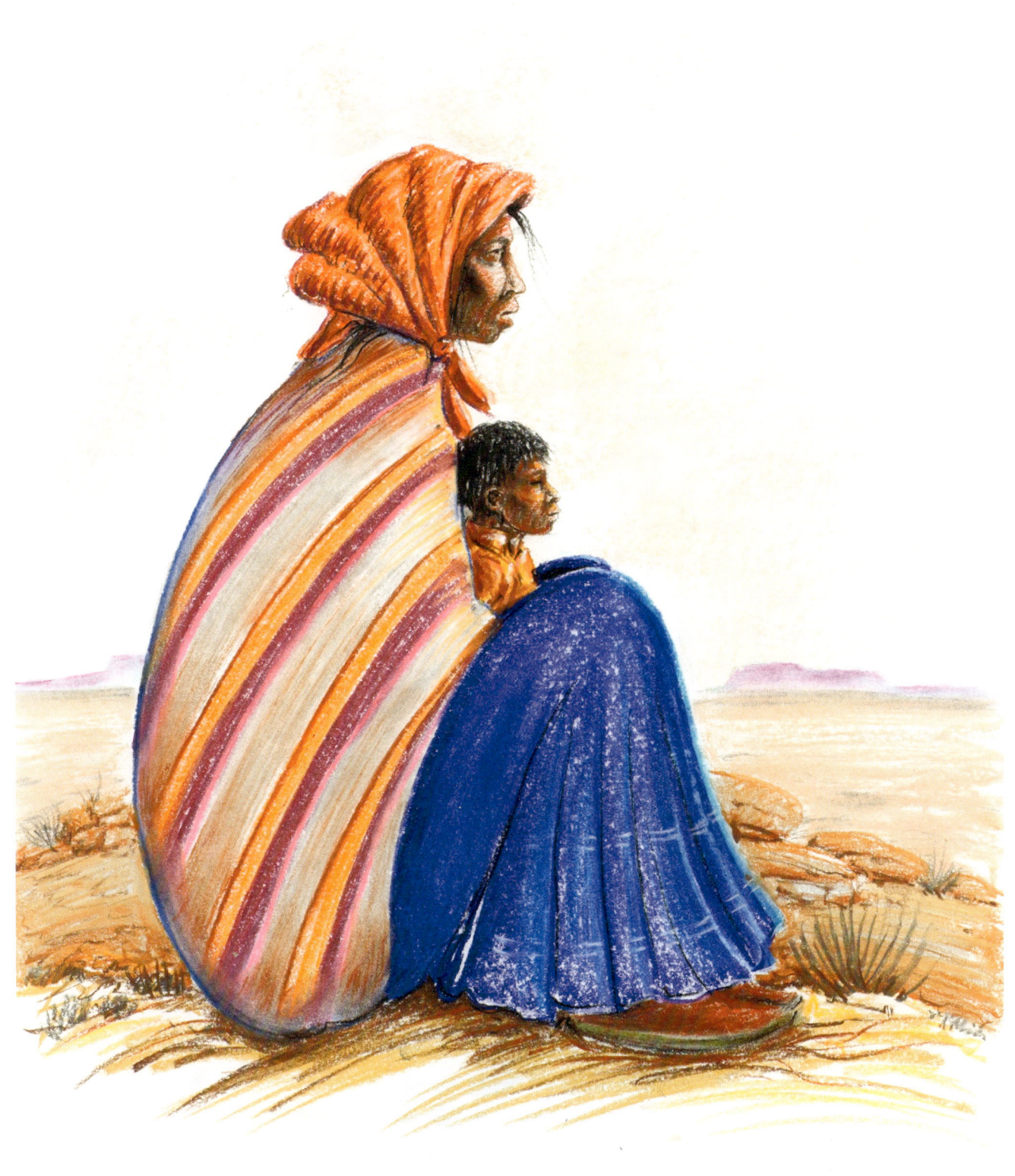

Plate 94
Mother and Son, c. 1992
Pastel, 18 × 24 in.
Chiinde, LLC.
HF1995.1-355.D

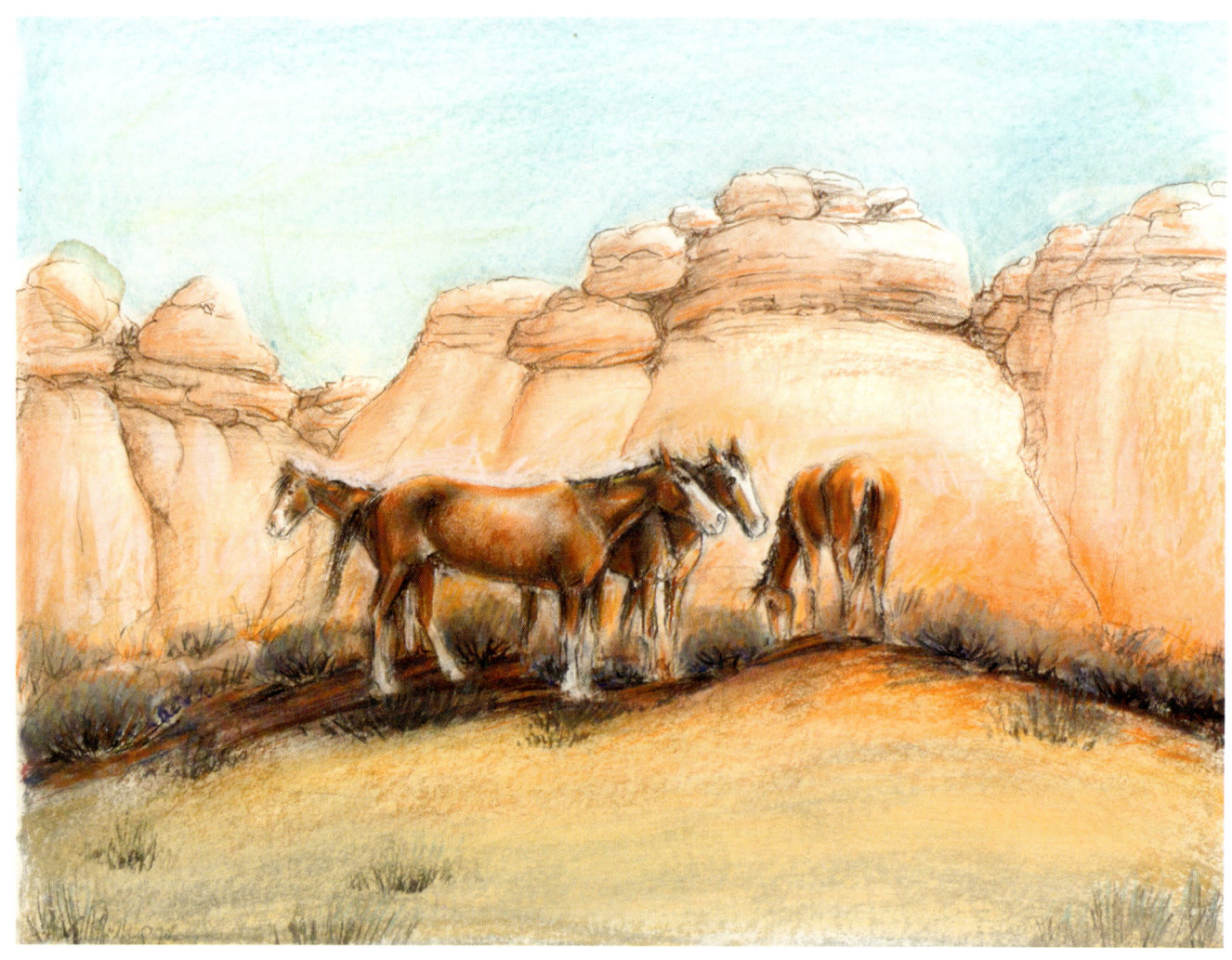

Plate 95
Horses Grazing, c. 1992
Pastel, 18 × 24 in.
Chiinde, LLC.
HF1995.1-358.D

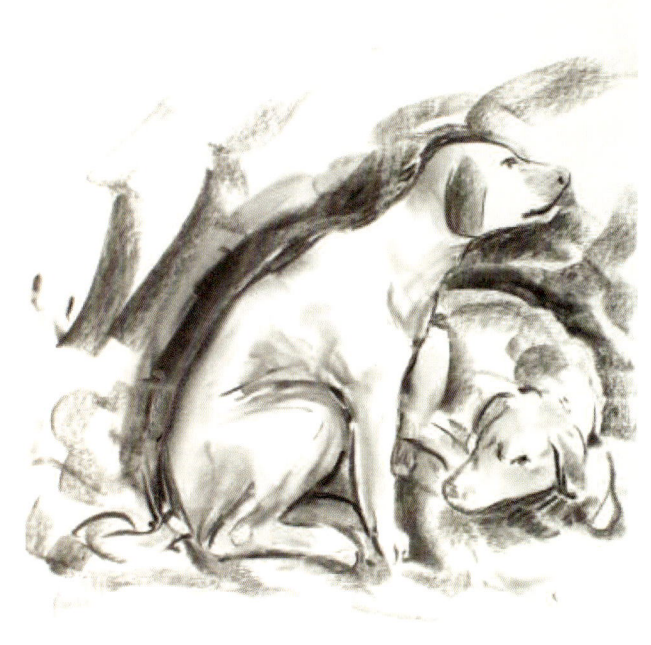

Plate 96
Study of Two Dogs, c. 1992
Charcoal, 17 × 14 in.
Allan Houser Inc.
HF1995.1-155

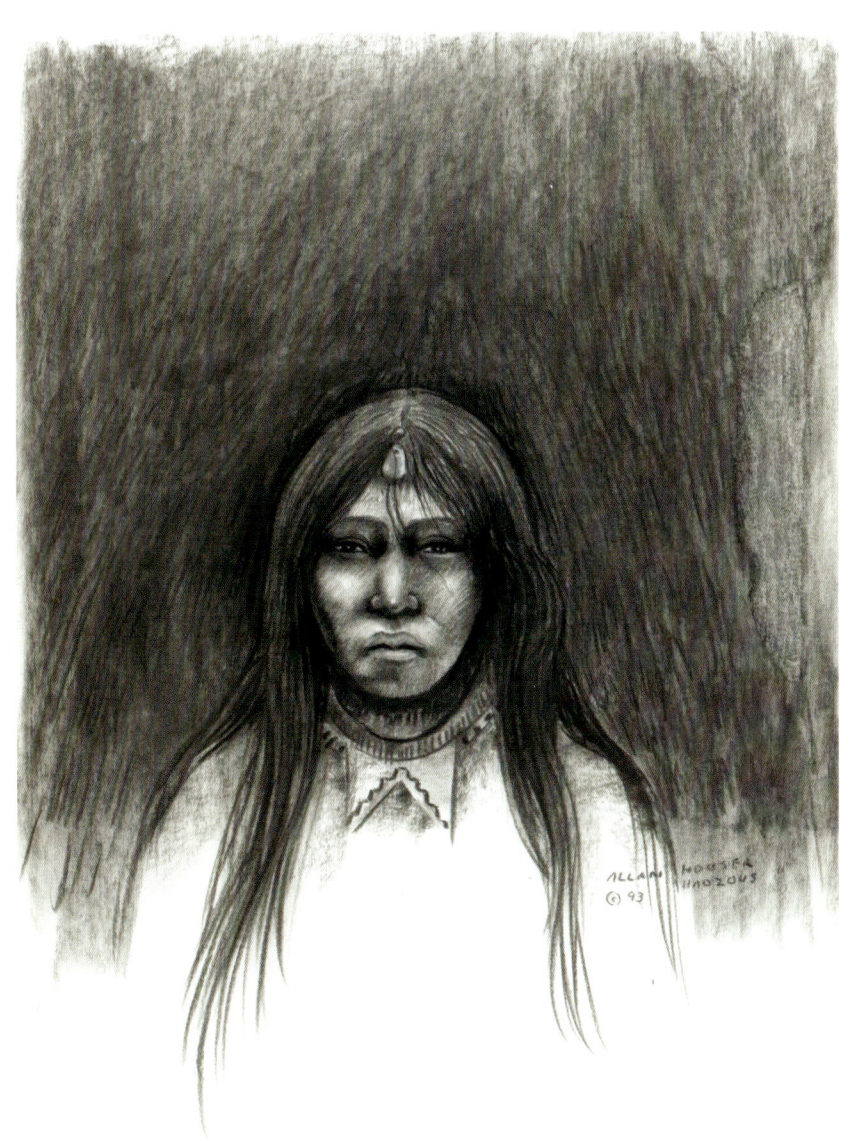

Plate 97
Bust of a Woman, 1993
Charcoal, 30 × 22 in.
Houser / Haozous Family Limited Partnership
HF1995.1-124.D

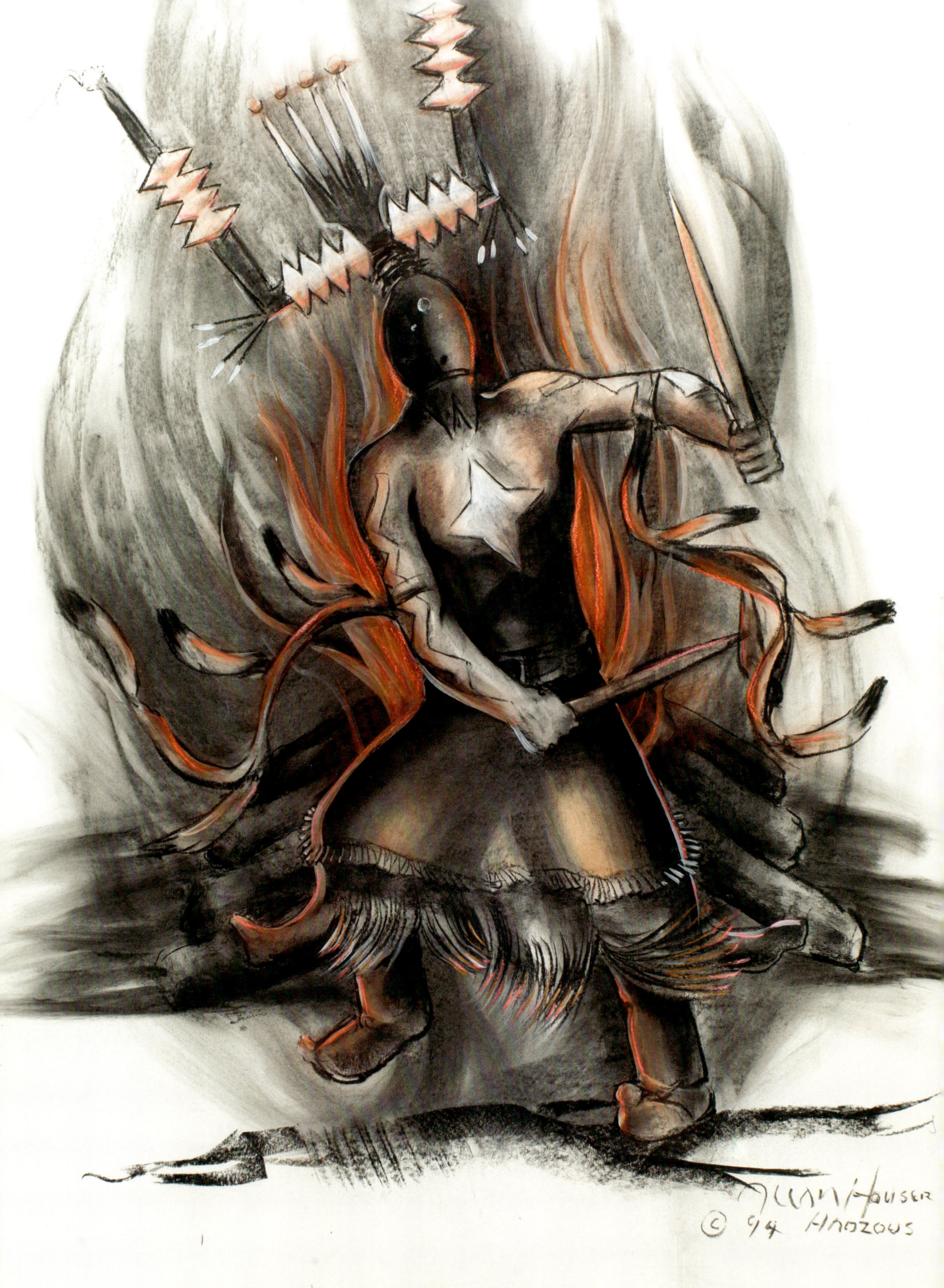

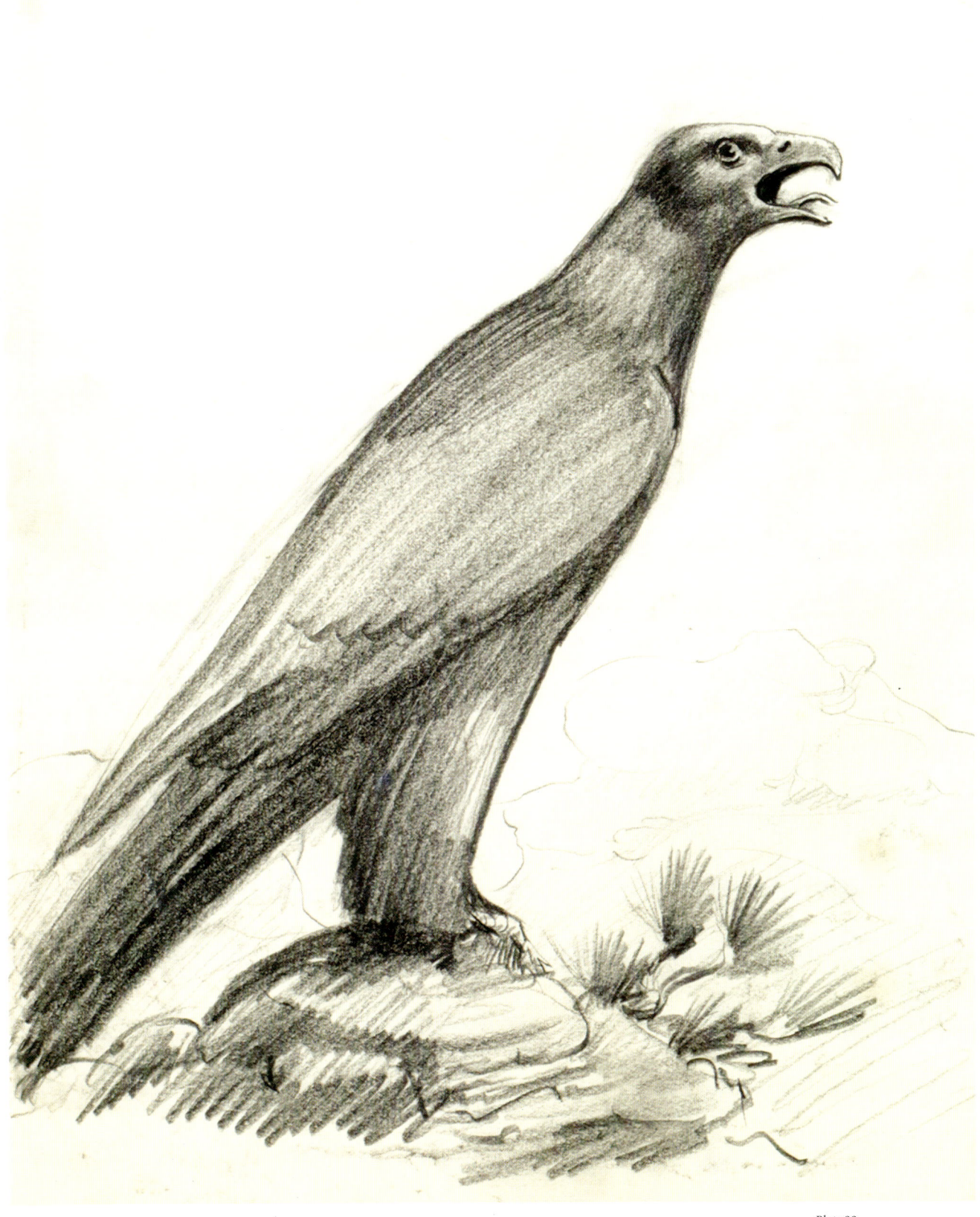

Plate 99
Eagle, c. 1994
Charcoal, 11 × 14 in.
Chiinde, LLC.
HF1995.1-334U.D

Plate 98
**Large Ga'an Dancer in the
Glow of a Fire,** 1994
Pastel and charcoal, 50 × 38 ¼ in.
Allan Houser Inc.
HF1995.1-262.D

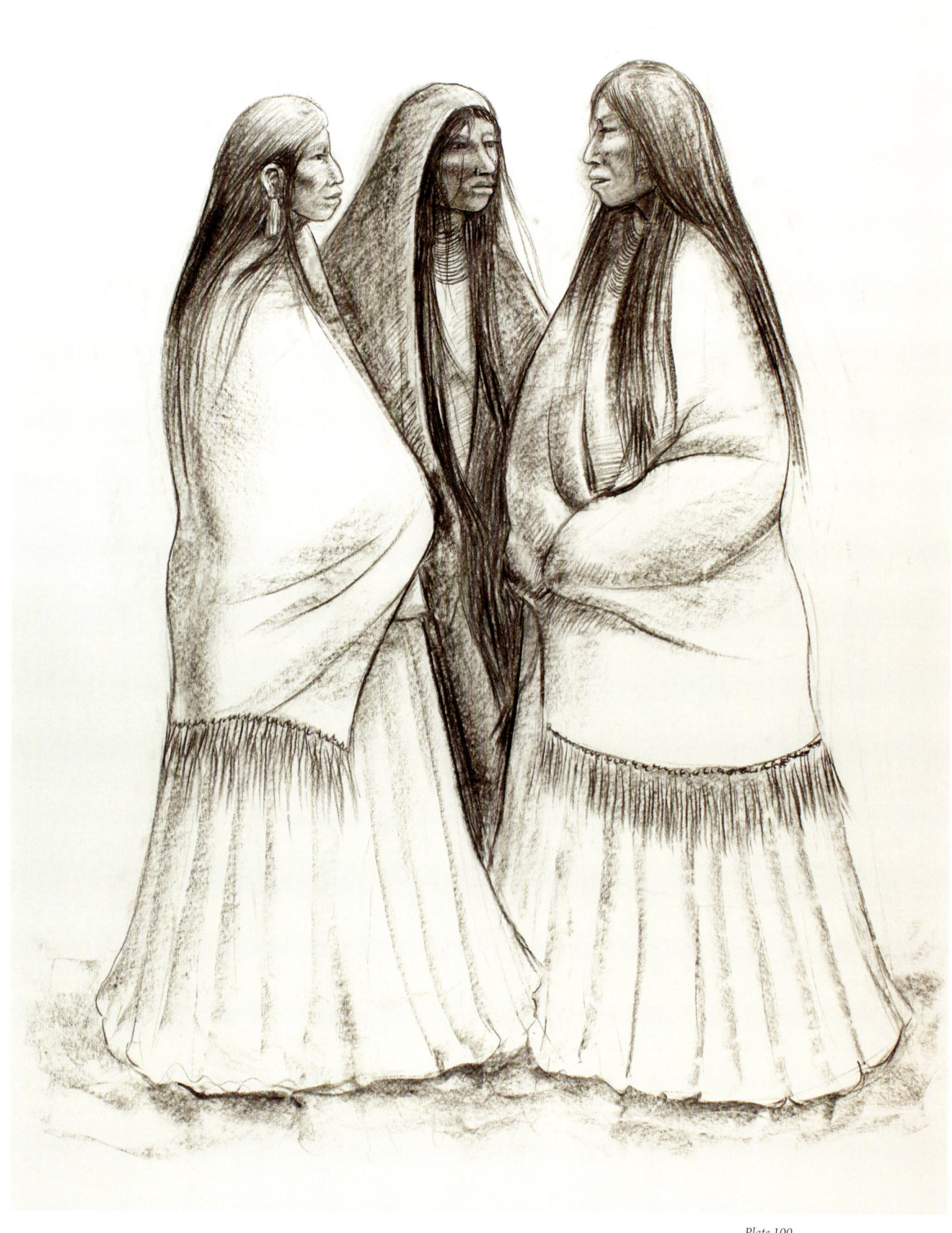

Plate 100
Three Women Talking, c. 1994
Charcoal, 38 ¼ × 50 in.
Allan Houser Inc.
HF1995.1-759.D

Notes

Preface

1. Allan Houser, sketchbook entry (c. 1989), Allan Houser Foundation Archives, HF1995.2-21K.N.

Apaches Forever:
One Hundred Years, One Hundred Drawings

1. See Barbara H. Perlman, *Allan Houser* (Ha-o-zous) (Boston: David R. Godine, 1987), and W. Jackson Rushing III, *Allan Houser: An American Master* (New York: Harry N. Abrams, 2004).

2. Bruce Bernstein and Sandra D'Emilio, *Allan Houser: A Life in Art*, exhibition catalogue (Santa Fe: Museum of New Mexico, 1991).

3. Rushing, *Allan Houser*, 11.

4. Truman T. Lowe, ed., *Native Modernism: The Art of George Morrison and Allan Houser* (Washington, D.C., and New York: Smithsonian National Museum of the American Indian, 2004). See also W. Jackson Rushing III, "Modern Spirits: The Legacy of Allan Houser and George Morrison," in Bruce Bernstein and Truman T. Lowe, eds., *Essays on Native Modernism: Complexity and Contradiction in American Indian Art* (Washington, D.C., and New York: Smithsonian National Museum of the American Indian, 2006), 53–65.

5. The FJJMA accession records link the work to the WPA. Other WPA-commissioned works by Houser are located in the Arthur Johnson Memorial Library in Raton, New Mexico. On the WPA and its support for Houser's work, see Jason Silverman, *Untold New Mexico: Stories from a Hidden Past* (Santa Fe: Sunstone Press, 2006), 97.

6. Personal communication (1996) from Ann Philbin, former director of the Drawing Center in New York City.

7. See the "Certificate of Authenticity" issued by the Allan Houser Foundation (July 30, 1999) in the accession file at the FJJMA.

8. The verso note indicates that that the drawing is figure 94 from Dunn's book and gives her name and return address; see Dorothy Dunn, *American Indian Painting of the Southwest and Plains Area* (Albuquerque: University of New Mexico Press, 1968), 256.

9. Rushing, *Allan Houser*, 41.

10. Frontispiece, *Indians at Work* (January 1940).

11. "Youthful Descendant of Geronimo Finds Paintings in Stories of His People," in ibid., 28.

12. Ibid., 29.

13. Ibid.

14. See Houser's comments in Bernstein and D'Emilio, *Allan Houser*, 15.

15. See Claude Cernuschi, *Jackson Pollock: "Psychoanalytic" Drawings* (Durham: Duke University Press, 1992), plate 81, p. 133

16. On Houser, Moore, and Pre-Columbian–inspired primitivism, see Rushing, *Allan Houser*, 142–43.

17. Ibid., 150

18. Ibid., 88.

19. Nelson Foss, *"Water": Allan Houser,* an educational guide (2001) written for the Palm Springs Desert Museum; www.tfaoi.com/aa/2aa527.htm, accessed July 18, 2013.

20. "Japanese Emperor Given Oklahoma Artist's Work," *The Oklahoman*, June 14, 1994, accessed July 7, 2013.

21. See Houser's comments in Bernstein and D'Emilio, *Allan Houser*, 16.

22. Pearlman, *Allan Houser*, 163.

23. On nobility and savagery, see my comments in W. Jackson Rushing III, "Native Authorship in Edward Curtis's 'Master Prints,'" *American Indian Art Magazine* 29 (Winter 2003), 62.

24. Barry Ace, e-mail to the author, July 17, 2013.

25. Rushing, *Allan Houser*, 129.

26. Ace, 2013.

27. Ibid.

28. Ibid.

29. Ibid.

30. Ibid. See also Jonathan Holmes, "Ponca Hethuska Society," July 31, 2012 www.powwows.com/2012/07/31/ponca-hethuska-society/#, accessed July 8, 2013.

31. Rushing, *Allan Houser*, 43, 45–46

32. Allan Houser, quoted in Jane B. Katz, ed., *This Song Remembers* (Boston: Houghton Mifflin, 1980), 102.

33. Ibid.

34. Cécile Ganteaume, e-mail to the author, July 10, 2013.

35. John G. Bourke, "Medicine Men of the Apache," *Ninth Annual Report of the Bureau of American Ethnology* (Washington, D.C.: Government Printing Office, 1892), Plates VII–VIII.

36. Ibid., 593

37. See Dunn, *American Indian Painting*, plate XXI.

38. Keith H. Basso, *Western Apache Raiding and Warfare* (Tucson: University of Arizona Press, 1971), 239–45. Thanks to Cécile Ganteaume for sharing this reference.

39. This drawing is clearly related to *Night Guard* (bronze, 1985).

40. See Tom Mashberg, "Where Words Mean as Much as Objects," August 19, 2013, www.nytimes.com/2013/08/20/arts/design/apaches-dispute-with-american-museum-of-natural-history.html.

Picturing Home: Allan Houser's Children's Book Illustrations, 1952–1962

Author's note: My analysis of Houser's book illustrations, focusing on his extant drawings and paintings, is based primarily on research I conducted at the Allan Houser Foundation in Santa Fe, New Mexico, in June 2013. I am indebted to David Rettig, curator at the Houser Foundation, for his time and expertise.

1. Namely, Viking Press, Whittlesey House/McGraw-Hill, John C. Winston and Co., and Little, Brown and Company.

2. Karin Williams and Phil Lucas, *Allan Houser Haozous: The Lifetime Work of an American Master,* VHS, prod. Phillip M. Haozous (Santa Fe: Allan Houser, Inc., 2001).

3. W. Jackson Rushing III, *Allan Houser: An American Master* (New York: Harry N. Abrams, 2004), 64.

4. Williams and Lucas, *Allan Houser Haozous,* 2001.

5. In the second storytelling scene, the primary difference between the drawing and the painting—besides the addition of color—is the addition of two more figures. The original color painting is housed at the Allan Houser Foundation Archives in Santa Fe, HF1995.1-617.I

6. Barbara H. Perlman, *Allan Houser (Ha-o-zous)* (Boston: David R. Godine, 1987), 58. Perlman reports Houser's father also served as an interpreter for Geronimo during the Apaches' internment at Fort Sill.

7. Rushing, *Allan Houser,* 57, 107.

8. Dorothy Dunn, *American Indian Painting of the Southwest and Plains Area* (Albuquerque: University of New Mexico Press, 1968), 352–53 and 252, 254, cited in Rushing, *Allan Houser,* 43.

9. Rushing, *Allan Houser,* 43. Rushing points out that it was the mimicking of American western painters like Russell or Remington that Dunn took issue with, more than the illustrative quality of Houser's images.

10. Ann Nolan Clark, *Blue Canyon Horse* (New York: The Viking Press, 1954), 14.

11. Tsianina K. Lomawaima and Teresa L. McCarty, *"To Remain an Indian": Lessons in Democracy from a Century of Native American Education,* Multicultural Education Series, edited by James A. Banks (New York: Columbia University Teachers College Press, 2006), 95. Lomawaima and McCarty specifically criticize Clark's "Little Herder" series published by the Department of Interior. The picture books, which follow a Navajo girl through the seasons were published between 1940 and 1942 in Navajo with an English translation.

12. The brainchild of Bureau of Indian Affairs Education Division director Willard Walcott Beatty, these picture books featured indigenous protagonists and illustrations by Native artists with the goal of increasing literacy among Native children. Dunn helped Beatty select Native illustrators for the readers. For an overview of the books, see Rebecca C. Benes, *Native American Picture Books of Change: The Art of Historic Children's Editions* (Santa Fe: Museum of New Mexico Press, 2004). See also Lomawaima and McCarty, "To Remain an Indian," 91.

13. For Houser's biography, see Perlman, *Allan Houser.* For *I am a Pueblo Indian Girl,* see Benes, *Native American Picture Books of Change,* 33. In 1939, Houser contributed four illustrations to Louise Abeita (E-Yeh-Shure', Blue Corn)'s *I am a Pueblo Indian Girl,* also illustrated by Santa Fe Indian School students Gerald Nailor and Quincy Tahoma, and published by William Morrow. In contrast to his book illustrations of the 1950s and 1960s, Houser's illustrations published in the 1939 book appear to have been paintings first, illustrations second. All are signed, one dated as early as 1937, two years before the book was published. The illustrations also vary from the text. The most obvious example is Houser's image accompanying a section titled "My Ponies." The mare in the text is described as "a buckskin color with white mane and tail," but Houser's mare sports a brown mane and tail, and the "frisky white" colt in the text is depicted as a dappled bay, nursing. This illustration, and Houser's depiction of a girl baking bread, reflect the Studio style in their lack of background, flat application of color, and heavy outlines. Houser's other two illustrations in the book depict entire scenes, much more similar to the landscapes he would create for children's books during the 1950s.

14. Houser's illustrations in *Geronimo* consist of small, quarter-page vignettes and occasional single-page illustrations. In *Cochise,* he was given multiple double-page spreads, with the smallest illustrations occupying entire single pages. The draftsmanship is better here, too—occasional stick figures in *Geronimo* don't appear in the later publication.

15. Houser's double-page drawings for the spread illustrations are approximately 10 × 8 inches; in the book they are split into two drawings isolated from each other by wide margins and the center binding (as opposed to a true double-truck or double-page spread that would "bleed" across the center binding). Lines that crossed the binding on Houser's original drawings were painted out, and in *Rider Entering Armed Village,* only half of Houser's original illustration was printed. The "rider" appears on page 127, but the village on the right half of the spread was omitted. In the published dust jacket, details (including Cochise's exposed left breast) were edited out from Houser's original tempera cover painting. The original cover design is located at the Houser Archives, HF1995.1-663.A.I.

16. *Battle Scene:* Houser Archives, HF1995.1-663.Q.I; *Apache Warrior Dragging Off Body:* HF1995.1-663.N.I. McGraw-Hill did, however, publish *Vigilantes Attacking Village of Women and Children* in *Cochise,* a disturbing image of soldiers brutalizing, shooting, and beating women and children in a burning village.

17. According to the book jacket for *Blue Canyon Horse,* their collaboration began when Clark became interested in

Houser's work while also working at Intermountain Indian School.

18. The book began as "Third Grade Home Geography," a project Clark worked on with her Tesuque students. Benes notes this book is probably best known of all the Indian Readers as Viking has kept it continually in print since 1941, and a special fiftieth anniversary edition was published in 1991. See: Benes, *Native American Picture Books of Change*, 3.

19. See Houser Archives, HF1995.1.631.I.

20. See HF 995.1-656-I, which is signed and dated "Allan Houser '54," along with a notation "Jacket Design" in the margin. Houser's cover choice is actually a more dynamic composition than the cover illustration that was used.

21. See Houser Archives, Viking Press Publisher's Label, HF1995.1-662.B.I.

22. Rettig estimated this amount based on a label on an existing painting sold in the 1950s. Rettig, e-mail to author, August 23, 2013.

23. See Houser Archives, letter from May Massee, Viking Press, to Houser, February 21, 1958. Houser Archives, HF1995.1-698.A-C.I.

24. In a letter dated May 9, 1958, Morris Colman at Viking indicated that Houser's working dummy for *The Cave* was received and that Houser should have received a check for his drawings. He requested a drawing for the cloth binding and asked if Houser might "suggest the colors of cloth and ink." Colman also indicated that in the enclosed jacket proof "the colors are not quite those of your sketch, and we intend to improve them when we print the edition. Even so, we think the effect is splendid." See Houser Archives, HF1995.1-698B.PE.

25. Colman indicated in a letter dated July 8, 1958, that the drawing for the cover was too detailed and lines too fine to emboss; he took Houser up on his offer (written in the margin of the same drawing) to provide a more simplified version. While Viking wrote to Houser on letterhead, Houser wrote to Viking in the margins of his drawings and paintings.

26. The image is *Boy Walking Ewe and Lamb*, 14⅛ × 20¼ inches; see HF1995.1-697.I

27. Nelson Foss and Rennard Strickland, "Selected Book Illustrations by Allan Houser," in *Education Guide for Museum Docents* (Santa Fe: The Allan Houser Foundation, 2003, unpublished), 7.

28. Although true in general for drawings reproduced in the book's margins, I am referring specifically to HF1995.1-603.BI, an illustration of a family getting into a wagon, which is more greatly reduced than any other of Houser's *Desert People* illustrations. Chock full of foreground, middle ground, and background details in lightly drawn ink, the illustration appears wedged in the upper margin of page 16 in Clark's text.

29. See HF1995.1-603.A.I. By contrast, neither of Houser's finished drawings of a ramada and two bedrolls were published; they were replaced instead with a color painting.

30. Williams and Lucas, *Allan Houser Haozous*.

31. Rushing describes Houser's distress at not studying anatomy and claims Houser "refused to apologize for admiring" nineteenth- and twentieth-century painters of the American West. Rushing, *Allan Houser*, 41, 43.

32. Foss, "Selected Book Illustrations," 7.

33. This statement is true of Houser's published book illustrations in general, but I focus on the Viking Press picture books and *Cochise* since those original illustrations are extant today.

34. For repeated landscape and vegetation forms in *Geronimo*, see pp. 66, 88, and 156. It could be argued that Houser used these repeated forms for the sake of time or economy. But if he were really interested in merely saving time, he might not have gone to the trouble of filling his illustrations with landscape elements in the foreground, middle-ground, and background.

35. See Edgar Wyatt, *Geronimo: The Last Apache War Chief* (New York: Whittlesey House/McGraw-Hill, 1952), 88, 92, 99. Illustrations rarely depict Apaches in the process of enacting violence in the book. More often, published images depict more humorous moments like Apaches tossing miners into a cactus (as opposed to tying miners to wagon wheels before driving the wagon off a cliff). It is possible that Houser illustrated more violent scenes for *Geronimo* but that they were not published, as was the case in *Cochise*.

36. Wyatt, *Geronimo*, 87.

37. Wyatt, *Cochise* (New York: Whittlesey House/McGraw-Hill, 1953), 184.

38. The Houser Foundation collection includes 239 of Houser's sketchbooks filled with 6,000 drawings in each. These books may date later than the 1950s and consist of many outdoor landscape sketches. Rettig, telephone interview, April 3, 2010.

39. Wyatt, *Cochise*, 8.

40. Wyatt, *Geronimo*, 173.

41. Williams and Lucas, *Allan Houser Haozous*.

42. Ibid.

43. Clark, *Blue Canyon Horse*, 7.

44. Ibid., 29.

45. Benes, *Native American Picture Books of Change*, 116.

46. Carl Waldman and Molly Braun, *Atlas of the North American Indian* (New York: Facts on File Publications, 1985), 144–45.

47. Joseph H. and Chava Schwarcz, *The Picture Book Comes of Age* (Chicago: American Library Association, 1991), 113.

48. Other John Ford films set in Monument Valley at mid-century include *My Darling Clementine* (1946), *Fort Apache* (1948), *The Searchers* (1956), and *How the West Was Won* (1962).

49. Elizabeth Coatsworth, *The Cave* (New York: The Viking Press, 1958), 30.

50. Ibid.

51. Ibid., 58.

52. Clark, *The Desert People*, 9.

53. Jackson Rushing notes that the church is lovingly referred to as the "White Dove of the Desert" by locals, and donations by its indigenous parishioners contributed to the

mission's restoration during the 1980s and '90s. See Rushing, *Allan Houser*, 101.

54. Rettig, telephone interview, April 3, 2010.

55. Donald Fixico, *Termination and Relocation: Federal Indian Policy, 1945–1960* (Albuquerque: University of New Mexico Press, 1986), 9.

56. Joe Sunpool, at Haskell, appears between identities.

In contrast to Houser's other illustrated protagonists, Joe is a character without a landscape. Houser most often depicts him indoors, or on the grounds of Haskell Indian School. When landscape is present in Houser's *Joe Sunpool* illustrations, it often appears bound by fences or sidewalks.

57. Lomawaima and McCarty, *"To Remain an Indian,"* 91.

58. Benes, *Native American Picture Books of Change*, 5.

Bibliography

Allan Houser Foundation Archives, Santa Fe, New Mexico.

Basso, Keith H. *Western Apache Raiding and Warfare.* Tucson: University of Arizona Press, 1971.

Benes, Rebecca C. *Native American Picture Books of Change: The Art of Historic Children's Editions.* Santa Fe: Museum of New Mexico Press, 2004.

Bernstein, Bruce, and Sandra D'Emilio. *Allan Houser: A Life in Art.* Exhibition catalogue. Santa Fe: Museum of New Mexico, 1991.

Bernstein, Bruce, and Truman T. Lowe, eds. *Essays on Native Modernism: Complexity and Contradiction in American Indian Art.* Washington, D.C., and New York: Smithsonian National Museum of the American Indian, 2006.

Cernuschi, Claude. *Jackson Pollock: "Psychoanalytic" Drawings.* Durham: Duke University Press, 1992.

Clark, Ann Nolan. "Ann Nolan Clark: A Handful of Days." *Something about the Author Autobiography Series,* vol. 16, 32–109. Detroit: Gale Research, 1993.

———. *Blue Canyon Horse.* New York: The Viking Press, 1954.

———. *The Desert People.* New York: The Viking Press, 1962.

Coatsworth, Elizabeth. *The Cave.* New York: The Viking Press, 1958.

Dippie, Brian W. "Drawn to the West." *The Western Historical Quarterly* 35:1 (Spring 2004), 4–26.

Dunn, Dorothy. *American Indian Painting of the Southwest and Plains Area.* Albuquerque: University of New Mexico Press, 1968.

Fixico, Donald L. *Termination and Relocation: Federal Indian Policy, 1945–1960.* Albuquerque: University of New Mexico Press, 1986.

Foss, Nelson, and Rennard Strickland. "Selected Book Illustrations by Allan Houser," In *Education Guide for Museum Docents.* Santa Fe: The Allan Houser Foundation, 2003 (unpublished).

Katz, Jane B., ed. *This Song Remembers.* Boston: Houghton Mifflin, 1980.

Lomawaima, Tsianina K., and Teresa L. McCarty. *"To Remain an Indian": Lessons in Democracy from a Century of Native American Education.* Multicultural Education Series, edited by James A. Banks. New York: Columbia University Teachers College Press, 2006.

Lowe, Truman T., ed. *Native Modernism: The Art of George Morrison and Allan Houser.* Washington, D.C., and New York: Smithsonian National Museum of the American Indian, 2004.

McNickle, D'Arcy. *Runner in the Sun: A Story of Indian Maize.* Albuquerque: University of New Mexico Press, 1987.

Perlman, Barbara H. *Allan Houser (Ha-o-zous).* Boston: David R. Godine, 1987.

Rushing, W. Jackson, III. *Allan Houser: An American Master.* New York: Harry N. Abrams, 2004.

———. "Native Authorship in Edward Curtis's 'Master Prints.'" *American Indian Art Magazine* 29 (Winter 2003): 58–63.

Schwarcz, Joseph H., and Chava Schwarcz. *The Picture Book Comes of Age.* Chicago: American Library Association, 1991.

Silverman, Jason. *Untold New Mexico: Stories from a Hidden Past.* Santa Fe: Sunstone Press, 2006.

Waldman, Carl, and Molly Braun. *Atlas of the North American Indian.* New York: Facts on File Publications, 1985.

Wilcox, Don. *Joe Sunpool.* Boston: Little, Brown and Company, 1956.

Williams, Karin, and Phil Lucas, *Allan Houser Haozous: The Lifetime Work of an American Master.* VHS. Produced by Phillip M. Haozous. Santa Fe: Allan Houser, Inc., 2001.

Wyatt, Edgar. *Cochise.* New York: Whittlesey House (McGraw-Hill.), 1953.

Wyatt, Edgar. *Geronimo: The Last Apache War Chief.* New York: Whittlesey House (McGraw-Hill.), 1952.

Contributors

Hadley Jerman is a Ph.D. student in Art History at the University of Oklahoma.

W. Jackson Rushing III is the Eugene B. Adkins Presidential Professor of Art History and Mary Lou Milner Carver Chair in Native American Art at the University of Oklahoma.

Mark A. White is the Eugene B. Adkins Senior Curator and Curator of Collections at the Fred Jones Jr. Museum of Art, the University of Oklahoma.

About the Venue

The University of Oklahoma's Fred Jones Jr. Museum of Art is one of the finest art museums in the United States. Strengths of this nearly 16,000-object collection (including the approximately 3,300-object Adkins Collection and the more than 4,000-object James T. Bialac Native American Art Collection) are the Weitzenhoffer Collection of French Impressionism, twentieth-century American painting and sculpture, traditional and contemporary Native American art, art of the Southwest, ceramics, photography, contemporary art, Asian art, and graphics from the sixteenth century to the present.

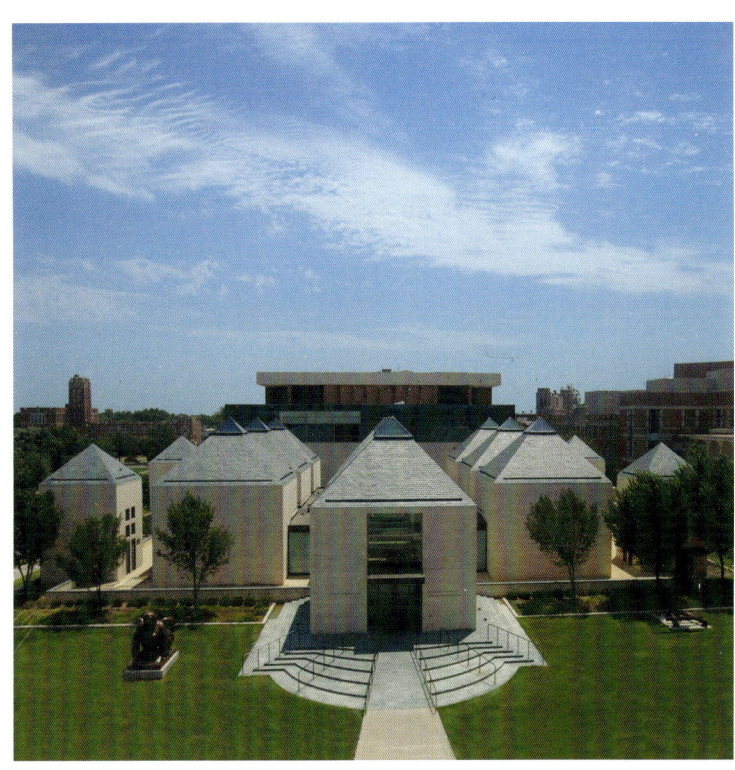

Publication Notes

The catalogue has been published in conjunction with the exhibition *Allan Houser Drawings: The Centennial Exhibition* at the Fred Jones Jr. Museum of Art, March 8–May 18, 2014.

Catalogue design: Julie Rushing
Copy editor: Alice K. Stanton
Photography: Todd Stewart, unless noted

Fred Jones Jr. Museum of Art
The Unviersity of Oklahoma
555 Elm Avenue
Norman, OK 73019-3003
Phone: 405.325.3272; fax: 405.325.7696
www.ou.edu/fjjma

Library of Congress control number: 2014930767
ISBN: 978-0-9851609-4-4

Credits:

(*front cover*)
Detail from *Apache Father and Son*, c. 1992, oil stick
Allan Houser Inc. HF1995.1-182.D. See plate 81 (p. 85).

(*back cover*)
Detail from *Non-objective Form*, c. 1992, pastel
Allan Houser Inc. HF1995.1-25.D. See plate 57 (p. 65).

(*pages ii–iii*)
Detail from *Non-objective Form*, c. 1992, pastel
Allan Houser Inc. HF1995.1-3.D. See plate 53 (p. 62).

(*pages iv–v*)
Detail from *Warrior in a Blanket with a Rifle*, c. 1992, charcoal
Allan Houser Inc. HF1995.1-206.D. See plate 84 (p. 87).

(*page 1*)
Detail from *Four Goats in Landscape*, c. 1992, pastel
Allan Houser Inc. HF1995.1-156.D. See plate 76 (p. 80).